WOMEN in Today's World

WOMEN in Today's World

Belle S. Spafford

Published by
DESERET BOOK COMPANY
Salt Lake City, Utah
1973

Lithographed by

DESERET PRESS

in the United States of America

Belle Spafford

Belle Smith Spafford, ninth general president of the Relief Society, is one of the Lord's chosen daughters. She is an elect lady of this day, and her coming to mortality was at a time and in accordance with the work she was fashioned to carry on as a wife, mother, teacher, writer, editor, executive, and spiritual leader.

She was born at Salt Lake City, Utah, a daughter of John Gibson Smith and Hester Sims Smith. Her parental home was conspicuous for its culture and refinement. The seven children were taught to work industriously, to be frugal, to be self-reliant and independent.

Upon Sister Spafford's mother devolved the entire responsibility of rearing this last child of her seven children —for the father of Sister Spafford died before she was born. A stern, but fair and righteous mother trained her five sons and two daughters. To be reared by a widowed mother with seven children would indicate thrift was practiced in the home. However, no matter whether or not there was much money everything was done properly and with decorum from the clothes worn by the daughters to the strict rules on proper party behavior and dating.

Often as situations arise, Sister Spafford will relate a pointed quotation of her mother's—always pithy—sometimes barbed or humorous. And when an appreciated compliment is received by Sister Spafford, she will remind herself of her Scottish grandmother's saying, "See that ye're desairvin'."

Sister Spafford graduated from the Normal School at the University of Utah, and afterward, continued her studies at the Brigham Young University Training School,

Provo, Utah. Following her marriage to Willis Earl Spafford, in 1921, she continued as special instructor in remedial work for retarded children at B.Y.U. Her employment there intensified her sympathy for the less fortunate, which has been reflected in later years as she gave general direction to Relief Society social service programs, first in the state of Utah and later in Arizona, Idaho, and Nevada, for unwed mothers, adoptive services, care of deprived and neglected children, and youth guidance services. She has also participated in an extensive foster-care educational program for Indian children.

In 1935, after moving to Salt Lake City, Sister Spafford, by then the mother of two children, was named a member of the governing board of Relief Society of The Church of Jesus Christ of Latter-day Saints. Shortly thereafter, she assumed the duties of editor of the *Relief Society Magazine*, a position she held until 1945.

In April of 1945, she was named President of the Relief Societies of the Church, a position which she holds today. This organization has grown steadily during her tenure of office, not only in membership and in the number of local organizations, but in its compassionate and welfare services, and in strengthened educational and cultural programs.

To be a great and beloved leader among the women of the Church requires certain attributes. The work accomplished by Sister Spafford and the regard in which she is held, highlight attributes which have aided in her achievements. She has a charming, forthright personality and a saving sense of humor; she is a hard worker, assuming her full division of "dog work"; she has a keen sense of the value of money and has exercised special watchcare over funds of Relief Society; she renders obedience to authority and seeks counsel as needed; she expects high performance from others; she is humble and just, and has been blessed with great discernment and wisdom; and she has a deep and abiding testimony of the truthfulness of the gospel.

The traits which she possesses are traits which her sisters in the Church everywhere could also practice with rich rewards both in their home lives and in their Church callings.

Sister Spafford early learned that life was earnest, that time was to be treasured and not to be frittered away. The preciousness of time is observed by her in her daily living and she expects it to be reflected in the work attitudes of those who are associated with her and with the work of Relief Society. She is ready to acknowledge her own shortcomings quickly and does not wish credit for that which is not her due. At one time she was asked, "Well, surely you will keep the title for yourself?" But she quickly answered, "As I will not be doing the work, I would not wish to retain the title."

Although her executive and managerial abilities are outstanding, the gospel is the motivating force in President Spafford's every action. She has been schooled by home training, study, and lifelong habits to be obedient to those in authority over her. This does not only apply to those who are in authority over the Relief Society, but she recognizes the Priesthood in her own home. Her devoted, unselfish, and considerate husband, W. Earl Spafford, until his death in 1963 was a tower of strength to her in all of the aspects of her busy life and important work.

Their two children, Mary Spafford Kemp, trained as a teacher and social worker, and Earl Smith Spafford, a lawyer, helped their mother hold the family in a closely knit unit, particularly after the death of their father. The daughter, now deceased, and her husband, Clarence W., made their home in Chicago with their five sons. The son, however, and his wife, Iris Montague, and their three boys and two daughters, who live in Salt Lake City, are constantly visiting back and forth with Sister Spafford.

The outstanding abilities of President Spafford are recognized in every endeavor to which she turns her attention, but as she is asked to participate, there is always the thought in the mind of President Spafford—how can this assist me to be a better President of Relief Society?

Sister Spafford served as a member of the National Advisory Committee to the White House Conference on Aging, which was held in January of 1961. She acted as chairman of the two sub-sessions of the conference having to do with volunteer service.

She was Second Vice-President from 1948 to 1956 of the National Council of Women of the United States, an organization in which Relief Society was a charter member in 1888. Sister Spafford was a member of the Executive Committee of that organization from 1956-62, and in 1954 she chaired the delegation from the United States at the triennial meeting of the International Council of Women at Helsinki, Finland. She was also a delegate to the triennial meetings of the international Council of Women held in Philadelphia in 1947, and in Montreal, Canada, in 1957. In May of 1966, she again served as a delegate from the United States to the triennial meetings in Teheran, Iran. In 1970, she chaired the delegation from the National Council of Women of the United States to the International Council of Women Conference held in Bangkok, Thailand.

In 1968, Mrs. Spafford was elected President of the National Council of Women of the United States, and served a two-year term. She is presently honorary president and chairman of its Constitutional Revisions Committee.

Mrs. Spafford was appointed, in 1965, as a Vice-President of the American Mothers Committee, Inc., and has recently been made a member of its advisory board. She was given a citation in New York City by the American Mothers Committee, Inc. for distinguished service to women's organizations.

She holds honorary life membership in the Utah State Conference of Social Work in recognition of her outstanding service and leadership to the people of the State of

Utah in the field of social services. She has been a special lecturer for the School of Social Work at the University of Utah.

Mrs. Spafford is a member of the governing board of the Latter-day Saint Hospital in Salt Lake City. She is also a member of the Board of Trustees of the Brigham Young University.

The Relief Society in its great humanitarian service has always been concerned with nursing; and the affiliation President Spafford has had with the National Association for Practical Nurse Education, as second vice president, has been of a two-fold benefit.

Through President Spafford's association with some of the outstanding women leaders throughout the world there has come friendship to her personally and an enhanced appreciation on their part for the work of the Church.

Many signal honors have come to Sister Spafford. She has been given the Distinguished Service Award for the Crusade for Freedom, to which she gave her active support for some years.

She was awarded the Alumni Distinguished Service Award by the Brigham Young University in 1951, and received the honorary Doctor of Humanities degree from that university in 1956. She has a Distinguished Achievement Award from Ricks College in Rexburg, Idaho; and, in February of 1967, was presented with a Distinguished Alumni Award from the University of Utah.

In June, 1971 she received the "Pursuit of Excellence" award from the Latter-day Saint Students Association, a world-wide group of college and university students who are members of the Church.

Sister Spafford has been well trained in Relief Society itself and has given great and valued service in ward, stake, and general board callings. Particularly noteworthy in her general board contributions, in addition to the regular work of the general board and previous to her being made the general president, was service as editor of the *Relief Society Magazine* for eight years from 1937 to 1945. During 1942, the one-hundredth anniversary of the founding of Relief Society, she and I were co-editors of the *Centenary*, a booklet which the general board published on the history of Relief Society during its first hundred years.

President Spafford sees Relief Society as a unique organization for women and the greatest woman's organization upon the face of the earth today, both by reason of its divine origin and the continuing guidance and direction it receives through the Priesthood of God. Its objective is to increase the testimony of the women of the Church both through learning and doing. Its motto is "Charity Never Faileth." It is her earnest wish that all Latter-day Saint women will join in the great work and obtain the rich blessings offered to them through Relief Society.

MARIANNE C. SHARP

Acknowledgments

Preparing this volume has been a delightful experience because of the encouragement and assistance of so many friends. To all whose efforts have blended together to make this book possible I express grateful appreciation.

Specifically, I am indebted to Elder Marvin J. Ashton, Assistant to the Council of the Twelve, for his initial suggestion that I prepare the volume, and for his patient prodding in its early stages.

Without the effort of Mayola R. Miltenberger, the general secretary of the Relief Society, this book could not have been produced. It was she who scanned the materials which I have written through the years and helped me select those which seemed worthy of publication. Her wise counsel is appreciated in so many ways.

I am also very grateful to my counselor, Marianne C. Sharp, for her advice and help in proofreading, and especially for the foreword and biography which she prepared.

Wm. James Mortimer, manager of Deseret Book, and his editors, have also given help in the various production phases.

Appreciation is also extended to Beth Burningham of the Relief Society staff who worked closely with Sister Miltenberger.

Most of all, I am grateful to the leadership of the Church for a quarter-century of opportunity to serve the good women of the Church, and to meet and work with many hundreds of capable women outside the Church. This blessing in my life will be cherished forever.

Belle S. Spafford

Contents

Section Three   Woman's Concern for Her Community
        and World

Section Four   The Woman's Role in the Eternal Plan

Section Five   Relief Society in a Priesthood-Governed Church

Section Six   National and International Reports and Addresses

Section Seven   Special Messages

SECTION ONE

Gospel Principles And Moral Values As They Relate To Women

THE SPIRIT OF THE GOSPEL, THE
SOUL OF RELIEF SOCIETY

MARCH 17, 1842 in the lodge room over the Joseph Smith store, the Prophet Joseph Smith uttered words of lasting import to Latter-day Saint women when he said: "I now declare this society organized, with president and counselors, according to parliamentary usages."

Addressing the 18 women present on that memorable occasion, Elder John Taylor said that he "rejoiced to see this institution organized according to the law of heaven . . . and to see all things moving forward in such a glorious manner." He prayed that "the blessings of heaven might rest upon this institution henceforth."

Today, 106 years since Elder Taylor so spoke, tens of thousands of women rejoice that this society was organized. They see it moving forward in a glorious manner. Grateful for the heritage of the past, faithfully and devotedly meeting the assignments of the present, sagaciously planning and building for the future, they acknowledge that the blessings of heaven do indeed rest upon this society.

There is within this society a great life-giving element —a spirit which reaches out to women from the eastern shores to the western shores of our own great country, into Mexico and on south to the Latin lands of South America;

it reaches into remote villages of Alaska and Canada; it extends into the continents of Europe and Asia, to South Africa and the islands of the sea, binding together women of all nationalities into a great sisterhood, unifying them in purpose and impelling them on to worthy accomplishment. This life-giving spirit is the spirit of the gospel; it makes Relief Society different from other women's organizations the world over. It gives to Relief Society its strength as well as its heart and soul.

The spirit of the gospel operating in the lives of Relief Society women causes them to reach out for immortal treasures; it leads them into experiences that bring enduring joy; it subdues selfishness and crowds out the spirit of criticism and fault-finding; it dissipates fear and builds confidence; it engenders a recognition of and a respect for an inspired Church leadership and bids them to render obedience to that leadership—not a reluctant, obligatory obedience, but a free, voluntary obedience actuated by love; it lifts them above the mean and petty things in life into the realm of that which is of good report and praiseworthy; it enables them to live useful, happy lives.

It was the spirit of the gospel operating in the life of Eliza R. Snow that caused her to travel the weary path across the plains bearing with her the sacred book of records—the first minutes of our beloved Relief Society, containing instructions from our inspired Prophet which for more than a century have guided the society. It was the spirit of the gospel within her that decreed that she go from door to door canvassing for students, who, according to the records, must be "possessed of nerve, energy, and ambition" to attend a school of medicine and surgery "for the instruction of females" in order that the medical and health needs of an isolated pioneering community might be met.

It was the spirit of the gospel alive in the heart of Zina D. H. Young that caused her to accept, without thought of dissenting, a mission to lead the Relief Societies of the Church in a new and untried venture—the production of silk "that the sisters might do all in their power to clothe themselves and their families, and that home industry might be promoted."

It was the spirit of the gospel active in the soul of Aunt Em that gave her the courage to lead the sisters in their strange mission of saving grain.

To say that these missions were accepted without feelings of trepidation would be to misrepresent truth. However, fear of failure was not its cause, for these sisters had faith in the inspired leadership of the priesthood authorities who directed them, and a courage born of testimony. These feelings were but the result of an intelligent sensitiveness to the magnitude of their tasks and all that was involved in their fulfillment.

At age 84 Aunt Em addressed the sisters in general conference on the grain-saving program, expressing her feelings in these words: "I felt very timid and I was just about trembling when I went to talk the matter over with President Wells." (President Wells was counselor to President Brigham Young.)

Praiseworthy success crowned the efforts of these sisters in their undertakings. Today, a symbol of this success, there rise toward the heavens great elevators filled with grain as a result of the garnering in the fields by the sisters, who sold not only Sunday eggs, but also quilts, rag carpets, and other products of their hands to earn funds with which to buy grain. They did it because the spirit of the gospel bade them accept their missions and render loving obedience to Church leadership.

This same spirit is active in the hearts of Relief Society women of this day. Only one year ago a Relief Society sister, president of a small branch of Mexican sisters, sat in this great Tabernacle and heard a plan proposed whereby the sisters of this day were to raise one-half million dollars for a Relief Society home. She, too, had feelings of trepidation because of the magnitude of the undertaking. But, strong in testimony, she said: "I don't know how we can do

it. But the First Presidency has authorized it. If they author-
ize it, it is right: If it is right, we can do it." And do it they
did. The response of this sister was typical of that of sisters
all over the Church—sisters imbued with the spirit of the
gospel.

Anxious hours have been my own lot in the planning
and conduct of this great fund-raising program for the
Relief Society home, but doubt has not been mine. Secure
in the approval of the First Presidency, mindful of the
support always given the sisters in their righteous undertakings by the priesthood authorities, fully aware of the
faithfulness and devotion of the sisters of this day, having
a strong inner conviction that the undertaking was right,
a deep-seated, calm assurance has been mine that success
would ultimately attend our efforts. And the future will
see a Relief Society home rise, a monument to the devotion
of the sisters of this day—evidence that the spirit of the
gospel has been with them.

The spirit of the gospel will always exist within this
Society in direct ratio to the strength of the testimonies of
the women who make up its membership. A knowledge of
the gospel, obedience to its teachings, a willingness to keep
the commandments of God on the part of Relief Society
women are prerequisites to their well-being as individuals
and to the well-being of Relief Society as an organization.

The Second Epistle of John, addressed to a woman,
"unto the elect lady," may appropriately be addressed to
Relief Society women today:

Grace be with you, mercy, and peace, from God the Father, and
from the Lord Jesus Christ, the Son of the Father, in truth and
love.

And now I beseech thee, lady, not as though I wrote a new
commandment unto thee, but that which we had from the beginning, that we love one another.

And this is love, that we walk after his commandments. This
is the commandment, That, as ye have heard from the beginning,
ye should walk in it.

Look to yourselves, that we lose not those things which we
have wrought, but that we receive a full reward. (II John 3, 5, 6, 8.)

In the gospel of St. John we read this message of the Master:

If ye love me, keep my commandments.

He that hath my commandments, and keepeth them, he it is that loveth me: and he that loveth me shall be loved of my Father, and I will love him, and will manifest myself to him.

. . . If a man love me, he will keep my words: and my Father will love him, and we will come unto him, and make our abode with him. (John 14:15, 21, 23.)

The Lord will come unto Relief Society; he will make his abode with us, and the blessings of heaven will rest upon our beloved society so that it will continue to move forward in a glorious manner if we who make up its membership will but love the Lord and keep his commandments. Our work will be accomplished with a glad heart and a cheerful countenance and we will receive the rewards of righteousness—even peace in this world and eternal life in the world to come.

I know that this gospel is true. This testimony sweeps over me at times with an almost startling reality. There is a Father to whom we may go in prayer and find comfort and sustenance, inspiration, and guidance. Joseph Smith was a Prophet of God, chosen to bring to earth in this dispensation the gospel of Christ, the only plan by which we may live and gain exaltation in the kingdom of God. God's chosen prophet is on earth today. Relief Society was organized according to the law of heaven. It has a work to do in the building of God's kingdom on earth. May we, the sisters of Relief Society, so live that we may do our part nobly and well is my earnest prayer, and I ask it in the name of Jesus Christ, Amen.

"AS FOR ME AND MY HOUSE, WE WILL SERVE THE LORD"

I SHOULD like to bring to your minds a message from an ancient prophet of Israel, the prophet Joshua. This message was of great significance in the day it was given, and it continues with us today of equal import.

The tribes of Israel had inclined their hearts toward a worship of strange gods. Joshua, fearing for his people, "gathered all the tribes of Shechem, and called for the elders of Israel, and for their heads, and for their judges, and for their officers, and they presented themselves before God." (Joshua 24:1.)

And Joshua warned them of what was happening among them. Earnestly admonishing them to put away their strange gods, he called upon them to repent, to serve the Lord, God of Israel, in sincerity and truth. Then, in the power and majesty of his calling as their prophet, he called upon them thus: "Choose you this day whom ye will serve . . . but as for me and my house, we will serve the Lord." (Joshua 24:15.)

The choice to be made by these tribes of Israel that day is a choice which men have had to make through the ages. Countless numbers have chosen, as did Joshua of old, to serve the Lord in sincerity and truth: tens of thousands among us today have so chosen.

For those who make this choice the path is straight and narrow, but the road is well marked. None who earnestly desire to follow it need go astray. If we would serve the Lord, we must love him, for it is not given to men to serve whom they love not. We must love our neighbors as ourselves. It is attendant upon those who choose to serve the Lord to obey the ordinances and keep the commandments of God. We must remember the Sabbath day to keep it holy; we must bring our tithes and offerings to the storehouse of the Church; we must fast and pray; we must keep ourselves pure in body and in spirit; we must keep the countless commandments which the Lord has given us for our well-being and for the establishment of his kingdom.

If we would have our households serve the Lord (and what parent who loves the Lord has peace of soul without this?), we must maintain homes of faith and righteousness, putting obedience and service to God foremost. We must ever hold before our families a vision of the greatness, the goodness, the power, and the love of God. We must help them to see the wisdom of his ways, the priceless worth of his words, and the precious values accruing to those who do his will, even though they may not fully comprehend his purposes. We must never be found compromising in the slightest degree with sin nor surrendering even in the smallest measure to that which runs counter to his teachings.

These requirements are contingent upon all who make the choice made by Joshua. In addition, the Lord makes special and individual requirements of almost everyone. Some of these are related to the work of the Church; others are highly personal. Some are fulfilled with comparative ease and rejoicing; others are difficult, testing the faith and trying the soul.

Such requirements are made by our Father of his daughters as well as of his sons. We remember the special requirements made of Hannah, one that would have sorely tested any mother. Hannah was without a child. So sad was her heart over this that "she wept and did not eat . . . she was in bitterness of soul." Then Hannah prayed unto the Lord, petitioning him that he should give unto her a man child. And the Lord heard her petition and answered it. To Hannah was born a son, who was called Samuel. Then Hannah rejoiced in the Lord, saying: "There is none holy as the Lord: for there is none beside thee: neither is there any rock like our God." (I Sam. 2:2.)

But it was required of Hannah that she should keep the vow she had made with the Lord, that she should give the child Samuel to the Lord as soon as he was weaned, that she should take him to the temple where, under the care and guardianship of Eli the priest, he should be trained to minister in the temple. What a severe requirement to be made of Hannah! What a test for any mother! Like any mother, she must have wondered how Eli would care for her baby. She must have wondered if the babe would waken in the night and miss her. She must have wondered how her own longing heart could be comforted.

But Hannah had chosen to serve the Lord. She loved the Lord. God had been good to her. He had taken away her reproach. He had assuaged her heart hunger by sending her the child. She stood ready to keep the covenant she had made with him. She bequeathed this most precious gift to the Lord, and mother-like, she found solace in each year making for her son a coat which she brought to him when she came up to the temple with her husband to offer the yearly sacrifice.

We remember the requirements made of the mother of Moses; of Deborah when she was called upon to lead the hosts of Israel in battle; of Mary, the mother of Jesus. We remember the requirements made of our own pioneer women of Nauvoo. Facing unspeakable hardships, they left the comfortable homes which they and their husbands had built with thrift and industry, and they courageously set out to establish new homes in a barren wasteland, driven thence because they had chosen to serve the Lord.

The Lord has always been mindful of those who serve him. Great and marvelous are his benefactions to his children. Did not Joshua remind Israel of this when he declared:

For the Lord our God, he it is that brought us up and our fathers out of the land of Egypt, from the house of bondage, and which did those great signs in our sight, and preserved us in all the way wherein we went, and among all the people through whom we passed. (Joshua 24:17.)

Did the Lord not bless Hannah for her righteousness so that she bore three sons and two daughters, and has her name not been perpetuated through the ages of time because of the righteous works of her son Samuel as a prophet and servant of the Lord? Of all the children whom she bore, it was the son whom she dedicated to the Lord who brought lasting honor to her name.

Did the Lord not bless the arid soil of this desert land that it would yield fruitful crops? Did he not preserve his followers from famine by sending the gulls?

Has he not blessed your household and mine even beyond our greatest hopes when we have served him in full righteousness?

The world today is moving at a fast and reckless pace. The problems, the struggles, the sorrows, and the heartaches press hard upon us. Few there are who are spared. At times, even though we may be living to the best of our knowledge and understanding, we are called upon to pass through experiences the reason for which we fail to understand. Big trials and little ones seem to be the lot of man. Evil influences are threatening our homes and our families. They are at times so subtle as to be almost unrecognizable, yet so powerful as to destroy. We hear on every side: Whither are we heading? Where will it all end? What is to become of us? What are we to do?

For our Relief Society sisters there is but one answer: "As for me and my house, we will serve the Lord." In this commitment lies our hope, our peace, our comfort, our strength, and our promise. In this commitment we fulfill our earthly mission, earning for ourselves exaltation in our Father's kingdom.

TESTIMONY, THE FIRST RESPONSIBILITY OF RELIEF SOCIETY

To search after objects of charity and administer to their needs, to pursue study that tends toward the elevation, development, and advancement of women, to enlarge homemaking talents and increase homemaking skills, to implant and nourish testimonies of the divinity of Jesus Christ and the divine mission of Joseph Smith—these are the fundamental purposes of Relief Society.

Among these purposes, the one of paramount importance is the development of testimony. Having this, all else falls into place, both in our individual lives and in our organization. The gospel of Jesus Christ encompasses all that is good. Charity toward one's fellows is part and parcel of the gospel of Christ. The sister filled with the spirit of testimony is impelled toward seeking after objects of charity and administering to their wants. Alma tells us:

> . . . if ye turn away the needy, and the naked, and visit not the sick and afflicted, and impart of your substance, if ye have, to those who stand in need—I say unto you, if ye do not any of these things, behold . . . ye are as hypocrites who do deny the faith. (Alma 34:28.)

The continued search for light and truth, eternal progression, is a basic teaching of the Church. The Latter-day Saint filled with testimony believes that:

Whatever principle of intelligence we attain unto in this life, it will rise with us in the resurrection.

And if a person gains more knowledge and intelligence in this life through his diligence and obedience than another, he will have so much the advantage in the world to come. (D&C 130:18-19.)

He follows the admonition of the Lord to "seek ye diligently and teach one another words of wisdom; yea, seek ye out of the best books words of wisdom; seek learning, even by study and also by faith. (D & C 88:118.)

If every Latter-day Saint sister had a sure knowledge of the divinity of Christ and the truthfulness of his gospel, she would do the will of the Father; and she would gladly serve as the handmaid of the priesthood in building the kingdom of God on earth; she would willingly work in any capacity in which the Church called her to serve.

To have a testimony contemplates that one accepts, without reservation, that Christ is the Son of God; that he came to earth to redeem God's children; that he suffered and died to atone for the sins of man; that he arose from the dead, bringing to pass the resurrection; that he will come again in his glory; "that all men shall stand before him, to be judged at the last and judgment day, according to their works." (Alma 33:22.)

Testimony contemplates a full acceptance of all of the doctrines taught by Christ and given again in this day through the Prophet Joseph Smith. A concise summary of the doctrines of the gospel was given by Jesus when he showed himself to the multitude gathered together in the land Bountiful.

And this is my doctrine, and it is the doctrine which the Father hath given unto me; and I bear record of the Father, and the Father beareth record of me, and the Holy Ghost beareth record of the Father and me; and I bear record that the Father commandeth all men, everywhere, to repent and believe in me.

And whoso believeth in me, and is baptized, the same shall be saved; and they are they who shall inherit the kingdom of God. (3 Nephi 11:32-33.)

Prophets, ancient and modern, have borne fervent

testimony of these things. Moses, the mighty lawgiver of Israel, sang of God's mercy and vengeance, declaring that "the Lord alone did lead him, and there was no strange god with him." (Deut. 32:12.)

Job, in the midst of the sorest of afflictions, remained steadfast, proclaiming, "I know that my Redeemer liveth."

Alma, in fervent appeal to his people, spoke thus: "Now behold, my brethren, I would ask if ye have read the scriptures? If ye have, how can ye disbelieve on the Son of God?" (Alma 33:14.)

The personal manifestation of God, the Eternal Father, and his Son Jesus Christ, in modern times to the boy Prophet brought forth a testimony that remained unshaken through martyrdom: ". . . For I had seen a vision; I knew it, and I knew that God knew it, and I could not deny it, neither dared I do it. . . ."

The Prophet Joseph Smith was martyred June 27, 1844, but apostles remained to bear testimony, and apostles and prophets have been raised up since that day to bear testimony and carry forward the glorious work of the Redeemer.

We of this day were favored and blessed in hearing President David O. McKay bear testimony in words which rang with conviction:

. . . acceptance of the divinity of Christ's mission and compliance with the principles of his gospel, give assurance of immortality and eternal life.

I testify that a knowledge of his existence and of the truth of his gospel is the source of the greatest comfort and happiness to man.

But testimony is not reserved for God's prophets alone; it is not alone for those who bear the priesthood. It is for all God's children, his daughters as well as his sons.

How then is this precious possession obtained? Alma says:

But behold, if ye will awake and arouse your faculties, even to an experiment upon my words, and exercise a particle of faith, yea, even if ye can no more than desire to believe, let this desire work in you, even until ye believe in a manner that ye can give place for a portion of my words. (Alma 32:27.)

Then he compares the word to a seed planted in the heart, a seed that must be nourished with great care that it may get root, that it may grow up and bring forth fruit.

In John 7:17 we read: "If any man will do his will, he shall know of the doctrine, whether it be of God, or whether I speak of myself." Here, the key is given by the Lord. Following closely the path he marked brings us to the light. If we do not know that Jesus is the Lord, it doesn't mean that he cannot be known to us. It means that it is our duty to find the pathway to the knowledge that Jesus does live. We are not justified in saying that we may not know until we make every effort to know the most important truth in the universe—the divinity of Christ.

The Lord has told us that we shall receive a knowledge of whatsoever things we shall ask in faith with an honest heart, believing that we shall receive. Those who seek in faith and sincerity are promised that the same conviction will come to them that came to Peter: "Thou art the Christ, the Son of the living God." (Matt. 16:16.) To know this is life eternal.

This knowledge comes to one through the Holy Ghost which shall come upon him and dwell in his heart.

A testimony of the divinity of the Christ and of the truthfulness of the restored gospel has within it the power to make us completely happy. The fruits of testimony according to Alma are:

> . . . most precious . . . sweet above all that is sweet . . . white above all that is white, yea, and pure above all that is pure . . . ye shall feast upon this fruit even until ye are filled, that ye hunger not, neither shall ye thirst. (Alma 32:42.)

A firm and unwavering testimony is of first importance to a mother, not for her sake alone but also because of her key position in the home and the potency of her influence upon her children. She is peculiarly situated to implant faith and build testimony, or to cause doubt and discount truth. Children are pliable, receptive to suggestion, direction, and teaching, but once habits of thinking and behavior are established, once beliefs are fixed, it is extremely difficult to modify or change them. Mothers everywhere today are seeking and praying for the safety and protection of their sons and daughters against the forces of evil and temptation so prevalent among us. The surest and strongest protective armor a child can possess is a testimony of the gospel of Jesus Christ. A personal testimony in the mind and heart of the mother is the beginning place in the establishing of it in the mind and heart of her child.

The Relief Society has always been concerned with testimony. The records of the days in Nauvoo report: "The women had recently accepted the restored gospel which stimulated study, discussion and testimony bearing, and directed their activities in accordance with the teachings of the Savior."

Of the early days in the West we read: "One meeting a month was devoted to sewing and caring for the needs of the poor; at the other meetings the members received instruction and encouragement from the discussion of elevating and educational themes, and were comforted and strengthened in their faith in the gospel by bearing their testimonies."

God grant unto you, my sisters, whom I love so dearly, the blessings of a testimony, that your burdens may be light and your souls at rest.

THE STRENGTH OF TESTIMONY

A TESTIMONY of the truth of the gospel of Jesus Christ is a priceless possession. He who has one is indeed blessed. His life has direction and purpose. He is fortified to meet the tempests, and his soul knows peace. He has an appreciation of the true and abiding values of life, while the glittering, shallow, superficial things which challenge the efforts and waste the energies of many men, do not trouble him. He goes forth to meet each day with a love of God and man in his heart and with the calm assurance that God whom he loves also loves him and will direct his course and bless his pursuits.

A testimony is a living, growing thing. It is nourished by faith, prayer, learning, and the application in our daily lives of the principles which we believe; it is strengthened by expression, while powerful testimonies borne by others lend conviction to our own.

Since the beginning of time, countless souls have possessed strong testimonies of the truth of the gospel of our Lord. The ancient patriarchs Adam, Seth, Enoch, Noah, and others, had the gospel. They, no doubt, bore testimony of its truth.

The testimony of Abraham was so strong that when the Lord commanded him to take his son Isaac, whom he

loved, and go to the land of Moriah and offer him there for
a burnt offering, "Abraham rose up early in the morning
and saddled his ass and took his son to the place which
God had told him of." He built an altar and kindled the
fire with his own hands and would have slayed his son in
obedience to God's command had not an angel of the Lord
stayed his hand, saying, "Lay not thine hand upon the lad
. . . for now I know that thou fearest God."

The disciples of Jesus knew for a certainty that he was
the Christ, the Son of the Living God. Jesus asked them,
"Whom do men say that I am?" and Simon Peter answered,
"Thou art the Christ, the Son of the Living God."

So powerful was Paul's testimony before King Agrippa
that the King said unto Paul, "Almost thou persuadest me
to be a Christian."

In the latter days, the truth of the gospel has burned
in the hearts of righteous men, and their testimonies have
strengthened the wavering and pointed the way to "light
and truth" for thousands of souls.

Today we have in our midst good men who are great
by virtue of the power of their testimonies. At our recent
conference, we were privileged to hear these testimonies,
and our own were strengthened because of them. Never in
the vigor of his young manhood was the testimony of President Heber J. Grant more impressive and more convincing
than when, in the full ripeness of his years, he declared, "I
know as I know that I live that it is God's work and that
Jesus Christ is the Son of the Living God, the Redeemer of
the World." This testimony penetrated the hearts and
touched the souls of all who heard it.

The conviction of President J. Reuben Clark, Jr., inspired the people with confidence in Church leadership
when he said, "Of these things I have the same knowledge
that I have that I live. Of all people, we are, with this
knowledge, the most blessed on the earth."

The sincerity of the testimony of President David O.
McKay was revealed in the concluding words of his ad-

dress: ". . . 'a more marvelous work about to come forth among the children of men.' I most sincerely bear witness that the Church of Jesus Christ is that marvelous work."

Testimony is not confined to men alone; women may possess it with equal conviction. The strength of the testimonies of the women of the Church was revealed in our own Relief Society Conference. President Amy Brown Lyman, in addressing the general session of the conference, said:

I believe the greatest motivation in stimulating men to righteous endeavor and living, comes from a testimony. A testimony is more than a collection of facts. It is a combination of knowledge, conviction, faith, and inspiration. It is dynamic and forceful in character. I am persuaded that it is the greatest armor one can have as a protection against temptation, weakness and sin, and the greatest sustaining force in trials and tribulations.

No one can doubt the need in our troubled world for an abiding testimony in the hearts of men and women everywhere of the truth of the gospel. No one can doubt the need for an application of the principles of the gospel in the lives of men and nations. Blessed are Latter-day Saints who are privileged to meet together in semi-annual conferences to learn of God and his ways and to have their testimonies nourished by the inspired wisdom of great souls whose own testimonies never waver.

TESTIMONY—A PRECIOUS HERITAGE

WE have been inspired by accomplishments which bear record that the Lord has had watchcare over his people and his kingdom in this beautiful land. We have had called to mind that from this land have come great and noble ones chosen of the Lord to hold positions of high leadership, influence, and trust in his kingdom.

We know that in addition to all that we have heard and felt today there has been a continuing flow of strength coming to the Church from an endless number of humble, devoted men and women of unwavering testimony whose lives have been unpretentious but whose contributions to the Church have been large.

My grandparents were among this group of faithful, unpretentious souls. My paternal grandparents were from Scotland as was my maternal grandmother. My maternal grandfather was from London.

When she was 17 years old, my maternal grandmother joined the Church in 1854 in Glasgow, along with her brother. Together these young people emigrated to Zion, walking across the great central plains and through the mountains into the Salt Lake Valley. Early snows and bitter cold overtook the little company in the mountains. Shoes were completely worn out and feet were frozen. Bleeding feet carried the Saints into the valley. But their faith remained strong.

When I was a growing, impressionable girl, grandmother lived in our family home. The Church was her life. She faithfully attended Relief Society and sacrament meetings. She was a visiting teacher, going about her district with a little basket on her arm to accept contributions to the poor, the custom at that time.

She always wore to Church on Sunday a black silk dress with a large gold watch which she had brought all the way from Scotland pinned to her blouse. The watch was attached to a somewhat heavy gold chain with a little clasp which her fingers would slide up and down as she attentively listened to the sermons. I would look at her in her silk dress and gold watch and think she was the most elegant woman in the meeting.

One day I said to her, "Grandmother, when you die will you will to me your gold watch that you brought all the way from Scotland?" Her reply has remained with me. She said, "By the time I'm gone, the watch will probably be gone also. I want to leave you something far more precious that I brought from Scotland. I want to leave you the memory of my testimony of the truthfulness of the gospel."

Her testimony, her teachings, the example of her life have been a precious heritage, as they were from my mother, as I feel they are for my children and grandchildren and as I pray they will be on through the generations which follow.

It may be of interest to you to know that descended from that Scottish girl who at age 17 recognized the light of truth in the gospel and whose testimony never wavered to the hour of her death at age 93, and from her faithful brother, there is in the Church today an Apostle and the General President of Relief Society. And descended from the family of which these young people were members, who also joined the Church, there is today a member of the

Presiding Bishopric and the wife of the senior member of the Council of the Twelve. There has been in the past a president of the First Council of the Seventy; there have been mission presidents, stake presidents, high councilmen, bishops, Relief Society presidents, and endless faithful members. There has been a large number of missionaries.

I tell you all this to illustrate the continuing and far-reaching influence of unwavering testimony, and the scope of the strength that may flow to the Church from humble converts.

Women are so positioned in life that what they believe, what they uphold, as a general rule, has pronounced bearing upon what their children believe and what they uphold.

Mothers of the Church must realize this and be firm in their testimonies and in their allegiance to the Church. They must keep their testimonies nourished through activity in the Church. Relief Society is the special organization given of the Lord to his daughters whereby this may be accomplished.

THE STRENGTH OF PRAYER

R ELIEF Society has not fully fulfilled its mission if its many activities do not combine in making of its members, regardless of where they may be located or the circumstances under which they may live, virtuous women and good wives, mothers, and homemakers.

I remind the sisters of the Church that it is a fundamental duty of Relief Society to help mothers to have the proper concept of the eternal nature of the family relationship; to awaken in them high ideals in their daily living; to inspire them with the greatness and joy of their mission as mothers and homemakers; and, continually, to give unto them constructive help in meeting the daily obligations of motherhood and homemaking.

There are two important aspects of motherhood and homemaking—the physical and the spiritual. Both must receive attention in order to assure the comfort, peace, happiness, and eternal well-being of family members. I think perhaps the physical aspects of our homes have never seemed to engage women more than they are doing at the present time. A clean, attractive, well-ordered home is something toward which every homemaker should strive. This does not mean extravagance in expenditures of money, but rather thoughtfulness in planning, skill in organizing, and wisdom in managing. The physical make-up of the home has been said to play an important part in creating and encouraging the spiritual. In fact, we are told by the Lord that ". . . all things unto me are spiritual, and not at any time have I given unto you a law which was temporal . . ." (D&C 29:34.) It is a truth that by her interest in the physical appearance of her home and through the orderly arrangement and conduct of home activities, a mother may influence her sons and daughters to attach great importance to the home.

Important as may be the so-called physical aspects of the home, however, we must never lose sight of the fact that the spirit of the home is the lasting element. Its influence goes on long after the physical is forgotten.

If mothers would have the spirit of the home right, they must maintain homes in which the Spirit of the Lord may dwell—homes that daily meet the requirements of righteousness. They must be obedient to the commandment of the Lord to teach their children "the doctrine of repentance, faith in Christ the Son of the living God, and of baptism and the gift of the Holy Ghost by the laying on of the hands, when eight years old. . . . And they shall also teach their children to pray . . ." (D&C 68:25, 28.)

It is my conviction that there is perhaps no single factor more important in a spiritual home and in building spiritual strength in our children, than the teaching and practice of prayer. Prayer is the medium through which we offer supplication and thanksgiving for the blessings bestowed upon us by the Father. It is the means whereby we confide in him the innermost desires of our hearts and present to him our needs. It is the way whereby we seek his guidance and help. President David O. McKay gave us this beautiful definition of prayer: "Prayer is the pulsation of a yearning, loving heart in tune with the Infinite. It is a message of the soul sent directly to a loving Father. The language is not mere words, but spirit-vibration." (Pathways to Happiness, p. 225.)

In all generations of time men have been admonished to pray. This instruction is not given to satisfy the whims or demands of an autocratic, imperious God who would make his children subservient unto him. Rather, prayer is a choice privilege granted by a kind and loving Father through which his children may obtain promised blessings. The Lord has told us he will be sought by his people for the blessings that they need. He has further said: "Ask, and it shall be given you; seek, and ye shall find; knock, and it shall be opened unto you. For every one that asketh receiveth; and he that seeketh findeth; and to him that knocketh, it shall be opened." (Luke 11:9-10.)

Failure to comply with this commandment has brought not alone a withholding of blessings, but at times severe chastisement, even to God's chosen leaders. The brother of Jared, a large and mighty man, highly favored of the Lord, was visited by the Lord in the land of Moriancumer. The Lord talked with him for three hours and chastened him because he remembered not to call upon the Lord. (Ether 2:14.)

As to the manner of our praying, the Lord has not left us in ignorance. In Matthew we are told "When ye pray, use not vain repetition, as the heathen do . . . for your Father knoweth what things ye have need of, before ye ask him." (Matt. 6:7-8.) Also, we have been taught the pattern of prayer in the simple, brief, worshipful Lord's Prayer.

The scriptures further tell us that our prayers shall ascend to our Heavenly Father as from a holy altar. When we offer prayer, our hearts must be right before him. As we are humble, fervent, submissive, yielding ourselves to the will of the Lord, we shall have his spirit to guide us and our prayers will be heard and answered by an all-wise Father for our greatest ultimate good.

Nor do we need to wonder for what we may properly pray, questioning in our own minds whether we are justified in bringing before the Father our everyday temporal needs as well as our spiritual needs. Amulek, in his teachings to his people, instructed them:

Cry unto him when ye are in your field, yea, over all your flocks.

Cry unto him in your houses, yea, over all your household, both morning, mid-day, and evening.

Yea, cry unto him against the power of your enemies.

Yea, cry unto him against the devil, who is an enemy to all righteousness.

Cry unto him over the crops of your fields, that they may increase.

But this is not all; ye must pour out your souls in your closets, and your secret places, and in your wilderness.

Yea, and when you do not cry unto the Lord, let your hearts be full, drawn out in prayer unto him continually for your welfare, and also for the welfare of those who are around you. (Alma 34: 20-27.)

I sometimes wonder if, as Latter-day Saint mothers, we frequently enough contemplate what our knowledge of the nature of God means in our lives and the lives of our children, how potently it affects our prayers, and how great is our responsibility to implant this knowledge in the hearts and minds of our children.

I recall being invited a few years ago in New York City, to sit in with representatives of other churches on the reading of a script from which it was proposed that programs be made for nationwide use on radio and TV. These programs were designed to increase Sunday School attendance of children. The opening scene of the script presented a majestic church building set in a beautiful garden. As the doors of the church slowly opened, sacred music came forth and the music was God inviting the children to enter the church. Then the flowers spoke and they, too, were God bidding the children to enjoy the beauty of Sunday School. Last, the singing birds called to the children as God, urging them to hear and love his voice. The entire presentation was beautifully written and impressive. However, I felt I could not endorse such a program. I would not wish my children to hear or to view it, since it would give to them a faulty concept of God as I know him, and as I knew it would be vital for my children to know him.

The present accepted view of the immateriality of God is entirely at variance with the scripture and contradicted by revelation. It must not be allowed to enter into the concepts of Latter-day Saint children. Mothers must see to this.

Just as we teach our children the true personality of God, and that he is a kind and loving Father, so also must we teach them that he is omnipotent, unlimited in power, ability and authority, and that they are accountable to him for their every act. They must be taught that they are his children.

Too often today we hear parents say, "Our lives are so complex. The varied duties of family members, with differing hours for performing them, make it difficult if not impossible to bring family members together at one time. Our work is driving us so that we have not time for family prayer."

In a world beset with temptations and the evils of designing men, what mother with a sincere desire for the right spirit to prevail in her home and a genuine concern for the well-being of her children would not make every effort to arrange a time for the family to kneel together in prayer, asking the Father for forgiveness of sins, for peace and rest through the night, and protection and preservation from temptation through the day, beseeching him for guidance in ordering their lives? An inscription on the motto scroll of the coat of arms of Lady Reading, a distinguished Englishwoman whom it is my privilege to know, might well be applied here: "Not why we can't, but how we can."

An impressive quotation comes to my mind:

All the duties of religion are eminently solemn and venerable in the eyes of children. But none will so strongly prove the sincerity of the parent; none so powerfully awaken the reverence of the child; none so happily recommend the instruction he receives, as family devotions, particularly those in which petitions for the children occupy a distinguished place. (*The New Dictionary of Thoughts*, T. Dwight, page 487.)

Important as are our obligations to family prayer, so also must we be conscientious in teaching our children to petition the Father in prayer in the silence of their own rooms for needed blessings, and to acknowledge his goodness unto them.

Fortunate indeed is the child whose mother kneels with him in prayer to petition the Father for help in meeting his little individual problems which may appear to him to be large and vexatious. Shame, I say, on any Latter-day Saint mother who puts her little ones to bed at night without being sure they have said a proper goodnight to their Father in heaven.

Through the ages countless honest and good men have borne testimony to the efficacy of prayer—Abraham, Isaac, Jacob, Moses, Noah, Peter, Paul, Lehi, Enos, Alma, Amulek, to mention but a few. In this dispensation we have the great testimony of the Prophet Joseph Smith, as well as of the prophets who have succeeded him, along with those of countless other righteous men and women. We have the testimony of good men and women not of our faith. There is no testimony so convincing, however, as the testimony within our own hearts. What mother among us could deny the power and blessing of prayer? Its fruits are too great and too numerous to enumerate at this time. Certainly we may say prayer unites every heart within the household. It brings composure to the home and peace to the soul. It offers comfort and guidance. It allays fears. It fortifies against evil. Evil has always been abroad upon the earth. The greatest fortress against it and the strongest defense weapon one may possess, has ever been and always will be good character—character developed through continually seeking to know and understand the will of God through daily communion with him and through obedience to his counsel and commandments. In the building of strong character, one of mankind's most powerful allies has always been prayer.

Brigham Young, early in the history of the Church, declared: "Whether we are poor or rich, if we neglect our prayers and our sacrament meetings, we neglect the Spirit of the Lord, and a spirit of darkness comes over us." (*Discourses of Brigham Young*, p. 170.)

What good mother would wish her children to live in darkness? Let her remember, then, that a person does not, as a rule, suddenly become a praying individual when he reaches adolescence or maturity. Prayer, born of faith, must be planted as a seed in infancy and carefully nurtured through the years. The mother is the person best positioned to do this for her child.

In conclusion, may I read a few lines from Alfred Lord Tennyson's *Morte d'Arthur.*

> More things are wrought by prayer
> Than this world dreams of. Wherefore, let thy voice
> Rise like a fountain for me night and day.
> For what are men better than sheep or goats
> That nourish a blind life within the brain,
> If, knowing God, they lift not hands of prayer
> Both for themselves and those who call them friend?
> For so the whole round earth is every way
> Bound by gold chains about the feet of God.

In this age of mechanical wonders, when the material things of life are absorbing the minds and hearts of men, may our Latter-day Saint mothers keep the spiritual balance and may this great God-given organization for women help them to do so.

PRAYER—OUR ANCHOR OF TRUST AND SAFETY

THERE probably has never been a time in the history of the world when the prayers of the righteous were more needed, and there has never been a time when humanity more needed to pray.

That evil is rampant in the world, none can gainsay. Its influences are so strong and its impacts so powerful that resistance requires fortitude and stamina. Things which are "not good for man" are not only allowed but are encouraged. Liberty has in too many instances become license. A spirit of recklessness characterizes our time, and an attitude of "what's the use?" prevails. A powerful restraining influence is needed.

We need to pray, our children need to pray, that we may constantly be reminded that a Supreme Father rules over all, that life has purpose and direction; that like David of old we may feel and know that there is no spot so dark and no place so far removed that the all-seeing eye of God is not upon us, and that we will be held accountable for our deeds. There is no finer, no more wholesome, no more powerful restraining influence than an unwavering belief in God, a God who is continually watching over us. Our belief in God becomes strong through prayer.

In today's world we are sorely in need of the comforting and sustaining influence of prayer. Distress is all about us; the very foundations of our social order seem to be shifting. Mankind feels insecure, wondering what the future holds.

When the conflicts of life are greatest, when we realize most of our own inadequacies, a belief in God is an unfailing source of comfort and strength. If we will but seek the Father in fervent and humble prayer, a God of understanding and love will sustain us in our trials and inspire and direct us onward. The Lord has said: "All victory and glory is brought to pass unto you through your diligence, faithfulness and prayers of faith." (D&C 104:36.)

Prayer is an expression of faith, and it is by faith, which impels to obedience, that we obtain our blessings.

The Savior commanded his disciples to pray unceasingly and always in his name. He had in mind their welfare. He loved his disciples and was concerned for their well-being. It was prayer that shook the heavens, turned the key in the lock, and opened up the glories of a new gospel dispensation—the prayer of a guileless, fourteen-year-old boy. It will be our prayers, our constant petitions, both in the silence of our chambers and as we kneel with our family groups, that will be our anchor of trust and safety in a disturbed world.

SEARCH THE SCRIPTURES

THROUGHOUT the sessions of any conference, as well as in most meetings of the Church, frequent reference is made to the word of the Lord to his children as recorded in the sacred scriptures. This teaching is one of the foremost functions of the Church. The Church has four volumes of scripture referred to as the standard works of the Church:

(1) The Bible, containing the Old and New Testaments, translated out of the original tongues.

(2) The Book of Mormon, an abridgement of the record of peoples formerly living on the American Continent. This book, according to the preface, is "to show unto the remnant of the House of Israel what great things the Lord hath done for their fathers; . . . And also to the convincing of the Jew and Gentile that *Jesus* is the *Christ*, the *Eternal God.*" This volume of scripture has a place beside the Bible as a spiritual guide to mankind. The Prophet Ezekiel made a significant prophecy relative to these two volumes being one in the hands of the Lord for his children in the latter days:

The word of the Lord came again unto me, saying,

Moreover, thou son of man, take thee one stick, and write upon it, For Judah, and for the children of Israel his companions: then

take another stick, and write upon it, For Joseph, the stick of Eph-
raim, and for all of the house of Israel his companions:

And join them one to another into one stick; and they shall
become one in thine hand. (Ezek. 37:15-17.)

(3) The Doctrine and Covenants, containing revelations given to the Prophet Joseph Smith, with some addi-
tions by his successors in the Presidency of the Church.

(4) The Pearl of Great Price, containing visions of
Moses revealed to Joseph Smith the Prophet, and the
translation of ancient records—the writings of Abraham
while he was in Egypt—which came into the hands of the
Prophet.

These are not the only scriptures, however. All scriptures are not found within the standard works. We believe
in continuous revelation and that those teachings which
come from our prophet today ". . . when moved upon by
the Holy Ghost, shall be scripture, shall be the will of the
Lord, shall be the mind of the Lord, shall be the word of
the Lord, shall be the voice of the Lord, and the power of
God unto salvation." (D&C 68:4.)

I wonder how often we contemplate the importance
in our lives of these sacred writings. How often do we ponder on what our lives would be if these volumes were
sealed against us. The loss would be incalculable. Conversely, I wonder how often we count the great blessings
which flow to us through having these scriptures readily
available for individual reading and study.

The Lord made clear to Nephi what it meant to possess the sacred record of the Jews which was in the hands
of Laban. When the Lord directed that Lehi and his family should possess this record and Laman sought to obtain
it, Laban grew angry and thrust Laman out of his presence.
Then by commandment of the Lord Nephi sought to obtain the record. The Lord delivered Laban into the hands
of Nephi, and it became necessary that Nephi should kill
Laban or fail in his purpose. Never at any time had Nephi
shed the blood of a man, and he shrank from so doing.

Then the Spirit said unto him: "It is better that one man should perish than that a nation should dwindle and perish in unbelief." (I Nephi 4:13.)

Nephi remembered the word of the Lord spoken to him in the wilderness:

> . . . Inasmuch as thy seed shall keep my commandments, they shall prosper in the land of promise.
>
> Yea, and I also thought that they could not keep the commandments of the Lord according to the law of Moses, save they should have the law.
>
> And I also know that the law was engraven upon the plates of brass. (I Nephi 4:14-16.)

Therefore, Nephi obeyed the voice of the Spirit, and the record was obtained.

Individuals have not always had the scriptures in their possession. At one time the people at large had to depend upon the teachings of their scribes and priests. Today we are abundantly blessed in that everyone who will do so may possess these valuable volumes containing the will of God for his children, the divine plan of life and salvation, the gospel of Jesus Christ. We may open them in our own homes and read the teachings and commandments of the Lord, ponder upon them and apply them to our own lives.

President Joseph Fielding Smith in a General Relief Society Conference said that there should not be a Latter-day Saint home in all the world where there would not be found a Bible, a Book of Mormon, the Doctrine and Covenants, and the Pearl of Great Price. This statement would apply, of course, only where these latter volumes are translated into the native tongues. These books should be conveniently at hand, inviting their use, and where family members may view them as a part of the make-up of the home. And it is mandatory upon us and to our eternal advantage that we search them diligently.

The Doctrine and Covenants counsels us: "Yea, seek ye out of the best books words of wisdom, seek learning, even by study and also by faith." (D&C 88:118.)

The best books are certainly those which contain the words of God, books that build faith in God—his holy scriptures.

The Prophet Joseph Smith admonished:

Search the scriptures—search the revelations which we publish, and ask our Heavenly Father, in the name of his Son Jesus Christ, to manifest the truth unto you, and if you do it with an eye single to His glory, nothing doubting, He will answer you by the power of His Holy Spirit. You will then know for yourselves and not for another. You will not then be dependent on man for the knowledge of God; nor will there be any room for speculation. (*Teachings of the Prophet Joseph Smith*, pp. 11-12.)

This admonition is for every individual. Each one must search for himself. Upon parents rests also an added responsibility to guide and direct children in their search, of implanting in the hearts of their children a love and a reverence for the word of God as set forth in the scriptures. It is their duty to train children in the use of the scriptures, for the Lord has made clear that it is the duty of parents to see that children are reared in light and in truth. How better can this be done than through familiarizing them with the word of the Lord as contained in the scriptures. While the Church with its priesthood quorums and auxiliaries plays a vital supporting role in teaching the gospel, the primary responsibility rests with parents.

Mothers are particularly favored in meeting this responsibility since they are with the children in the home for more hours of the day than is the father.

Brigham Young said:

Education commences with the mother and the child . . . It depends in a great degree upon the mother, as to what children receive in early age, of principle of every description pertaining to all that can be learned by the human family. . . . The character of a person is formed through life, to a greater or less degree, by the teachings of the mother. The traits of early impression that she gives the child, will be characteristic points in his character through every avenue of his mortal existence. (*Journal of Discourses*, Vol. 1, pp. 66-67.)

The scriptures themselves bear testimony of the truth-fulness of the influence of the mother in these matters. Paul, writing to his dearly beloved Timothy, speaks of Timothy's childhood training as follows:

When I call to remembrance the unfeigned faith that is in thee, which dwelt first in thy grandmother Lois, and thy mother Eunice; and I am persuaded that in thee also. (II Tim. 1:5.)

Paul further wrote:

But continue thou in the things which thou hast learned and hast been assured of, knowing of whom thou hast learned them;

And that from a child thou hast known the holy scriptures, which are able to make thee wise unto salvation through faith which is in Christ Jesus. (II Tim. 3:14-15.)

I know of one young mother whose familiarity with and love for the scriptures came to her largely after her marriage to a returned missionary. So meaningful did they become in her life that she has conscientiously devoted herself to helping her children to know and appreciate them. Today her ten-year-old girl and eight-year-old boy have their own copies of the standard works. At first, as very little ones, they were provided with illustrated stories from the Bible and Book of Mormon. Mother read these to the children. Later the children, as they learned to read, would read the stories back to Mother. Then as they read from their story book Mother would read the same story, in whole or in part as the children were able to comprehend, from the scripture itself, explaining to the children the dif-ference between the book from which she was reading and the story book from which they read. Always she empha-sized the greater value of the scripture, implanting in the children a special regard for it. Later as the children be-came ready they would read to mother a familiar story from the scripture itself. It was then they were given their own volumes. When a simple verse had special meaning for the children Mother would take time to help them mem-orize it and mark it in their own books.

When the children are given opportunity to talk in Sunday School or other Church gatherings they select their subject from their own books, with mother's interested help and guidance. The selection is usually a principle of the gospel such as prayer, sabbath observance, or Word of Wisdom, rather than a story.

A regular practice in the home is for the father to inquire at dinner on Sunday, "What was your Sunday School lesson about?" Then after dinner the father makes a practice of helping the children find something about their lesson in their books. Mother teaches Primary. The children and their scriptures are brought actively into her lesson preparation. Thus acquaintance with the scripture has been handled in a way that has brought happy companionship with mother and father as well as light and truth into the lives of the children, along with an acquaintance with these great books.

In addition, the hours spent together with the word of the Lord are bound to develop a close family unity, which in itself will bring rich rewards.

In this day of intensified missionary effort, Latter-day Saint mothers, imbued with a testimony of the gospel, strive earnestly to prepare their sons and daughters to receive a call to missionary service. Is not a knowledge of the scriptures and training in how to effectively use them a vital part of this preparation? The scriptures are without doubt the great proselyting tools of the missionary. Fortunate indeed is the young man or woman who goes into the mission field knowing his tools and how to use them. He is able to speak with power and authority to the convincing of his hearers.

The Book of Mormon points this fact out with reference to the missionary labors of the sons of Mosiah who, along with Alma the younger, persecuted the Church and then were miraculously converted, as was Paul. Following their conversion the sons of Mosiah filled a mission to the Lamanites. One day as Alma was journeying in the Land of Gideon southward he met with the sons of Mosiah. He rejoiced to see his brethren and,

. . . what added more to his joy, they were still his brethren in the Lord, yea, and they had waxed strong in the knowledge of the truth; for they were men of a sound understanding and *they had searched the scriptures diligently,* that they might know the word of God.

But this is not all; they had given themselves to much prayer, and fasting; therefore they had the spirit of prophecy, and the spirit of revelation, and when they taught, they taught with power and authority of God.

. . . by the power of their words many were brought before the altar of God, to call on his name and confess their sins before him. (Alma 17:2-4, italics added.)

The vast content of the scriptures cannot be mastered in a moment or a day. It is a lifetime labor. I recall that several years ago when Relief Society sisters were studying the Book of Mormon every sister was expected to read the book in its entirety. As a special feature of the general conference and to encourage the sisters in their efforts, a brother was invited to speak to them on the subject of the Book of Mormon. Last minute circumstances, however, made it impossible for him to attend the conference. It became necessary to obtain another speaker the morning of the day on which the address was scheduled. Elder Matthew Cowley was enlisted. He delivered a masterful address, in which he bore this impressive testimony:

I would like to bear my testimony to you about the book which you are studying in Relief Society, the Book of Mormon. I know nothing about archaeology. I have not studied the maps which apparently relate to the Book of Mormon, the travels of the Lehites, the Lamanites, and so forth. I know very little about the outside evidences of the Book of Mormon, but I have a testimony of the divinity of this book, and that testimony has come to me from within the two covers of the book itself. ("Testimony Through Reading the Book of Mormon," *The Relief Society Magazine,* Jan., 1953, pp. 7-8.)

In appreciation I said to Brother Cowley, "I marvel that you could give such a magnificent and convincing address with so little time in which to prepare!" To this Brother Cowley responded, "What do you mean by little time in which to prepare? I had plenty of time. I have had a lifetime. My preparation for that address began when I was a little boy at my mother's knee."

The Lord has said: "He that seeketh me early shall find me, and shall not be forsaken." (D&C 88:83.)

In Second Timothy, we read:

All scripture is given by inspiration of God, and is profitable for doctrine, for reproof, for correction, for instruction in righteousness:

That the man of God may be perfect, thoroughly furnished unto all good works. (II Tim. 3:16-17.)

May the Lord bless us to love and appreciate these sacred writings and to follow their admonitions. May he help us as mothers to train our children to do likewise I sincerely pray.

THOSE WHO ENDURE TO THE END

"T HE race is not to the swift, nor the battle to the strong, but to him that endureth to the end."

To *endure* is to maintain the capability of holding out, of lasting, of continuing in the same state without weakening or perishing. It is the power to continue under pain, hardship, discouragement or suffering without being overcome.

History is replete with goals that have been realized and battles that have been won, not by those who made a brilliant beginning or an impressive first stand but by those who had the power to remain firm, patiently to overcome obstacles, to be constant in their efforts.

The scriptures offer a priceless blessing to those who accept the gospel of Christ and who endure to the end. The scriptures refer to this fact not once but a number of times. One of the numerous passages dealing with this admonition and its blessing reads as follows: "And, if you keep my commandments and endure to the end you shall have eternal life, which gift is the greatest of all the gifts of God." (D&C 14:7.)

Eternal life is a gift every Latter-day Saint worthy of the name desires. Yet in this complex world of trouble and testing, and handicapped as we are with human weaknesses and imperfections, it is not always easy to endure throughout life. To do so requires firm faith, strong convictions, sterling character. Failure often comes to us because we are insensitive to the fact that faulty attitudes have developed and behavior counter to the will of God has gradually been adopted. Then, we tend to justify these attitudes and actions without being aware that they are adversely affecting our lives.

May I relate an experience. Authorization, as many of you know, has been given by the Brethren for Relief Societies, under specified circumstances, to be organized in nursing or residential homes for older sisters. One day I visited such a Relief Society. The members were between 75 and 90 years of age. They were ambulatory, bright of mind, and enthusiastic over their Society. The lesson was from the Doctrine and Covenants and was followed by testimony bearing. The sisters contributed intelligently to the lesson discussions. Their offerings reflected a knowledge of Church doctrine and familiarity with the gospel, as well as rich life experiences. It was a delightful meeting. Then came the testimony period. Each sister who spoke, one by one, prayed that she would endure to the end. As I contemplated their intelligent understanding of the gospel as demonstrated in the discussion, and as I considered how late in life it was for most of them, I thought, why would they pray that they might endure to the end? Surely they have already proved themselves.

Later, however, in private conversation with some of them, I was made aware that they were not entirely above reproach, that they had a tendency to excuse themselves for failures to comply with the laws of the gospel because of age and circumstances.

These are a few comments made by these sisters as I talked with them:

One sister said, "We have sacrament meeting here at the home, as well as Relief Society, but I never go to sacrament meeting. I am too old to be preached to." I inquired, "Don't you feel a need to partake of the sacrament?" "No," the sister indifferently replied. "I don't think it matters at my age."

Another sister said, "I want to move to a little better home. I have enough money to do so. I have no one on whom to spend my money but myself. My family does not need it, and I am no longer interested in doing things for others that cost money. I don't even pay tithing. I don't think the Lord expects it of one my age."

Still another sister, who was drinking tea as I called, said, "I almost live on tea. When I was a younger woman, you couldn't have hired me to drink a cup of tea, but I don't think it will be held against me now."

Yet another said, as we heard footsteps near the door, "I hope that's not my daughter. She only comes because she fears criticism if she doesn't. She has very little love for me, and I have very little for her."

One more comment: "I seem to be growing weaker every day, suffering as I do with pain. I used to have the elders administer to me, but I don't believe in that anymore."

Attendance at sacrament meeting, partaking of the sacrament, renewing one's covenants, the payment of tithing, observance of the Word of Wisdom, love of family, priesthood administration—all basic laws of the gospel—had been abandoned by one or the other of these sisters with a feeling of justification; yet each had earnestly prayed that she might endure to the end.

Sympathetic as we may be toward these sisters and toward their circumstances, and understanding as we may be of their actions, yet we must recognize that with clear minds they were justifying the nonobservance of God's laws. I am led to ask also, "Has the Lord ever set a retirement age for keeping his commandments?"

Nor is it during the later years of life only that people grow careless. During the younger years there are those who violate their covenants, weaken in defense of right, disobey commandments which they know to be important, and rationalize their nonallegiance to Church teachings. Social pressures, the enticements of fashion, the desire to be like others whom one would cultivate but who do not have the same light to guide them, adversity, unfulfilled expectations, disappointment—all of these sometimes press hard upon one and break him down at a weak point, opening the door for Satan to step in.

Sometimes we engage in behavior counter to the teachings of the Church with the feeling, "I know it's not right, but I don't intend to make a practice of this. Once or twice won't hurt." The once or twice, however, soon become more frequent until the behavior develops into a habit. Also, as one weakens at one point, it becomes easy to weaken at another. I ask, "Wouldn't it be easy for one who discontinues regular attendance at sacrament meetings to lose sight of the importance of keeping the Sabbath day holy?" I fear that it would. Thus, error subtly creeps into our lives, and the promised blessings for those who endure to the end are in jeopardy.

How then may we avoid the pitfalls which lead us away from the straight and narrow path? How may we muster the strength to endure to the end?

First, I would suggest continuous Church activity to the full measure of one's opportunities and capacities.

I would recommend a study of the scriptures with meditation upon the promised blessings of obedience to the respective commandments. What is more desired than the blessings promised by the Lord for obedience to the Word of Wisdom?

And all saints who remember to keep and do these sayings, walking in obedience to the commandments, shall receive health in their navel and marrow to their bones;

And shall find wisdom and great treasures of knowledge, even hidden treasures;

And shall run and not be weary, and shall walk and not faint.

And I, the Lord, give unto them a promise, that the destroying angel shall pass by them, as the children of Israel, and not slay them. (D&C 89:18-21.)

Consider the promise to the tithe payer:

Bring ye all the tithes into the storehouse, that there may be meat in mine house, and prove me now herewith, saith the Lord of hosts, if I will not open you the windows of heaven, and pour you out a blessing, that there shall not be room enough to receive it. (Mal. 3:10.)

For those who must be convinced through personal experience, let them heed the words of Alma:

But behold, if ye will awake and arouse your faculties, even to an experiment upon my words, and exercise a particle of faith, yea, even if ye can no more than desire to believe, let this desire work in you, even until ye believe in a manner that ye can give place for a portion of my words. (Alma 32:27.)

I remind you that spiritual strength comes through worthily partaking of the sacrament. This we do as we attend the meeting required of us by the Lord—the sacrament meeting.

Would it not be well occasionally to let our minds dwell upon the blessings rather than upon the adversities of our lives? Let us consider the countless times our prayers have been answered against the few times when the Lord in his wisdom may have given a negative answer.

Let us avoid the tendency to justify disobedience to God's commandments because of circumstances as we would avoid a plague.

It may be useful, also, to remember that strength grows with practice and that the Lord helps those who earnestly seek his help through fasting and prayer.

Regardless of the adversities of life and the difficulties encountered in striving faithfully to endure, success can be achieved; people can overcome obstacles, and they can be constant in their faith and in their obedience to the laws of the Father.

The Bible gives us an impressive example in the account of Joseph, son of Jacob. Joseph was born when his loving father was in his old age. He found himself, through the chicanery of his brothers, finally living in Egypt in the court of Potiphar. Imagine this boy, sent by his father on a mission to his brothers, advancing toward them in all the unsuspecting openness of brotherly affection, finding them to be his unnatural assailants, consumed with hatred toward him and determined to rid themselves of him. A Bible commentary says,

> It is impossible that mere envy . . . or the doting partiality of their common father could have goaded them on to such a pitch of frenzied resentment. . . . Their hatred of Joseph must have been produced by a dislike . . . of his excellencies which made his character and conduct a constant censure upon theirs. . . .

In the Egyptian household of an idolator, the boy had to contend with strange conditions. Though separated from his father, Jacob, he was not separated from his Heavenly Father. He faithfully and zealously served God and kept his commandments. This sometimes brought him earthly advantages. At other times, however, it brought him extreme suffering—even imprisonment. (Genesis 41: 14.)

But the Lord blessed Joseph all the days of his life because of his faithfulness, and through him he blessed his father's household as well. Joseph's words in remonstrance to Potiphar's wife when she made the most infamous advance a woman can make toward a man, was characteristic of his response to every evil that beset his path: "How then can I do this great wickedness and sin against God?" (Genesis 39:9.)

Joseph lived 80 years after his elevation to the chief power of Egypt, giving continuous proof of his faith and the assurance of the promise of the Lord to those who keep his commandments. His entire life was characterized by righteous professions supported by conscientious and righteous conduct.

In the New Testament we learn of Paul—first a persecutor of the Christians, then a devoted follower of Christ, a teacher, a missionary, an apostle—who at the close of life could say with confidence:

I have fought a good fight, I have finished my course, I have kept the faith:

Henceforth there is laid up for me a crown of righteousness, which the Lord, the righteous judge, shall give me at that day: and not to me only, but unto all them also that love his appearing. (II Tim. 4:7-8.)

The Book of Mormon gives many striking examples of men who kept the faith and endured to the end: Lehi, Jacob, Mormon, Enos, Abinadi, and others.

May I refresh your minds with regard to Abinadi, a Nephite prophet whom the Lord raised up to reprove the wicked people of King Noah for their sins. His bold denunciations of their abominations ended in his being cast into prison. The evil priests clamored to slay him,

And they stood forth and attempted to lay their hands on him; but he withstood them, and said unto them:

Touch me not, for God shall smite you if ye lay your hands upon me, for I have not delivered the message which the Lord sent me to deliver . . . therefore, God shall not suffer that I shall be destroyed at this time. (Mosiah 13:2-3.)

The scripture tells us further that they had no power to slay him because he was protected by divine power. In his humility, Abinadi reveals his complete surrender to the work of the Lord: "But I finish my message; and then it matters not whether I go, if it so be that I am saved." (Mosiah 13:9.)

Faithful unto martyrdom, surely the promise of salvation made to those who endure to the end would be the blessing of Abinadi.

This dispensation, too, offers many examples of those who have had the strength to endure in the face of great trials and suffering. To each of our minds come examples of women, as well as men, some of them simple, unpretentious souls; others, those holding places of prominence and trust.

Let us keep these faithful souls in remembrance as an example. They were not fictitious characters from an imaginary past. They were human beings living in the world of reality, just as are we. Let each of us strive to be among those who remain faithful. True, it is hard to resist temptations, to rise above trouble and keep our faith strong. It is easy to succumb to those evils that temporarily comfort the flesh, particularly in our declining years; it is not always easy to remain constant and to avoid the human weakness of justifying the error of our ways. But this we can and must do if we would enjoy the blessings promised by the Lord to those who endure to the end.

How wonderful it would be, what a good world this would be if each one of us would so live as to be able to say at the close of life as did Paul, "I have finished my course, I have kept the faith."

OUR AVAILABLE WEALTH

A LOCAL newspaper recently published an interesting item titled "Woman Lives in Poverty But Leaves Two Million." While this woman lived as though in destitute circumstances and obtained advantage of low rates intended only for the poor, she was worth nearly $2,000,000.

This was indicated when her safety deposit boxes were opened. Among deeds to valuable properties and deposit slips for money in American and foreign institutions, there was $125,000 in U.S. government securities for which the coupons had not been clipped since 1935.

She had $900,000 in foreign securities and 404,358 francs on deposit in Paris; $25,000 on deposit in the Toledo Trust Company, and parcels of valued Toledo land, examination of her papers indicated.

It was learned that a Toledo attorney, believing she was poor, had charged her only $8 for legal services recently.

We saner mortals not only pity this woman but wonder at her lack of wisdom in not using her available wealth to secure the good things of life. Having at her command sufficient wealth to satisfy any normal desire, to live in ease and comfort, we are aghast at her judgment in choosing to live a life of poverty.

Such a philosophy of life is almost beyond our understanding. Yet, the worldly wealth to which this woman had access was paltry compared to the wealth offered to the humblest Latter-day Saint. The Lord has said,

The kingdom is yours and the blessings thereof are yours, and the riches of eternity are yours.

And he who receiveth all things with thankfulness shall be made glorious; and the things of this earth shall be added unto him, even an hundred fold, yea, more.

And he that is a faithful and wise steward shall inherit all things. (D&C 78:18-20, 22.)

The securities listed here are unlike those found in the safety deposit boxes of this unfortunate woman. Here is a promissory note given by the one infallible banker. Here is a promise to pay not $2,000,000 but all the riches of eternity. Are we wisely making use of the wealth available to us, or, like the foolish woman, do we prefer to live impoverished? We clearly see her lack of wisdom. Yet, many Latter-day Saints are neglecting to take advantage of the spiritual wealth freely offered them and are content to live spiritually poor. They choose for associates those who are spiritually undernourished.

All this woman had to do to benefit from her wealth was to go to the safety deposit box, convert her securities into cash, and buy according to her desires.

Latter-day Saints must go to the scriptures, our safety deposit box of knowledge, then must our knowledge be converted into good acts, and lo! the riches of eternity are ours.

FRIENDLINESS IN CHURCH GATHERINGS

A POPULAR magazine recently published an account of a little orphan girl, eight years of age, who journeyed nearly 8,000 miles alone, to the United States from Norway, her name and destination stitched on the inside of her coat. Her knowledge of the English language was limited to two words, "Mickey Mouse." After landing in New York, the little traveler rested a few days and then was placed on a train by an attache of the Traveler's Aid Society and sent an additional 3,155 miles to San Francisco, where the gentleman who had adopted her received her at the final terminus of a long trek. Greeting her in her native tongue, the gentleman asked, "How do you like America?" Enthusiastically the little girl answered, "I am glad I came to America. Everybody adopted me." The memories of her long trip were of kindnesses received along the way. She was alone and yet not alone. Everyone she had met had extended the hand of friendliness, and the long road had been made bright by human kindness. The magazine concludes the story by saying: "It is comforting in times of universal turmoil to read of something wondrously beautiful, something not yet perished from the souls of men."

Friendliness and human kindness are universal needs of mankind. Without them one is lonely and embittered with them one's spirit is light and he rises above the things that would defeat him. However, in every community, in schools, churches, clubs, or social organizations, there are those who are denied these things. For one reason or another they stand on the edge of things. Sometimes it is because they are critical and bitter, condemning other people as snobs, blaming circumstances, feeling that they are unappreciated and misunderstood, that people are unfair to them. Sometimes they remain on the outside because they feel inadequate—financially, socially, or otherwise. Sometimes something has occurred in their lives that makes them withdraw. Sometimes they are not a part of things merely because they are by nature diffident and retiring. Wistful people, they innately yearn to be a vital part of the group, to be friendly and to win friends, but they remain lonely because they do not know how to freely mingle with others.

No matter what the cause, he who feels outside the group and who remains on the edge of things is to be sympathized with, and understanding effort should be made to bring him in and to make him feel an integral part of the whole.

Too frequently those who should be alert to his situation, those who are in a position to draw him in, either fail to recognize his need or are so absorbed in other (and often less important) things that they do not take time. In some instances they thoughtlessly contribute to his feeling of loneliness.

This frequently happens in our Church gatherings, even in Relief Society. A letter received at the general office a short time ago read: "There are a few things that have been fretting me which I mention for your consideration. A lady who has been active and lived in the ward most of her life said she had bet her family that she could go to Sunday School and sacrament meeting and not have one person speak to her, except perhaps the bishop at the evening meeting. She claimed this happened. It has also happened on other occasions."

Church gatherings should be the most friendly gatherings in the world because the Church is built upon the divine principle of brotherhood. The terms "brother" and "sister," so universally used in the Church are symbols of the fellow feeling that should characterize us upon all occasions and under all circumstances as The Church of Jesus Christ of Latter-day Saints. There is no organization more concerned with the well-being and happiness of mankind.

Elder Melvin J. Ballard said upon one occasion, "The future growth and strength of the Church depends upon our ability to win and hold and save our fellowmen." Friendliness wins and holds as do few other things. The Prophet Joseph Smith, in addressing the Relief Society sisters, said: "When persons manifest the least kindness and love to me, oh what power it has over my mind."

Through cooperative effort, the spirit of "gladly meeting, kindly greeting" should distinguish all Church gatherings. Everyone attending any of our meetings should feel as did that little Norwegian girl, that "everybody has adopted" him.

"FEED MY SHEEP"

WHEN Peter, deeply repentant, asked his Lord what he should do to prove himself, he was told, "Feed my sheep." The importance of this behest was made manifest by repeated emphasis: "Simon, son of Jonas, lovest thou me?" Then, "Feed my sheep."

Even as Peter was to show his love for the Master by giving the "bread of life" to all who would partake, so we in latter days must demonstrate our love.

In the world today there are thousands of souls hungering for the "bread of life," seeking the nourishment that only it can give. Those having this precious food are under obligation to share it, no matter where they may be, no matter what may be the work they are engaged in.

In counseling the Relief Society sisters, the Prophet Joseph recalled the Master's words to Peter, saying, "If the sisters love the Lord, let them feed the sheep." And he further counseled: "Let your labors be mostly confined to those around you, in the circle of your own acquaintance."

The women of the Church have endeavored to follow this counsel. Their love of the Master has been manifested by the service they have rendered "to those around them." Reaching out and touching the hearts of women in communities throughout the world, they have drawn them in to partake of the bounteous feast of the Lord; and these women, having in their turn partaken, have become dispensers of the food to others until from a humble beginning of 18 members, we now visualize 300,000 women feeding his sheep.

There are, however, in every community many indifferent shepherds and many unfed sheep. Though each week the table is spread, there are still those who do not partake of the feast because they do not know of it or because they are waiting for someone to fetch them to it.

Those who have had the good fortune to sit at the table and partake of the feast know the bounteousness and benefits of it. They also know their responsibility to share it with others. It is not enough to say to our sisters, "Come, join us." We must go into the highways and byways seeking and searching, even as did the Savior when he dispensed the "bread of life," until all have been brought in to the fold. Indifferent shepherds must awake, and all who know the truth must carry the message to those who know it not.

Peter grew great in the service of the Lord; so has Relief Society grown in greatness through service; so will it continue to grow as it feeds his sheep.

SOURCES OF SPIRITUAL REFRESHMENT

T HESE days should find us often in the house of worship. It is inevitable that we gain composure and inward strength through Church attendance. Even though the surroundings may not be entirely to our liking, the sermon not appeal to us, and the music leave much to be desired, it is there that we commune with the Father, it is there that we partake of the sacrament and renew our covenants, it is there that we contemplate the eternal plan and see life in its true perspective. Those who attend church in a true spirit of worship leave better fortified to cope with conditions, no matter how serious they may be.

These are days when time spent reading the scriptures brings spiritual renewal. Five minutes a day spent with the scriptures would instill hope and build a faith that would be a power in meeting our trials. Who would not be comforted by reading of David's confidence in God's grace when he said, "The Lord is my shepherd, I shall not want"? (Psalms 23:1.) Who would not have his confidence restored by the words to latter-day Israel, "Therefore, fear not, little flock; do good; let earth and hell combine against you, for if ye are built upon my rock, they cannot prevail." (D&C 6:34.) Who could remain utterly helpless and discouraged after reading such passages as: "God is our refuge and strength, a very present help in trouble. Therefore will not we fear, though the earth be removed, and though the mountains be carried into the midst of the sea." (Psalms 46:1-2.)

Yes, in the scriptures there is comfort, encouragement, and hope. In them one finds that which uplifts, builds, and strengthens.

Conditions in the world today are serious—sufficiently serious to demand our supreme effort in maintaining self-control and morale. Conditions are so unusual as to tax our greatest powers of adjustment. But Latter-day Saints can remain composed, they can calm the frenzy of others, they can still purposefully direct their lives and intelligently adjust to whatever comes if they place confidence in their leaders, if they study the word of God and do his bidding, if they commune with him often, both in their homes and in the house of worship. These are the sources from which we may draw courage and strength to meet these precarious times.

SPIRITUAL STRENGTH THROUGH SABBATH OBSERVANCE

S uch times are upon us today that anxiety is the present lot of mankind, and only those who are spiritually strong can triumph.

"But," we ask, "how may one grow strong in spirit? What are the foods which nourish this part of man?" President Joseph F. Smith gives answer in these words: "It is the purpose of the Gospel and the holy Priesthood . . . to benefit mankind spiritually." (*Gospel Doctrine*, p. 261.) He further states that the Lord designed that all Latter-day Saint people should become the richest of all people in heavenly gifts—in spiritual blessings.

We must remember, however, that even though the richest of spiritual blessings are designed for Latter-day Saints, they will not come to us as individuals through inertia or indifference—they will come only as the result of faithfulness and diligence. They come through knowledge and obedience, sacrifice and service. They come through keeping ourselves attuned to the mind and will of the Father.

The Father has commanded us to "remember the Sabbath Day and keep it holy." He has also told us through modern revelation: "It is expedient that the Church meet together often and partake of bread and wine in remembrance of the Lord Jesus." (D&C 20:75.) "And that thou mayest more fully keep thyself unspotted from the world, thou shalt go to the house of prayer and offer up thy sacraments upon my holy day." (D&C 59:9.)

Obedience to these commandments brings a renewal of both physical and spiritual strength.

The week days of the average individual today are crowded with new and unusual tasks. The majority of us are overworked. How easy it is, particularly for mothers who during week days are employed outside the home, to leave for the Sabbath day odd jobs that they have been too busy to attend to on other days. Because the work demands of week days are so strenuous, they feel justified in using the Sabbath as a day for catching up on undone work rather than a day of rest and worship. But there is no excuse for robbing the Lord's day of its sanctity. Work should be so planned and affairs so managed that on the Sabbath we may lay aside our week-day tasks, pay our devotions to our Heavenly Father, and obtain needed physical and spiritual refreshment.

To attend sacrament meeting on the Sabbath should be regarded by Latter-day Saints not as a burdensome requirement, but as a glorious privilege. The sacrament meeting provides opportunity for us to partake of the sacrament, thereby renewing our covenants with our Heavenly Father and testifying that we are willing to serve him and keep his commandments; it is a period wherein we may worship the Father in humility and prayer; it is an hour of repentance and a time for meditation upon God's great plan of life and salvation.

A proper observance of the duties and devotions of the Sabbath Day will give us the best rest that we can obtain, as well as a great renewal of spiritual strength.

THOSE WHO ARE CHOSEN

THOSE who have taken upon themselves the name of Christ have a great responsibility in maintaining his organization and furthering his work upon the earth. The Master has said, "For Behold, this is my work and my glory—to bring to pass the immortality and eternal life of man." (Pearl of Great Price, Moses 1:39.) The accomplishment of this great purpose requires the devoted service of all who will accept the call. Not only must we strive to live the law ourselves, but we must enlist others. The Lord has need of every one of us, each according to his own endowments.

Too often when a call to serve comes to us we disparage our own abilities, refusing to trust the inspiration and judgment of those appointed over us. Sensitive to our human weaknesses and shortcomings, and conscious of our limitations, we would deprive the great Church organization of our strengths and gifts.

An important lesson is to be learned from a study of the calling of Christ's first apostles. They were men with human imperfections and many limitations. The Master recognized these, but he saw beyond them to the great strengths which could be utilized in the building of the Kingdom of God upon the earth.

And Jesus, walking by the sea of Galilee, saw two brethren, Simon called Peter, and Andrew his brother, casting a net into the sea: for they were fishers.

And he saith unto them, Follow me, and I will make you fishers of men.

And they straightway left their nets, and followed him.

And going on from thence he saw other two brethren, James the son of Zebedee, and John his brother . . . and he called them.

And they immediately left the ship and their father and followed him. (Matt. 4:18-22.)

And as Jesus passed forth from thence, he saw a man named Matthew, sitting at the receipt of the custom: and he saith unto him, Follow me. And he arose and followed him. (Matt. 9:9.)

Thus, so simply, is recorded the calling and response of these men to the greatest work ever given to men.

Books have been written explaining the qualifications of these men for their work; their probable reactions to their call, and their preparation for the work have received much speculation. Men have pondered over why these certain ones were selected, men who ofttimes stumbled on their way to greatness—who learned the hard way. Yet with all the writing, with all the surmise, we come back to this simple account: The Savior bid them, "Follow me," and they arose and "followed him."

How well these men succeeded in their callings is borne out by scripture. Peter, despite his impulsive nature, grew to such stature as to become the head of Christ's earthly organization. Matthew, a hated publican, has given to the world a record of Christ's ministry that has directed the lives of millions. John, referred to as a son of thunder because of the force of his wrath, is today universally accepted as "John, the beloved."

Had these apostles stopped to count all the reasons why they were unfitted for their callings, how would the work have gone on? Christ had need of all the strengths they possessed. Despite their weaknesses and limitations, he called them to lend their strengths to his work. But after they "followed him," it became their responsibility to conquer their weaknesses and develop additional strengths that they might be fitted to labor in his vineyard.

Had Peter said, "I am so impulsive—there are many better qualified than I," how great would have been the loss to both the Church and to Peter himself. Had Matthew said, "But Master, think, I am a publican and the Jews hate me," or had he said, "I have a prosperous business, and if I leave it now I will lose all," even we today would have suffered great loss.

The Lord's call, "Follow me," comes to us in this day as truly as it came to his early disciples. True, he does not call us directly, as he did in their day, but he calls us through his appointed agents here on earth. His work must go on. Its progress depends upon the strength we lend it. Needing our strengths, he is tolerant of our weaknesses. Each of us is called to a particular work because of some strength we possess. It is our responsibility to accept his calls, to grow in his service to such stature that our weaknesses and our limitations will not impede the progress of his work. We must not be so sensitive to our shortcomings that we fail to recognize and magnify our strengths. As we magnify our strengths our weaknesses will become submerged.

In response to their callings, the Apostles manifested a willingness to follow, to learn by being with the Master and by doing his bidding. Thus, they became qualified for their work, and their efforts brought the blessings needed to carry it on to fruition. So we today may measure to the stature expected of us in our callings, remembering always the words of the Master:

"Ye have not chosen me, but I have chosen you, and ordained you, that ye should go and bring forth fruit." (John 15:16.)

"WHEREFORE HAVE WE FASTED?"

I N a day when tragic war encircles the globe and new
trials and sorrows must be met almost daily, Latter-day
Saints may well turn with renewed zeal to those principles and practices which build the Church and bring
spiritual strength to the individual. Among these is the
fast observance, a practice too often neglected or not fully
adhered to, a practice whose blessings and power many of
us minimize.

The principle of fasting is ancient. The prophet Joel
instructed the people: "Sanctify ye a fast, call a solemn
assembly, gather the elders and all the inhabitants of the
land into the house of the Lord your God and cry unto
the Lord." (Joel 1:14.) Zechariah 7:1 records: "Speak unto
all the people of the land, and to the priests, saying, When
ye fasted and mourned in the fifth and seventh month, even
those seventy years, did ye all fast unto me, even to me."
The Savior taught us the great principle of fasting when
for forty days and forty nights he fasted in the wilderness.
Paul spoke of the fourteen-day fast of those who were with
him in the boat as he journeyed to the courts of Caesar.

The word of the Lord came to Latter-day Israel
through revelation given to the Prophet Joseph Smith in
1831 and again in 1832: "Also, I give unto you a command-

ment that ye shall continue in prayer and fasting from this time forth." (D&C 88:76.)

Brigham Young, referring to the institution of the fast day in modern times says:

> Before tithing was paid, the poor were supported by donations. They came to Joseph and wanted help in Kirtland, and he said there should be a fast day which was decided upon. It was to be held once a month . . . and all that would have been eaten that day, of flour, or meat, or butter, or fruit, or anything else, was to be carried to the fast meeting and put into the hands of the person selected for the purpose of taking care of it and distributing it among the poor.

President Joseph F. Smith, in *Gospel Doctrine* tells us, "that the Lord has instituted the fast on a reasonable and intelligent basis," and that the "leading and principal object of the institution of the fast among Latter-day Saints was that the poor might be provided with food and other necessities."

The prophet Isaiah recognized this value in the fast. He taught, as do all men inspired of the Lord, the necessity of those who have, sharing with those who have not; and he saw the fast as a means whereby this might be done— not in a spirit of "strife and debate" but with a spirit of brotherly love and self-sacrifice to "undo the heavy burdens." Speaking of the principle of fasting, Isaiah said: "Is it not to deal thy bread to the hungry, and that thou bring the poor that are cast out to thy house? when thou seest the naked, that thou cover him; and that thou hide not thyself from thine own flesh?" (Isa. 58:7.)

Latter-day Saints are admonished to abstain from two meals one day each month and to give the full equivalent to the bishop as a fast donation for the care of the worthy needy of the Church. President Heber J. Grant has told us that, "The fast day donation alone, if we were absolutely honest with the Lord, would take care of the poor among us." He said: "You cannot get a good meal for less than ten cents, and twenty cents a month for every man, woman, and child in the Church would take care of those who need care and are not chronic beggars."

The difficulty with most Latter-day Saints is that while they believe in the principle of fasting, recognizing the worth of the purpose for which the fast fund is created, yet they fail to conscientiously appraise their own expenditures for meals and are inclined to be content to contribute the amount set by the Church as the minimum amount per capita—or even less.

I would suggest that on the Sunday preceding next fast day each mother keep close account of what she spends for the two Sunday meals, and that on fast day at least that amount be contributed as a fast offering.

I sometimes wonder how we would like to have the Lord, who provides all things, give us our portion according to our own recorded fast-day contributions.

While temporal necessities make a fast day advantageous, the greatest value of the fast is spiritual. Those who have need of great spiritual strength have ever sought the Lord fasting even as did the Savior when he fasted in the wilderness; and many there are who attest to receiving through fasting and prayer increased spiritual strength sufficient to their needs.

Alma rejoiced in the spiritual power of the sons of Mosiah, declaring it to be the result of fasting and prayer:

Now these sons of Mosiah were with Alma at the time the angel first appeared unto him; therefore Alma did rejoice exceedingly to see his brethren; and what added more to his joy, they were still his brethren in the Lord; yea, and they had waxed strong in the knowledge of the truth; for they were men of a sound understanding and they had searched the scriptures diligently, that they might know the word of God.

But this is not all; they had given themselves to much prayer, and fasting; therefore they had the spirit of prophecy, and the spirit of revelation, and when they taught they taught with power and authority of God. (Alma 17:2-3.)

Fasting engenders a love for the Lord and for one's fellow men. Those who neglect to fast neglect to fully develop within themselves the true spirit of love for God and man. Isaiah sets forth the rewards of righteous fasting thus:

Then shall thy light break forth as the morning, and thine health shall spring forth speedily: and thy righteousness shall go before thee; and the glory of the Lord shall be thy reward.

Then shalt thou call, and the Lord shall answer; thou shalt cry, and he shall say, Here I am. (Isa. 58:8-9.)

SECTION TWO

The Personal Development Of The Woman

THE QUALITIES NEEDED FOR GREATNESS

I WELL remember my call as president of Relief Society. I had been serving as a counselor to Sister Amy Brown Lyman in the presidency. One day the First Presidency called me to their office. Just before I left for their office, Sister Lyman advised me that she was to be released at the forthcoming general conference and a new president was to be appointed, and she said offhand, "It is my understanding that from now on the auxiliary heads are to be called for a period of five years only."

I went to the office of the First Presidency and was told that the next morning in the opening session of the general conference my name would be presented for a sustaining vote of the Church membership as the new general president of Relief Society. All I could think of was *five* years, and I thought if I could stand it for five years maybe I could get by. So I said to the Brethren, "Am I to understand, Brethren, that this is to be a five-year calling?" Whereupon President Clark, who was inclined to lower his glasses and peer above them when he wanted to look through you, lowered his glasses and said, "Five years? Why you may not last that long, Sister!"

Well, I assure you that the twenty-four years have been choice and rewarding.

In recent months I have had three or four invitations to speak to college students. In each instance no subject has been designated. I have asked for suggestions either from the person issuing the invitation or from some person whom I knew would be a listener, in the hope that they would give me some good guidance. The responses have been interesting and, in some instances, surprising. I would like to refer to a few.

I recall several months ago being invited to the Brigham Young University to speak at a summer school devotional. I met an alert young man and I asked what subject he thought might be of interest. Promptly he replied, "Well, we get quite a lot of faith and repentance. Why don't you give us a little hope?" Then in a more serious vein he said, "On the whole I think the students at Brigham Young are pretty good. Most of them are here through effort on their own part and sacrifice on the part of their families. I think most of them want to make good. In fact," he said, "I think most of them want to be a little above average and I believe a few of them would like to be great. Why don't you tell us how to be great?"

On another occasion I was invited to speak to the women students at Ricks College. In acknowledging the invitation, I asked for a suggestion as to subject, and I received this reply from the young woman:

I think there is a growing need for true greatness in women of the Church today because of the growth of the Church and the confused world in which we live. I think there will be even greater need for greater women tomorrow. Why don't you point out to us the qualities that will help us to be among the great women of tomorrow?

About three weeks ago, I was invited to speak to students at the Utah State University. I was advised that the theme was "Happiness Is the Full Life," but no reference was made to the part of the theme they desired me to treat. I telephoned one of the students and asked if she had a suggestion. She said, "Oh, I don't think so."

Then I said to her, "Tell me what you regard as 'the full life.'"

She said, "Well, to me it's being as good, and as useful, and as great as one's capabilities and opportunities will permit. Then, of course, one can enjoy the accompanying satisfactions."

Whereupon, she perked up and said, "I think I'd like to hear you talk along these lines."

Day after tomorrow, I am invited to speak to a social group of young men and women who are graduate students. The majority of them are Latter-day Saints, most of them are enrolled at the University of Utah. When I pressed them for a subject, one of the boys said, "Don't talk about the evils of the day such as drugs, college riots, and deplorable moral conditions. We know these things exist and we know their dangers. Say something that will inspire us and strengthen us to use our efforts and our training so that we will be worthwhile. Help us to see what it takes to rise above the common herd. Help us to see what it takes to make the most of what we have."

Every one of these comments and suggestions reflect high aspirations on the part of our Latter-day Saint college-trained youth. They are promising for our young people as individuals, and they are promising for the Church in a day when many young people are confused, some are in open rebellion, and others are feeling, "What's the use, you can't win anyway." Our young people seem to justify the confidence which the Church leaders feel in the youth of the Church today.

I do not wish to pose as an authority on what will help you to become superior people in life or to achieve greatness, but I offer a few personal viewpoints.

First, I turn to the dictionary, which defines greatness as, "being much above the average in magnitude, intensity, importance, and eminence." I love the word intensity. I don't think anyone ever achieved anything very out of the ordinary without putting intensity into what he was doing. I would add to the dictionary definition, "being above average in worthwhile accomplishments."

Greatness is not synonymous with worldly prominence or with occupying a position of influence and power. Many people have been prominent and held positions of power and yet they have been anything but great. I think some have been even ignoble. Also, greatness is not confined to accomplishment in a few selected fields of endeavor, such as science, medicine, or government. It can be achieved, I believe, in *any* field of human endeavor, and it draws upon a wide variety of talents and skills. Nonetheless, greatness or superiority is never achieved without effort and without unselfish purpose. A single act of human compassion or devotion may place one in the realm of the great. Scripture contains many examples.

I refer to Hannah who, according to the Book of Samuel in the Bible, had no children. She prayed to God to give her a son, promising that if he would do so, she would dedicate the child to the Lord. The Lord granted her request, giving her a son whom she called Samuel. When the child was weaned, obedient to her promise, she took him to Shiloh and placed him in the custody of the high priest, Eli, that he might thereafter serve God. That this was hard for Hannah is without question. This mother loved her son with a rare devotion as is evidenced by the record that every year she went to the temple to worship and carried with her for her son a little coat made by her own hands. Her willingness to submerge her own longings and to keep her promise to the Lord immortalized her.

Now I would like to tell you another story. One day a baby boy was born to hardworking, intelligent, God-fearing parents living on a small and somewhat unproductive farm in Utah. He was the eldest of a family of ten children. Naturally he had to work hard on the farm, but he was taught to respect work.

His parents also taught him to love his Church and to be obedient to its teachings. They taught him further to love his country with its great freedoms and endless opportunities. The boy had a good mind and as he grew to young manhood, he determined to study law in order that he might understand civil government and perhaps contribute toward good law and its proper use. His education entailed extreme sacrifice and tremendous self-effort, for it was necessary for this boy to meet the expenses of his education himself. Added to this, the boy had had the responsibility of helping to support his father on a mission.

And then he fell in love. He met a delightful young Mormon girl and he decided that he would get married. This young girl later told me that she had longed for a diamond ring. She said, "I didn't care how tiny the diamond was if I could just have a diamond ring. But," she said, "he was so pinched for money that it was simply out of the question." She also told me that it was twenty years before she received a diamond ring from him.

After he graduated from law school, his brilliant mind, his training, his integrity, and his dependability soon placed him among the foremost of the nation's international lawyers. At length, he was made an ambassador to one of our great, neighboring nations, and the doors of opportunity leading to future national honors and great financial success opened wide for him.

Then came an unexpected test. He was notified by the First Presidency of the Church that he was being called to a high office in the Church which would require all of his time. Acceptance of that call meant foregoing the national honors and personal advantages which appeared so imminent in favor of humbly serving the Lord. In secret prayer he appealed to the Lord to help him make the right decision. He made his choice; he would serve the Lord.

Today his earth life is over but his teachings and his example remain. His writings are the basis for Melchizedek Priesthood lessons. Scarcely a day passes that I do not hear some distinguished Church leader quote him.

His brilliant mind has given us new insights into Church doctrine. His contribution to God's kingdom is beyond measure and paces him high among the great leaders of this dispensation. He did not acquire great financial wealth during his lifetime; indeed, he came to feel that wealth was not particularly important. He said to me one day when we were discussing appointments to the general board, "I suggest that you call to the board a few financially poor women. You need them."

This man closed his earth life not financially wealthy, but honored and wealthy in things of eternal value.

In front of the Relief Society Building is a perfectly designed and proportioned flagpole from which waves, on appropriate occasions, a glorious silk American flag. Both were purchased from royalties on a book written by this man and given to the Relief Society as a gift for the Relief Society Building, to be used as the presidency saw fit. We could think of no more appropriate use for the money than to erect a flagpole.

When the pole was completed and we were ready to raise the flag, we invited this man to the service. It was to be his surprise. As the flag waved aloft in the breeze, I saw this powerful man break down and weep. Then he turned to me and said, "Sister Spafford, you could not have done anything that would have been more pleasing to me. I love my Church and I love my country."

This was a great churchman, a great American, a great man—President J. Reuben Clark, Jr.

Every student here today possesses elements of greatness. A wise man has said:

If one would attain stature above the ordinary, there must first be within him desire, but desire alone cannot bring fulfillment. He must have goals, faith, discipline, training. He must be willing to work patiently and persistently toward his goals, refusing to be diverted from his course or weakened by self-indulgence. He must know that no true greatness ever accompanied selfish ambition or a desire for personal recognition or reward.

There must be in one's makeup a strong spiritual fiber out of which there grows nobility of character—character that is elevated above anything selfish, degrading, or uncharitable; character that squares with the principles of truth and righteousness. The Savior put it in these simple words:

> . . . If any man desire to be first, the same shall be last of all, and servant of all. (Mark 9:35.)
> . . . But whosoever will be great among you, let him be your minister;
> And whosoever will be chief among you, let him be your servant: (Matthew 20:26-27.)

A few years ago, it became my responsibility to arrange an interview with President McKay for a distinguished British woman visitor to Salt Lake City. She had come for the purpose, in her own words, "of finding out what made the Mormons tick." I was privileged to sit in on the interview at the invitation of President McKay. It lasted less than one hour. Conversation centered upon the work of the Church as directed by President McKay and upon the work which the visitor was doing. Viewpoints were exchanged, opinions were expressed and, I might say, at times opinions were challenged. There was a delightful exchange of sharp wit.

At the conclusion of the interview, President McKay accompanied us to the door and as this woman stepped ahead through the doorway the President turned to me and said, "We have been in the presence of true greatness. That is a great woman." Scarcely had the door closed behind us when the woman locked arms with me and with great depth of feeling said, "I know you regard your President as a great religious leader. He is far more than this. He is a great man, judged by any standard. I think I have never met a greater one."

Here were two people who had never met before, who had little previous knowledge of one another, who had been together less than one hour, each pronouncing the other great. That their evaluation of one another was accurate there is no doubt. All of us here today confirm the validity of the visitor's opinion of President McKay, while women throughout the world attest the greatness of this British woman, esteeming her as one of the foremost women of this era. She has headed for many years the most advanced women's volunteer welfare organization in Great Britain. It was under her leadership that families were evacuated from London during the German blitz of World War II. She has been a leader in the development of social welfare programs that have been adopted by many nations. She serves today in the House of Lords where, uninfluenced by political party, she has been instrumental in the adoption of some of Britain's finest social legislation. She has received honorary degrees from great universities of many nations.

Let me read a paragraph from a letter I just received from her which, to some extent, reveals her character:

At this moment I am very occupied with an important speech I have to make on the 15th of April in connection with the After-Care of prisoners and of Borstal boys (these are boys who have been in a home for correction). Some of us have an idea that there is a plan we could introduce which could give very great help to the whole of the criminal class of Great Britain, and if it were possible to get everybody to pull together to bring in this new program, it would be of great value, not only to this country, but I think eventually it could serve as a pattern for others. But as you know well, these things are not easy to do, and I always doubt myself as the one best prepared to do them. I am so frightfully apprehensive before I undertake anything of the sort in the House of Lords, that I feel anybody in the world could do it better, and anybody in the world should be preferred to do it. But the task is mine and with hard work and the help of God, I may succeed.

In the light of what you know about President McKay, in the light of what I have told you about this woman, I ask you to determine for yourselves the qualities which each recognized in the other which led each without hesitancy to call the other *great*. In the light of what I have said and told you about President Clark, I ask you to define for yourselves those qualities which lift one above the average toward greatness.

I would like to conclude with this question: Should we strive for greatness? If we mean greatness for greatness' sake I would say, "No." Rather I would say, "Let us strive for those virtues which tend toward goodness of soul and nobility of character." Let us make the most of our inborn capabilities and earnestly work toward unselfish accomplishments, with the Church and its teachings and its opportunities as the staff upon which we lean. I believe then that greatness will take care of itself. I believe that in this group today there are countless young men and women who will achieve true greatness.

"FOR AFTER MUCH TRIBULATION COME THE BLESSINGS"

R ECENTLY I read a short biographical sketch of Giacomo Leopardi, a great Italian poet and a distinguished scholar of his day. Though somewhat tinged with pessimism, his writings were noted for their perfection of style. Leopardi lost his love of God and, eating his heart out in reasoning despair, ended with these desolate lines: "Life is but the privation of the pleasurable; it is destroyed illusions and wounded pride. Tiresome and bitter is life— never aught but that."

Mr. Clarence Darrow, one of the nation's great criminal lawyers of a few years ago, an eminently successful man judged by the standards of the world, wrote that to him "the outstanding fact of human life is the utter futility of it all." He said that "no life is of much value . . . the most satisfying part of life is the time spent in sleep when one is utterly oblivious to existence, and the next best is when one is absorbed in activities."

Such futilism as expressed by these two men is one of irreligion's commonest effects. The soul who knows true religion, who has a belief in God, views life hopefully as an opportunity and a blessing. To the Latter-day Saint, possessed of revealed truth regarding God's great plan of life and salvation, the divine purposes of God in the earthlife of man and how man may fulfill these purposes are clear. God has made known to us in positive terms the "why" of human existence and the ultimate destiny of man. In the light of this knowledge, life as we live it here upon the earth from day to day assumes its true significance.

We know that we are sons and daughters of God; that our spirits had an existence before they tabernacled in the flesh; that there we dwelt with our Heavenly Father and Mother and the Son, that there we were given our free agency to act as we saw fit and that we exercised that agency and proved ourselves valiant. As a reward for that valiance, the Lord permitted us to come to earth, to take upon ourselves mortal bodies that we might further our progression. Moreover, we were given a special blessing to come to earth through the lineage of the faithful, in the dispensation of the fullness of times, heirs to salvation.

This knowledge should be a constant source of inspiration, strength, and confidence to us as we continue our earthly existence.

The Lord showed Abraham the intelligences that were organized before the world was.

And there stood one among them that was like unto God, and he said unto those who were with him: We will go down, for there is space there, and we will take of these materials, and we will make an earth whereon these may dwell;

And we will prove them herewith, to see if they will do all things whatsoever the Lord their God shall command them;

And they who keep their first estate shall be added upon; and they who keep not their first estate shall not have glory in the same kingdom with those who keep their first estate; and they who keep their second estate shall have glory added upon their heads forever and ever. (Abraham 3:24-26.)

One cannot be proved by walking only the easy road, nor does he become valiant without struggle. Through a mastery of the difficult the character of a man becomes strong. Lehi, speaking to his son Jacob, declared: "For it must needs be, that there is an opposition in all things. If not so . . . righteousness could not be brought to pass, . . ." (II Nephi 2:11.)

Doctrine and Covenants, Section 136:31, tells us:

My people must be tried in all things, that they may be prepared to receive the glory that I have for them, even the glory of Zion; and he that will not bear chastisement is not worthy of my kingdom.

History is replete with accounts of the children of men who have been tried, tested, and refined in the furnace of life—men whom the Lord loved dearly.

There is no more striking example than the story of Job. Job was perfect and upright. He feared God and eschewed evil. The Lord blessed the works of his hands and his substance increased. Then the Lord permitted Satan to try Job as a test of his faith. His prosperity turned to calamity; his honor to contempt. Sore bereavement came upon him, physical suffering, loss of substance, taunting by his friends. So great were his trials that he cried:

Oh that my grief were thoroughly weighed, and my calamity laid in the balances together!

For now it would be heavier than the sands of the sea; . . . (Job 6:2, 3.)

My days . . . are spent without hope. (Job 7:6.)

My soul is weary of my life; . . . (Job 10:1.)

Yet, withal, he steadfastly refused to accept sin and, with sublime faith and trust in God, he met the test, declaring:

For I know that my Redeemer liveth, and that he shall stand at the latter day upon the earth;

And though after my skin worms destroy this body, yet in my flesh shall I see God: (Job 19:25-26.)

Scripture tells us: "The Lord blessed the latter end of Job more than his beginning." (Job 42:12.)

Even that great Prophet, chosen of the Lord to open this last dispensation, was not spared. When the Prophet Joseph Smith was incarcerated in Liberty Jail, he was called upon to endure hardships which were revolting to his refined and sensitive nature. Not only were high-handed injustice and cruelty practiced upon him, but the food was filthy. He was compelled to hear blasphemous oaths and to witness scenes of drunkenness and debauchery. Out of the midst of his tribulations, he called upon God in passionate earnestness:

> O God! where art thou? And where is the pavilion that covereth thy hiding place? . . . How long shall thy hand be stayed, and thine eye . . . behold from the eternal heavens, the wrongs of thy people, and of thy servants, and thine ear be penetrated with their cries? . . . O Lord . . . stretch forth thy hand . . . let thine heart be softened, and thy bowels moved with compassion toward us.

And God answered the cries of the Prophet, and said:

> My son, peace be unto thy soul; thine adversity and thine afflictions shall be but a small moment; and then, if thou endure it well, God shall exalt thee on high . . . . If thou art called to pass through tribulation, if thou art in perils among false brethren, if thou art in perils among robbers, if thou art in perils by land or by sea, if thou art accused with all manner of false accusations, if thine enemies fall upon thee, if they tear thee from the society of thy father and mother and brethren and sisters, and if with a drawn sword thine enemies tear thee from the bosom of thy wife and of thine offspring . . . if thou shouldst be cast into the pit, or into the hands of murderers, and the sentence of death passed upon thee, if thou be cast into the deep, if the billowing surge conspire against thee, if fierce winds become thine enemy, if the heavens gather blackness, and all the elements combine to hedge up the way; and above all, if the very jaws of hell shall gape open the mouth wide after thee, know thou, my son, that all these things shall give thee experience, and shall be for thy good. (*DHC* III, p. 291 ff.)

Surely, the Prophet is "exalted on high."

Zion's Camp furnishes us another striking example of testing. In the year 1834 there came a day of calling and a day of choosing. A little band of brethren set out to aid their brothers in Jackson County. The hardships of that journey beggar description. Spied upon, tortured by mob threatenings, wading through mire and stream, half-fed, suffering the plague of cholera, they pushed toward their goal. Some murmured and found fault, were disobedient to the authority of the Prophet; others were loyal and true, facing hardships with unwavering faith.

In a revelation to the Prophet on Fishing River, Missouri, in June of 1834, the Lord said:

But the strength of mine house have not hearkened unto my words.

But inasmuch as there are those who have hearkened unto my words, I have prepared a blessing and an endowment for them, if they continue faithful. I have heard their prayers, and will accept their offering; and it is expedient in me that they should be brought thus far for a trial of their faith. (D&C 105:17-19.)

Essentials in Church History tells us:

While the object for which Zion's Camp was organized and for which they made the journey, as understood by the members, was not attained, yet without question they did accomplish all that the Lord expected of them . . . . Their faith was tried; experience had been gained by which men were to be chosen for responsible positions in the Church in days to come. (p. 149.)

But, you say, these are trials which came to the great and chosen of the Lord. What of the more humble among us? We too must be proved. All must face trials. These trials are not given us by an unkind providence to crush us. Many of them are man-made, the result of man's weaknesses and imperfections. But, regardless of their source, by a mastery of them we rise to our fullest stature.

Paul Speicher has said:

Cripple him and you have a Sir Walter Scott. Put him in a prison cell and you have a John Bunyan. Bury him in the snows of Valley Forge and you have a George Washington. Have him born in abject poverty and you have an Abraham Lincoln. Deny her sight and speech and you have a Helen Keller. Bind him down with bitter racial prejudice and you have a Disraeli.

And we might add: "Have him reared by a widowed mother under the hardships of desert pioneer life and you have a Heber J. Grant."

The women of the Church must prove themselves a steadying and unwavering influence in their homes and on their children. Driven by our own anxieties, it is so easy to project fears, to implant bitterness, to impair hope, to destroy faith. This, Latter-day Saint wives and mothers must not do. Rather, they must build faith and enlarge their own understanding and that of their families, so that when the bitter experiences of life come the doctrines and teachings of the Church will be a sustaining influence and power. Courage and a hopeful heart must be ours. Wisdom and intelligence must dictate our course, and our emotions must not be allowed to run unbridled. The Lord has admonished us, "Live near unto me," with the promise, "I will live near unto you."

Let us make of our homes a sanctuary, a place where the sweet spirit of the Lord may dwell, regardless of the confusion in the world about us. Let each of our homes be a place of such faith, peace, and understanding companionship that wherever family members may go, or whatever experiences they may pass through, the sweet memory of home will bind them to it, buoy them up, and help them to endure without yielding.

I beseech you, sisters, during these days of stress to maintain your homes as normally as is humanly possible. Safeguard your own health. Do not dissipate your physical strength, for a troubled spirit takes its toll of physical strength, and, in turn, the spirit is more readily crushed when the body is weak. Know this, that being children of the Father we have within us resources of power and strength great enough to enable us to meet valiantly whatever adversities this earth life may bring; and "after much tribulation come the blessings," (D&C 58:4.) if we meet them with faith, retaining our testimonies strong as did Job when he said, "I know that my Redeemer liveth."

And now, my sisters, I leave with you my blessing. I bless you for the righteousness of your lives, for the faithfulness of your service to Relief Society, for the quality of your wifehood and your motherhood, that as you order your lives according to the teachings of the Church, the stern days ahead will not find you disconsolate and crushed in spirit, but strong in faith and testimony, more worthy of exaltation in our Father's kingdom because of the manner in which you have met the tribulations incident to your day.

The Lord has promised:

Wherefore, I now send upon you another Comforter . . . that it may abide in your hearts, even the Holy Spirit of promise . . . This Comforter is the promise which I give unto you of eternal life, even the glory of the celestial kingdom.

May this be your blessing, sisters, I pray.

THE BLESSINGS OF EXPERIENCE

C HURCH history records many accounts of the trials and tribulations that beset the Prophet Joseph Smith—he who was chosen of the Lord to open this dispensation. No account, perhaps, reveals more graphically the personal hardship endured by the Prophet than the account of his incarceration in the Liberty Jail, where indignities to his refined and sensitive nature were heaped upon him.

Out of the midst of his tribulation he called upon God in passionate earnestness.

And God answered the cries of the Prophet, enumerating various adversities which could befall him and concluding that "all these things shall give thee experience, and shall be for thy good." (*DHC* III, p. 291ff.)

This leads us to ask, "What really is this thing which the Lord called experience, and what are the values to be found therein, not alone for the Prophet but for each of our Father's children?"

Experience, I believe, is the actual living through of an event or events; it is personally undergoing enjoyment or suffering which directly affects one's feelings, one's judgment, and one's character. The dictionary says, "Experience is the sum total of the conscious events which compose an individual life." Experience has been referred to as "Life's greatest teacher, one's sure source of knowledge."

A gifted writer, Donald Culross Peattie, says that life is an adventure in experience and "as one's head is silvered o'er with age, his variable experiences make him sage."

Another writer has said that a strong and well-constituted man digests his experiences (deeds and misdeeds all included) just as he digests his meats, even when he has some tough morsels to chew and swallow, and from these well-digested morsels comes nourishment by which his character is formed.

Latter-day Saints know that earth life is a proving ground for the Father's children; that experiences, both pleasant and difficult, come to all; that each will be tested by the experiences of his life and that his character and accomplishments will be measured by the manner in which he meets testing.

The Doctrine and Covenants, Section 136:31, tells us, "My people must be tried in all things that they may be prepared to receive the glory that I have for them, even the glory of Zion; and he that will not bear chastisement is not worthy of my kingdom."

I recall being authorized several years ago by the First Presidency, as is the usual custom, to interview a sister relative to her call to become a member of the general board. She was an intelligent and talented woman, devoted to the Church and to Relief Society. Her quick mind readily grasped the importance of the call and what, in general, would be expected of her as a board member and as a leader of Latter-day Saint women. She was reluctant to accept the call because, she said, she felt she had not had experiences in life which would make her sufficiently understanding of the problems and needs of the sisters or wise in her counsels to them. She said her life had been practically devoid of trial or hardship, and she feared her lack of kinship of experience with most Relief Society sisters would keep them from drawing lovingly to her. This she could not bear. Then she said this, which has remained with me through the years, "Insofar as experiences which test and develop one are concerned, my life has been quite impoverished."

This beautiful woman who, at that moment, felt her life had been impoverished was the daughter of one of our most prominent and financially successful Church leaders. She had long enjoyed the prestige as well as the other advantages of belonging to such a family. Her husband, too, held high office in the Church and was professionally and financially successful. She had a beautiful home and a lovely family of bright children. She, herself, was personally attractive, healthy in mind and body, gifted far beyond the average woman. Yet she felt unqualified to accept a wonderful Church calling because of the ease of her life experiences.

I suggested that she delay decision for a few days, that she talk the matter over with her husband and her father. The next morning she returned to the office and humbly accepted the call. She said her father had told her not to worry about her lack of hard and testing life experiences. She would not be denied these, nor would any of our Father's children.

He had quoted to her the teachings of the Lord to Abraham wherein he said they would make an earth whereon the spirits God had created might dwell, and he would prove them herewith to see if they would do all things whatsoever the Lord their God should command them. (Abraham 3:24-25.) She said her father had told her that the way of trial was ordained of God, even for his most favored sons and daughters. It was a means of development and purification, a means whereby man would be proved in earth life. To some persons, trial came early in life; with others, it was withheld until later years, but in due time it came to all. Furthermore, her father had indicated to her that acceptance of the call would bring a strength that would sustain her in adversity when it came.

In time, life did bring to this sister, in rapid succession, trial, hardship, sorrow, disappointment, even physical suffering.   She proved herself capable of rallying the forces which enabled her to meet each experience with patience, faith, and fortitude, devoid of bitterness or a spirit of rebellion.   And there emerged from these experiences a woman of rare spiritual strength, a compassionate and understanding woman, a woman wise in counsel, an example to the women of the Church of one's power to rise above adversity, a loving and beloved Relief Society leader, a soul refined.

Truly, it is not what comes to us by way of experience but how we meet the difficulty that counts.   In meeting the adversities of life one's greatest strength is a firm and abiding testimony of the gospel, a knowledge of God's great plan of life and salvation.   This knowledge enables one to determine the true values of life and directs him in the pursuit of that which is of eternal worth.   Life's denials, hardships, and tribulations, small or great, are then viewed in true perspective, and one is lifted above them and sustained in going forward.

Strength to meet adversity comes through seeking counsel of the Lord as contained in the holy scriptures. Counsel and the comforting power of the Lord are always available through this source.   True, the scriptures speak to us as a collective body—his Church—but they speak also to us as individuals if we will but let them.   We must be on familiar terms with them, having full faith and applying divine wisdom to our individual problems and circumstances.

To one in sorrow do they not say, "Blessed are they that mourn for they shall be comforted"? (Matt. 5:4.)

To one engulfed with fear over the perplexities of the times they say, "Fear not, little flock; do good; let earth and hell combine against you, for if ye are built upon my rock, they cannot prevail" (D&C 6:34.)

To one who must make a troublesome and far-reaching decision is not this wise counsel given: "You must study it out in your mind; then you must ask me if it be right, and if it is right I will cause that your bosom shall burn within you; therefore, you shall feel that it is right." (D&C 9:8.)

Wise, indeed, is the woman who fortifies herself to meet the vicissitudes of life through a knowledge of the scriptures.

Inspired guidance and increased strength are also available to us through prayer. The Lord mercifully invites us to lay our burdens at his feet. In Alma 37:37 we are admonished, "Counsel with the Lord in all thy doings, and he will direct thee for good." These are not idle words spoken by man. They are the words of the Lord to his beloved children—to you and to me.

As we review our lives and those of others about us, we become aware that, generally speaking, there is a fair balance between the pleasant and difficult experiences of life; that with breadth of experience lives are enriched. We know that difficult experiences make us more understanding of others and more compassionate towards them. We recognize that through self-mastery in rising above the trials of life, character is developed and refined. We know that in none of the tribulations of life do we stand alone. Always the Lord is near to comfort, guide, and sustain us, to raise up friends unto us. We know that we must be tested if earth life is to fulfill its purpose. We see the truth and the wisdom of the words of the Lord when he tenderly said to the Prophet Joseph Smith, ". . . know thou, my son, that all these things shall give thee experience, and shall be for thy good."

Latter-day Saint mothers, obedient to God's commands, may ever find comfort in this blessed promise of the Lord, whether their path be through green pastures or over rocky roads:

And now, verily I say unto you, and what I say unto one I say unto all, be of good cheer, little children; for I am in your midst, and I have not forsaken you. (D&C 61:36.)

SERVING WITH FULL INTENT OF HEART

Through the consideration of the First Presidency, it has been my opportunity to have a number of unique and impressive experiences related to, but not necessarily a part of, the work of Relief Society. These experiences have brought me into contact with many people not of our Church—persons of wide experience, broad influence, and generally speaking of good motive. I have had opportunity at least to glimpse in wide focus, conditions in a number of places in our own and foreign lands.

These experiences have left me impressed with the fast pace at which the world is moving—the tremendous changes that are taking place in home, family, and community life, the strange standards by which people judge acceptable behavior, the struggle that is going on for the possession of worldly goods.

Materialism appears to be enthroned, with the best efforts of some of the ablest of people being directed toward enhancing it and attracting to it a worshipful following. The acquisition of worldly goods seems to be the paramount goal of the masses and the measure of success to be what one gets rather than what one gives. All too often the attitude exists that for each effort made in behalf of another, one should be paid, that only the foolish would give of himself without seeking some personal advantage.

The imbalance in the lives of people seems to call for a re-evaluation of what makes life poised, happy, and genuinely successful. It appears that there is need for society to be more responsive to the enduring, deep-seated, spiritual needs of mankind—the need for inner peace, emotional satisfaction, and strengthened character.

These values do not accrue through the acquisition of material goods and the enjoyment of a so-called prosperous life, nor through the pursuit of self-interests. Rather, they accrue through subordinating our private interests to the interests of our fellow men. They come through utilizing a portion of our time and energies in uplifting others and making their path a bit more smooth.

In the Doctrine and Covenants, Section 6, verse 7, we are admonished: "Seek not for riches but for wisdom, and behold, the mysteries of God shall be unfolded unto you, and then shall you be made rich."

In the light of present-day trends and conditions, it would be wise for people everywhere to exercise stricter self-discipline, to be more considerate of the needs and interests of others, and to use their energies and abilities for the things that really matter in the long run of life—to put them to uses that train the mind, enlarge the soul, promote the spiritual health of the individual and society, and make character strong.

The Lord has told us by way of commandment: "Thou shalt love the Lord thy God with all thy heart, and with all thy soul, and with all thy mind. This is the first and great commandment. And the second is like unto it, Thou shalt love thy neighbor as thyself. On these two commandments hang all the law and the prophets." (Matt. 22:37-40.)

From the beginning of recorded time, warm-hearted, good, generously inclined human beings have lived the great law of brotherhood. They have shared their friendship, their strength, their hospitality, and their abilities.

They have fed the hungry, cared for the sick, comforted the bereaved, and befriended the lonely, with no thought of personal recompense. Yet, while seeking no recompense, they have tapped the deep well springs of true happiness and received rewards of eternal value.

Today, there is urgent need to intensify this selfless free-will service. It is being called for on every hand. It is referred to in the popular vernacular as "voluntary service," the giving of one's time and service to a specific activity of one's own free will and choice without any financial compensation. Such service may be given by the professionally trained or the non-professional. It tolerates no age limits. The child with his boundless energies, the teen-ager of good will, the mature person of wisdom and experience—all may devote themselves to it and find satisfaction. To countless retired persons, it is the happy, constructive answer to the question: "What may I do with my spare time?" Voluntary service lays no claim on any specified block of time that must be applied equally to all. Each person may give each bit of time and each type of service that he is willing and able to give.

It is true that many factors enter into the quality of one's service. Service given from a sense of duty or with restraint and reservations, service given grudgingly, service given for personal recognition or for other selfish ends, falls short of its greatest good.

I was interested in reading recently that every volunteer's orientation should include a stern warning on what was called "creeping professionalism." The charge was made that every now and then, especially in large organizations using many volunteers, the volunteer sometimes becomes so capable at her work and so at home in the work situation, that instead of bringing to the task at hand a warmth and gentleness, such valuable elements in the work of the volunteer, she tends to adopt an impersonal efficiency. When the volunteer at the hostess desk begins to give short answers and the woman at the message counter is in such a rush that she gives no answer at all, it is time for a frank appraisal of her worth as a volunteer, it was stated.

Excellence, of course, should imbue the volunteer in her free-will service, just as it should in any other activity. And excellence can be achieved in human relations and in free-will service. Individuals must accept the need for high standards of performance and try to achieve those standards within the limits possible for them if they would enjoy the full rewards of their labors.

I know of no more important element of excellence in the giving of service than to give with full intent of heart. In Moroni 7:6-8, we read:

> For behold, God hath said a man being evil cannot do that which is good; for if he offereth a gift, or prayeth unto God, except he shall do it with real intent it profiteth him nothing.
> For behold, it is not counted unto him for righteousness.
> For behold, if a man being evil giveth a gift, he doeth it grudgingly; wherefore it is counted unto him the same as if he had retained the gift. . . .

Just as there should be excellence and full intent of heart in the performance of free-will service, so it is equally important that it be discriminately rendered and wisely directed; otherwise it could be unfair to the giver, the recipient, and to the cause one is trying to serve.

That which is given impulsively and prompted by strong emotional feelings but is undirected, often falls short of its goal. Also, the limitations of the individual working alone, regardless of how willing, competent, and resourceful he may be, often precludes the possibility of full service.

So it has been found that exclusive of the little loving acts of personal kindness which we all perform as individuals from time to time for those about us, free-will service is most productive of good when it is organized and well directed.

Blessed indeed were the women of the Church when the Lord gave to them an organization through which their humanitarian impulses might find expression in an organized and divinely directed way. It is my conviction that in founding Relief Society and assigning to it humanitarian and compassionate service, the Lord's plan was not alone for the relief of the distressed and the amelioration of human woes, but for the soul growth and life enrichment of all of his daughters.

The intent of heart on the part of the sisters is shown in the following:

First, a quotation from a recent letter from a mission Relief Society president:

It is a pleasure to give such a favorable report of the part the Relief Society organization played during our recent tidal wave, that was such a disaster in Hilo, Hawaii.

As you probably know, the wave hit the city at one o'clock in the morning. By daylight the Relief Society sisters had their blankets and clothing from their welfare projects on the way to the presidency of the South Hawaii District. Each Relief Society on the outside islands had called to offer help in every way possible for those in need.

We lost one member of the Church. Six families lost the homes they were living in. Sixteen members were taken into the Church building and temporarily housed until homes could be made ready for them by the week end. Others are living with family members.

I feel I have done so little to warrant my membership in the Relief Society organization after seeing how united the sisters become in time of disaster.

A Relief Society president of a ward made up largely of young mothers reports:

Three years ago in March a mother in our ward was stricken with a severe case of crippling arthritis. At the present time she is practically bedridden.

Since she was first afflicted, the Relief Society sisters have taken her, at first once a week and now twice a week, to the hospital for therapy. In the beginning I assumed this responsibility. Later, other sisters were called upon to assist. As it was realized that this would be a long-time service, the sisters who had cars and were willing to help were organized with one sister being placed in charge, so that each in turn could perform the service. So many of the sisters have been willing to assist that their service is required only about once each four months. In the three-year period only one sister has shown the least reluctance to take her turn, and that because she couldn't stand to see the pain of the ill sister if she hit a bump or had to come to a short stop.

Now this mother is so sorely afflicted that the one taking her to the hospital must call at the home sufficiently early to help her dress. They leave for the hospital at 12:30 and return about 4 P.M.

The afflicted sister eagerly looks forward to the days when she goes to the hospital, not alone for the physical relief of pain it brings her but because it is her only opportunity to get out. She enjoys the ride and the association with her sisters of Relief Society.

One Relief Society sister who lives nearby looks in on her every day. She often takes her family hour program into the home of the afflicted mother. Housekeeping help is given from time to time, and one Relief Society member takes special food and fruits as needed into the home.

In reporting this service, the president made an interesting observation. She said, "This service has had a tremendous influence upon the sisters of our Relief Society."

A letter of appreciation for the opportunity to serve was recently received by the general board. The sister states:

I am sixty-four years old. I have been a member of Relief Society since I was twenty. I live alone and for the past few months I haven't felt very well, although I must confess I have not been sick.

Early this week, the Relief Society president asked if I would help out a little in the home of a widowed mother in the ward who has six small children. The mother had an injured leg and had to keep off it for two days.

I spent both days in this home. I think I have never worked harder in my life, and I know I have never been more needed.

Today I am home and expected to be completely worn out. Instead, I feel fine. I have not felt so good in spirit for months. I am so glad I could be helpful that I felt I should write to you and let you know my feelings. Relief Society has been a blessing to me ever since I joined it more than forty years ago.

Latter-day Saint mothers open their homes to one or more Indian children for the school year on an entirely free-will basis. These children are participating in the Indian Student Placement Program. The program provides the children opportunities for schooling as well as bringing to them other benefits not available on the reservation.

At the recent health clinic held for the children, there were 151 volunteer workers consisting of doctors, dentists, laboratory technicians, practical and registered nurses, Relief Society sisters, and others. Some of the Relief Society sisters were at their posts of duty as early as four o'clock in the morning in order to have breakfast ready for the children upon their arrival at the center at five A.M. The Relief Society sisters alone gave a total of 925 hours of service.

In compliance with the directive of the Prophet Joseph Smith that the Society should "seek after objects of charity," visiting teachers visit Latter-day Saint homes on a monthly basis. They are concerned with the spiritual and temporal well-being of the home. The requirements of no Latter-day Saint family need go undiscovered as long as this program fully functions.

Thus, Relief Society presses on in its work of service, and there redounds to those who willingly give of themselves a sweetness and richness of life, the inner peace that companions well-doing, and a spiritual and character strength that is a fortress to them in meeting the vicissitudes of their own lives. Thus Relief Society builds a great sisterhood united in a day of trouble.

Relief Society must continue on, ever building on the great record of the past. In view of present day trends and conditions, however, Relief Society must give alert and thoughtful attention to safeguarding its long and honored tradition of human helpfulness. As the Church grows in numbers, the calls for help are bound to increase. As changes continue in individual, family, and community life, Relief Society undoubtedly will be required to enter into new and expanded programs of helpfulness.

The Society can meet its obligations only insofar as its

individual members are willing to submerge self and with full mind and heart give of their time and energies in response to the calls made of them by the Society.

The trends of the times, the ever-growing tendency for people to consider their material well-being above all else, the countless false values crowding in upon women demand that Relief Society women evaluate their thinking and conduct. Each might well ask herself, "For what am I really striving in life? Are the values which I hold dear those which the teachings of the Church, time, and experience have proved to be of genuine and enduring worth?"

The first and second great commandments given by the Father—Love the Lord thy God and thy neighbour as thyself—have not been rescinded, nor will they ever be because they are fundamental for man's eternal well-being.

Someone has wisely said, "At the close of life the question will not be how much you have got, but how much have you given; not how much have you won, but how much have you done; not how much have you saved, but how much have you shared; not how much have you been honored, but how much have you loved and served?"

President Joseph F. Smith said, "The important consideration is not how long we can live, but how well we can learn the lessons of life, and discharge our duties and obligations to God and to one another" (*Gospel Doctrine,* 6th ed., p. 27.)

My earnest prayer is that the work of Relief Society may kindle in the heart of every one of its members the spark of desire to love and to serve, and that it may fan it into full and glowing flame so that every one of us may enjoy the attendant blessings.

LEARNING TO LIVE

L IVING wisely and well in this day is not always easy. Yet it is a day when opportunities for helping us to so live are abundant. It is no mere platitude to say this is a glorious day and age and land in which to live. Indeed we might say as did the Psalmist David ". . . the earth is full of the goodness of the Lord." (33:5.) This is a day foretold by the prophets of old. Nephi more than 500 years before Christ foreshadowed the present America, saying:

And I beheld the spirit of the Lord, that it was upon the Gentiles, and they did prosper and obtain the land for their inheritance; and I beheld that they were white, and exceeding fair and beautiful. . . .

And I beheld that the power of God was with them. . . .

And it came to pass that I, Nephi, beheld that they did prosper in the land. . . . (1 Nephi 13:15, 18, 20.)

We, in America, are highly favored in living under the protection of that great document to which the Prophet Joseph Smith referred as "a glorious standard . . . founded in the wisdom of God"—the Constitution of the United States. Calvin Coolidge said of this document: "To live under the Constitution of the United States is the greatest political privilege that was ever accorded to the human race."

For 166 years the strengths and blessings of the Constitution have been proved. Through years of social and economic change it has stood the bulwark of American life, safeguarding liberty and happiness. As Latter-day Saints we know that liberty is a law of God. Without it there can be neither happiness nor advancement. Without it man cannot rise to his fullest stature.

The Constitution of the United States made it possible for the ancient gospel which Jesus brought to the earth to be restored in full glory on the American continent. Blessed with the protection of that great document, the Church has been permitted to grow and expand in the dominions of liberty. The gospel of Jesus Christ adheres to the sacred truth that man was not created to live in ignorance, doubt, and uncertainty upon the earth. "The gospel plan declares the everlasting existence of the spirit of man, that this life upon earth is a precious and essential part of his upward progress, his increasing knowledge, his unending opportunities, his eternal life."

Under divine favor, America has prospered. We in America today have comforts, standards of living, educational opportunities beyond anything our forefathers ever dreamed. We have newspapers, radio, and television to keep us informed and to enlarge our understanding of the world and its people. We may sit comfortably in our own homes and see nominees chosen for president, and a president inaugurated. We may see a queen crowned. We have complicated machines to do our grueling labor; we have medical science and wonder drugs to protect health and prolong life. We have scientific marvels almost beyond comprehension.

No child or adult in America need go without the discipline of mind and character that comes through study and instruction. Of America we might say, as did Ecclesiastes of old: "Of making many books there is no end." (12:12.) America offers free schooling to its children; its secondary schools and institutions of higher learning are legion. Its adult education program is varied and extensive.

We also have a marvelous free public library system with extension service to villages and farms. Learning opportunities are available to all who will accept them.

The leaders of our Church from the Prophet Joseph Smith to the present have shown great faith in education, accepting its divine approval and extending its influence into eternity.

Whatever principle of intelligence we attain unto in this life, it will rise with us in the resurrection.

And if a person gains more knowledge and intelligence in this life through his diligence and obedience than another he will have so much the advantage in the world to come. (D&C 131:18-19.)

From the beginning of the Church, education and salvation have gone hand in hand in the restored gospel plan of exaltation. The Prophet set a good example. He not only taught from the pulpit the importance of education but he attended and organized schools. Josiah Quincy in his account of his visit to Nauvoo said that the Prophet read from the Hebrew Old Testament in order to make clear a theology point. How did Joseph learn Hebrew? He hired a teacher, sat in beginners' class, and applied himself to study just as we do when we want to master a difficult subject. There was always a close association between education and the most sacred activities in the life of the Prophet.

Many times in support of education we quote from the dedicatory prayer given by revelation and uttered by the Prophet at the completion of the Kirtland Temple:

And do thou grant, Holy Father, that all those who shall worship in this House may be taught words of wisdom out of the best books, and that they may seek learning even by study and also by faith. (D&C 109:14.)

To the Church, education is not an end in and of itself but a tool to an end—the end of learning how to live and progress, how to conduct our lives in conformity with truth and righteousness and according to the will of the Lord as set forth in the scriptures and taught by his prophets.

In the business of living, the activity that brings to the normal woman the greatest fulfillment is homemaking —which means a mate, children, friends, and all the radiating obligations, joys, and burdens these relationships imply. The home is our primary educational institution and homemaking is woman's highest and most important calling.

To bear and rear children, to feel the dependence of husband and family, to know that upon her rests, in large measure, the health, the character, and the happiness of human beings whom she loves, to see herself laying and preserving the foundations of so imposing a thing as a family, to so build that this family will be of service to the Church, society, and republic is a responsibility of great magnitude. To contemplate it leaves one impressed that no other work to which she might set her hand could be so broad and inspiring, so filled with interest, and so demanding of intelligence and ability.

The problems of homemaking are of delicate social and spiritual import. If a child is anchored to religious truths and sound moral principles, it is usually because the home from which he comes is built on them. A mother can direct the ideals, influence the concepts, cultivate the tastes, and affect the habits of her children.

A mother can also direct the wants of her children. Families today become too often driven by one goal— getting material things. The mother holds a strategic position from which she can hold in check this tendency as well as counteract habits of wastefulness and attitudes of getting something without paying the price in personal effort. The mother can cultivate simplicity, independence, and thrift in her family. I ask you to consider the effect of these upon the character and well-being of an individual.

> The ones who seek their happiness
> By buying cars and clothes and rings,
> Don't seem to know that empty lives
> Are just as empty filled with things.
>
> —Anonymous

Today we have gotten away from much of the long hours of drudgery which so easily grind down the human spirit. Woman's work in the old-fashioned family was literally never done. Today's woman has far more freedom to enrich her life by activities and diversions which make her a better wife and a more capable mother. Release from certain kinds of labor which modern science has granted woman puts upon her the obligation to apply ingenuity, imagination, time, and learning in making her home fulfill its function as a molder of character.

Woman must realize that business careers, political and industrial activities, or academic learning should not lure her from her basic work as mother and homemaker. It is rather startling to learn that married women increasingly outnumber single women in the U.S. labor force. I do not wish to be misunderstood. I would not deter a woman from entering the professions, going into fields of endeavor that are useful and remunerative, that will contribute to the fullness of her life and increase her influence for good. But always she should be sure that she does not do so at the sacrifice of home and family. She should be sure that her family is gaining more than it is losing from her so doing. The working mother who hopes to achieve happiness must always put that objective first.

I know a competent young mother; she has a brilliant mind, is well trained, and is a good manager. She has two children, six and eight, to whom she is deeply devoted. She holds a responsible position in industry as does her husband. I said to her the other day, "Why do you work?" Quickly she answered, "I like to. I have an interesting job and the people I associate with are stimulating—they are doing things in the world." I pressed her further: "Do you feel your children are in any way handicapped because you work?" "I think not," she replied, "I have a girl in the home during my absence. The children are kept clean, fed well, sent to school, put to bed on time, and they have a well-equipped play area in the back yard. In fact," she said, "I think they are better cared for than the neighboring children whose mothers do not work."

I persisted a bit further. "When do you find time to read to them, listen to their little troubles, help them with their prayers? How often do you have an entire day when you may be with them hour by hour observing and directing their actions? Are you able to take them with you to church services on Sunday?" To this she answered: "As a matter of fact, I don't very often. There just aren't enough hours in the day or days in the week to do everything. I put first things first and do other things if and when I can. As for Sunday, I simply have to use Sunday to get caught up. I do take the children to sacrament meeting occasionally."

I leave to your judgment the measure whereby this mother is meeting the obligations of motherhood.

Mothers must learn to distinguish those things which are of greatest value to their children.

Elder Ezra Taft Benson, in addressing the graduates of the University of Utah said:

> We must come to the realization that it is PEOPLE—not things—that are all-important. Material things may contribute much to our comforts, our opportunities, our safety. Qualities which make for sterling character and true leadership, however, can be and have been developed in all ages regardless of the physical things with which men have been surrounded.
>
> Let us, therefore, examine carefully some of the basic principles and standards—the eternal verities of life—which build self-reliant, honorable, courageous people and their by-products—strong families, healthy communities, and glorious nations.

Next to homemaking a woman finds her greatest life fulfillment in humanitarian service. Kind, helpful service to those in need is a realm wherein God and nature destined woman to serve and bless mankind. The Prophet Joseph Smith recognized this, for in organizing the work of Relief Society he said, ". . . it is natural for females to have feelings of charity and benevolence." Love of woman for her sister, love of woman for humanity, love of woman

for that which is pure, ideal, and sacred is God-implanted
in her heart. This love is the most potential service power
known to society.

There has never been a time in the history of the
world when this service was not needed, and conditions
today seem to warrant a re-emphasis on this fundamental
work of women. Advanced as we are in many fields,
today's world is not free from distress, sorrow and suffering. There are countless situations which call upon woman
to freely exercise her love in intelligent, skilled humanitarian service. Through this service she strengthens community virtues and wins for herself an important place
in the community.

A great mission of Relief Society is to help women
in these two vital aspects of living—homemaking and
humanitarian service. As I contemplate the encouragement, guidance and direction Relief Society has given
women in these fields through the years, I recognize anew
the divinity of the work.

Long before formal classwork as we know it today
was conducted in Relief Society, the women were engaged
in educational activities. They attended classes conducted
outside the Relief Society and some of them sponsored
classes themselves. Relief Society members were urged
by their leaders to take an interest in educational matters
so that they might be better wives, mothers, homemakers,
community builders, and better Latter-day Saints. President Zina D. H. Young in remarks at the first general
conference of Relief Society held in Salt Lake City in 1889
said: "In all things possible let us endeavor to cultivate
our home talents and stimulate our sisters to read and
write that they may be intelligent wives and mothers. Read
good books, especially the Bible, the Book of Mormon,
and the Doctrine and Covenants." For more than half a
century formal class instruction has been offered the general membership in the weekly meetings of the Society.

Individual, family, and community welfare have enlisted the interests and best efforts of the Society since

its inception. In recent years the Church Welfare Program has engaged the talents and time of countless numbers of Relief Society women, providing inspired, well-directed avenues of expression for their humanitarian urges.

Relief Society recognizes that motherhood is divine, that the home and love of neighbor are of eternal value. It accepts its responsibility to help the women along these lines.

THE POWER OF COMPOSURE

A T various times and under different circumstances special character traits seem particularly desirable. The pioneer would be helpless without courage; the man in business finds dependability a requirement; in the social group affability is important. In today's strife-swept and insecure world, a character trait of paramount importance is composure. Composure implies a settled state of mind, calmness, tranquility, self-possession. This trait enables the individual to face facts squarely, to think clearly, to reason intelligently, and to arrive at sound conclusions. Composure does not imply that an individual is less sensitive to the seriousness of a situation, nor does it lessen the evil or make the condition less grievous, but it enables the individual to draw fully upon his inner resources in meeting a situation and is the first step in the intelligent solution of his problem.

Too often when we face a grave situation, when our accustomed way of life is interrupted, when some unexpected calamity sweeps down upon us, or even when we are overworked or face tasks for which we feel inadequate, a sort of hysteria takes possession of us; our normal poise is upset and we "go to pieces." We exhibit imperfect self-control and indulge in destructive emotional outbursts.

Thus, we lose mastery of both self and the situation. Though we recognize the power of composure, we argue, "Anyone would be upset facing what I face." We genuinely believe it would be more than human to remain calm and serene. But the emotions need education as well as the mind. We should strive constantly for emotional stability. We should form habits which utilize our emotional energy in constructive ways. When we are not able to change a situation, we should try changing our attitude. While it is probably true that some people naturally possess a greater degree of emotional stability than others, an honest effort to be less sensitive to disturbing stimuli and to remain self-possessed under trying circumstances usually results in improved behavior.

There is no place where composure is more essential than in the home. A composed father, a serene mother, means the meeting of family problems with reason and intelligence and the creation of happy, restful home life for all.

The Prince of this world was the great emissary of love and peace. Facing difficulties greater than any other, he went about his work with a composure which accomplished his purposes and preserved his dignity to the last.

Composure does not prevent strained relations, but it is invaluable in the wise solution of difficulties.

The Church is proud of its record of composed leadership; it is equally proud of its numerous examples of outstanding group composure. Recall with me the terrible experience of the saints at the time of the martyrdom. It was expected that the outraged and grief-stricken people would burn the town. The people of Carthage fled in all directions. Even the governor and his posse took flight. But there was no uprising or violence on the part of the Saints. Elder Willard Richards stood before eight or ten thousand Saints at Nauvoo and advised them "to keep the peace." He stated that he had pledged his honor and his life for their peaceful conduct. When the multitude heard that, notwithstanding the scene of outraged justice under which they labored and the cruel invasion of the rights of liberty and life—in the very midst of their grief and excitement, with the means at their hands to wreak a terrible vengeance, they voted to a man to follow the counsel of their leader. Such composure is scarcely paralleled in the history of our country—if in the world.

Brigham Young displayed the same type of composed leadership. On July 24, 1857, President Brigham Young and 2,587 persons were encamped at the head of Big Cottonwood Canyon, celebrating the tenth anniversary of their entrance into the Salt Lake Valley. A spirit of peace, joy, and patriotism prevailed when men bearing "war news" rode in upon the scene. The United States Army was about to invade the Utah territory; everything the Saints owned would be destroyed. Yet, there was no hysterical nervousness. President Young received the message quietly, and the Church history records: ". . . the afternoon's merriment went on as if no messengers . . . had arrived. At about sunset the camp assembled for prayers. President Wells made a few remarks in relation to 'the latest news from the states,' the order of leaving ground in the morning, and concluded with prayer." The calm, wise leaders evolved a plan whereby the invading army proved a blessing to the struggling settlers. The confidence of the people in their leaders, their knowledge of the gospel, and their unwavering faith in God, gave them an almost superhuman composure.

An understanding of the plan of life and salvation, which can come to the meekest and most humble of us through consistent effort to learn and live the gospel of Jesus Christ, is the greatest power in the world to equip us to meet whatever life has to offer with reason and intelligence, to remain composed and unafraid—come what may.

UNDERSTANDING HEARTS

"I CAN tell *you* this, because *you'll* understand." These are words which we both hear and speak. They are words which imply the capacity to comprehend, the ability to appreciate, and the ability to form reasoned judgments; they are words which imply a confidence in one's ability to see a situation in all its ramifications and to arrive at wise and just conclusions; they are words which indicate a sympathetic, understanding heart.

How many of us really have "understanding hearts" when approached by a friend or neighbor? How many of us have a friend or neighbor with an "understanding heart" to whom we may unburden our souls in times of stress? The "understanding heart" is the great alleviator of vexation, worry, and distress. Just to recite the trivial irritations of the day into a sympathetic ear will often clear away the annoyance and leave one undisturbed, while the more serious problems of life are almost insurmountable without the assistance that comes from an "understanding heart."

Whether we be young or old, rich or poor, obscure or prominent, we need someone who understands—someone who sees not only what we do but why we do it; someone who is acquainted with our motives as well as our conduct; someone who appreciates the obstacles we have encountered and who recognizes the struggle we have had; someone who fully comprehends all that is involved in our situation and consequently has a tolerant, sympathetic attitude toward us; someone who has compassion for our weaknesses and who recognizes our strengths and appreciates our achievements.

Who does not value the "understanding heart"? Yet how much does any one of us really try to cultivate it within himself? We are complimented when people say, "You are so understanding." Yet we make little conscious effort to develop this trait. We are not sensitive to all that another is up against; we fail to recognize all that is involved in his situation; we are too frequently biased, prejudiced, or otherwise unfair; we do not take time to learn another's problems or to hear his story through. The greatest obstacle to understanding, however, is usually our own selfish interests and ambitions. Our vision is obscured by our own purposes, and we lose the larger view.

The life of the Savior is a recital of perfect understanding. He understood the Samaritan woman and the woman taken in adultery; he understood Mary and Martha. In the selection of his apostles he evidenced perfect understanding, not only of the men and their capabilities but of the needs of the people to whom they must minister. His final scene on the cross is the superb example of perfect understanding: "And when they were come to the place, which is called Calvary, there they crucified him and the malefactors, one on the right hand, and the other on the left. Then said Jesus, Father, forgive them; for they know not what they do." (Luke 23:33-34.)

The Prophet Joseph was concerned lest Relief Society women should lack understanding, and through this lack lose fellowship with one another. He said: "It grieves me that there is no fuller fellowship; . . . by union of feeling, we obtain power with God." Union of feeling comes in no other way than through understanding.

When time and experience have declared the worth

of anything, why not exert ourselves to make it ours? While some people seem to be born with greater capacity to understand than are others, kinship of experience and conscious effort are twins which will open the doors of understanding to anyone. Experience comes with living, but effort is dependent upon ourselves alone. Why not put forth effort? Why not occasionally go behind the scenes and see what makes the play progress? Then we would better understand the actor's rendition of his lines. Why not endeavor to learn the problems which confront our fellowmen? Why not pause to lend a listening ear to a neighbor in distress? Why not seriously strive to gain an "understanding heart"? In Proverbs we are admonished: ". . . with all thy getting get understanding." (4:7.)

Lack of understanding erects barriers and impedes progress; understanding generates love and furthers accomplishment. Of all organizations in the world, Relief Society should be an organization of "understanding hearts."

JUDGING VALUES

T HE great difficulty with humankind is that it knows so poorly how to pursue its own best interests. However, this isn't a thing for which we should be too severely criticized, for after all, we are still but children; the fine qualities of God-like judgment are in us as yet undeveloped.

A small child allowed the choice between an ice cream cone and a ten dollar bill would not hesitate in choosing the ice cream cone. We who are more sophisticated, counting ourselves mature in our judgments, smile indulgently at such a choice.

But we may well look to ourselves and see if we, like the child, are not seeking present gain rather than future good. Given a choice between such things as worldly pleasure, association which brings excitement, power, or material gain on the one hand, and on the other the opportunity for service in the kingdom of God, which brings incitement to do good and results in development of spiritual strength, we too frequently show the immature judgment of a child and like him choose the thing of lesser value which satisfies our immediate selfish desire—we choose the ice cream cone.

The Lord recognized this tendency in man when he said: "Verily, verily, I say unto you, ye are little children, and ye have not as yet understood how great blessings the Father hath in his own hands and prepared for you." (D&C 78:17.)

A LOOK AHEAD

Be ashamed to die until you have achieved some victory for humanity.—*Horace Mann.*

S OMEONE has likened the mind to a closed room in which we live all of our lives. We walk about in this closed room day after day, year after year. On its walls we hang pictures representing our efforts. We naturally key our lives to these pictures. If we shut our minds in this dark room with only pictures of our weaknesses and our failures before us, we lose confidence in our own abilities, increase our weaknesses and our fears. Thus we lose our power to DO.

Why not then emphasize our *strengths?* Why not in this mind room hang pictures of the best things we have done, the successes that have been ours, holding before us the fine lesson we have given, the life we have enriched, the strengths we have developed. Think of all the things we have done of which we may be proud. What we have done we can do again with even greater success because of the experience behind us.

Latter-day Saints realize that our strengths are God-given. Our Father has told us that we cannot all have all gifts but that each is given his special gift and is expected to use it for the good of man.

For all have not every gift given unto them; for there are many gifts, and to every man is given a gift by the Spirit of God.

To some is given one, and to some is given another, that all may be profited thereby. (D&C 46:11-12.)

In recognizing that we have a strength we take the first step in its development. The second step is putting it to active use. The Church provides abundant opportunity to put to use all of the strengths of all of its members for the good of all mankind.

GOOD MANNERS

INTERESTING, challenging, demanding, life today moves forward with speed and aggressiveness. Its driving force is so pronounced that individuals cannot relax and keep pace. All are constantly faced with struggle— struggle in the home, in business, and in social pursuits. The spirit of present-day living is making people self-assertive, thoughtless of the rights of one another, and often genuinely selfish. More or less unconscious of this trend, most of us if accused would deny it. However, conditions all about us bear testimony of its existence. The high accident rate on the highway, the lack of reverence in our churches, crowding and jostling for positions of vantage in public gatherings, handling of merchandise in shops, care of books in libraries, and the general disrespect for the rights and possessions of others cry out for control of our selfish impulses and increased courtesy and good manners.

Using good manners after all is the suiting of our behavior to the greatest benefit, comfort, and ease of others. Human felicity is produced not so much by great pieces of good fortune as by little considerations every day. Genuine courtesy comes from the heart and is based on morality, decency, and consideration. Good manners involve the art of adjusting our behavior to all. They transcend the habits of clique, caste, or period of time.

Too often we think of good manners in rather a restricted sense, interpreting them as a knowledge of what constitutes "good form." Time, place, and situation dictate correct form. There are continual revolutions in social forms according to prevailing fashion. What is "the right thing to do" today may not be so tomorrow. What is right in one situation may not be so in another. "Good form" changes with more or less frequency and must be learned, while good manners come from within and never go out of fashion.

Emerson it was who said, "A beautiful behavior is better than a beautiful form; it gives higher pleasure than statues or pictures; it is the finest of fine arts."

Every one of us should consciously endeavor to develop perception of the best interests of one another. We should avail ourselves of every opportunity to learn what constitutes acceptable behavior. We should constantly teach and exercise good manners until they become fixed habits.

There are few other things that will tend to unite people more or pay higher dividends on time and attention invested.

SECTION THREE

Woman's Concern For Her Community And World

OUR RIGHTS VERSUS OUR RESPONSIBILITIES

Early in April of this year, it was my honor and privilege to be the guest speaker at a meeting held in New York City in honor of the 80th anniversary of the founding of the National Council of Women of the United States and the International Council of Women. These two great councils were established in 1888 primarily in the interest of woman's suffrage with two so-called giants of the early suffrage movement, Elizabeth Cady Stanton and Susan B. Anthony, as the key figures. Today millions of the world's women are identified with these councils.

More than 700 women attended this anniversary meeting, with 61 countries represented. These were capable, serious-minded women leaders who had distinguished themselves in varied fields of human endeavor in their respective countries. They were women of conscience, concerned with ways to alleviate the strains under which we are living and anxious to bring about a more just, orderly, and peaceful way of life.

I was advised that the aim of the program was to recognize the past in the world of woman, with particular emphasis upon her work in woman's suffrage, her place today, and what may be expected of her tomorrow.

Three strong impressions emerged from the considerable research involved in preparing my address: First, the dedication of women of the past to the cause of suffrage and their conviction of its rightness. So strong were Mrs. Stanton's convictions that according to one of her biographers, Theodore Tilton, ". . . she would willingly have given her body to be burned for the sake of seeing her sex enfranchised." While Susan B. Anthony, according to one of her biographers, Ida H. Harper, ". . . stood ready to sink all personal feelings . . . for the sake of promoting this cause which she placed above all else in the world."

Second, I was impressed with the long and hard struggle of the women, the patience and persistence with which they overcame almost inconceivable obstacles in order to achieve their goal.

Third, I was impressed by the worthy motives which prompted early day leaders to work for woman's suffrage. I found nothing in my reading which indicated in any way that the struggle was in order that women might be competitive with men in public life; rather, suffrage was seen as an avenue through which women might have voice in public affairs, might use their talents and exercise their judgments in the achievement of a better life for all. They saw it as a way to enlighten women for the enhancement of the society in which they were destined to live.

It is of interest that once a nation grants suffrage to its women, there is, as a rule, a favorable response. For example, so delighted was Iran when suffrage was granted its women a few short years ago that the International Council of Women was invited by the Empress Farah and the Princess Ashraf (twin sister of the Shah) to hold its triennial meeting in Teheran in honor of the event.

When in comparatively recent years the women of Chile won suffrage, there appeared in the International Council of Women Bulletin an account of the event. I quote the following:

The formal announcement of this law was attended by brilliant and important personages. After an eloquent speech, the President of the Republic designated this day as a historical date to commemorate this great event for the democracy of the country, when a new and an inspired contingent—the women—would begin to participate in the responsibilities of citizenship. With this, a new day dawns for Chile.

The president of the National Council of Women of Chile had this to say:

The task which awaits women is as great as the difficulties they have overcome; but it is not only Chile that is confronted with this terrifying dilemma, but the entire Western civilization. And it is today that woman should take on her share of responsibility on a par with man in the destiny of a world hungry for faith in eternal, spiritual values, impoverished by crises and economic conflicts, bleeding from the wounds of war, frightened by the possible disintegration of the universe—this is the opportune moment. At this time we must collaborate, men and women unitedly, if we want a . . . ray of hope to dispel the clouds that obscure the future.

And indeed it does seem that the time has arrived when the focus of woman should no longer be on her rights but rather upon her responsibilities. The same dedication that characterized the winning of suffrage should characterize the achievement of the goals envisioned for it by the pioneer leaders of the cause, namely, the use of woman's talents and the exercise of her judgments, the use of the ballot, in making a better world.

The times demand on *all* sides a new degree of public mindedness—an awakened conscience, a penetrating appraisal of those factors which have made nations great, along with re-dedicated allegiance to them. The times call for a greater degree of individual responsibility on the part of men and women alike in preserving the free way of life, together with the self-discipline that marks its wise and orderly use.

As I looked out at the 700 women assembled for the Council's anniversary meeting and considered for a brief moment the vast body of organized women which they represented, I was struck with the power and influence now in the hands of women. This power, properly directed and wisely used, could and would bring about great changes for good.

Democracy is a precious heritage. It has been defined as government by the people, government in which the supreme power is retained by the people and exercised directly and indirectly through a system of representation. Its base is liberty. Its expression is the voice of the people. The law of liberty is a law of God.

Considering democracy a little more intimately, it means the right to go to the church of our choice unrestricted; the right to express our opinions without danger to ourselves; the right to own property, to work and save and make provision for our future; the right to maintain our homes and rear our children according to our own desires and standards; the right to go forward and improve our own conditions and pursue the interests which make us happy without unnecessary restraints or restrictions; the right to realize our potential as individuals—rights guaranteed us by a government in which we have voice.

This democratic way of life did not have its inception with the American colonies, nor is it peculiar to America. The ancient Greeks advocated it. History records that Aristotle taught that a state should be but the joining together of people for the happiness of themselves and families, each one being allowed as much independence as possible without interfering with the rights of others. He declared that laws would be made and must be sovereign. Modifications in the law would be made by established processes.

As early as 1215 Magna Carta was conceived, the foundation and pillar of English constitutional law. It placed limitations on the exercise of arbitrary powers of the king and was a charter of individual liberty for the people. The Bill of Rights set forth in the Constitution of the United States was patterned after Magna Carta.

As Latter-day Saints, we know that God's prophets

have taught the importance of freedom through representative government. About 90 B.C. King Mosiah on the American continent admonished his people:

> Now it is not common that the voice of the people desireth anything contrary to that which is right; but it is common for the lesser part of the people to desire that which is not right; therefore this shall ye observe and make it your law—to do your business by the voice of the people. (Mosiah 29:26.)

It is highly disturbing that today certain influences are making inroads upon our democracy and its happy, productive way of life. Women properly should be concerned with these. May I suggest a few such influences:

(1) the moral lassitude on the part of people in private and public life

(2) the ascendency of materialism over spiritual values

(3) the growing disregard of law and order

(4) the various social devices and programs now being offered which tend to stifle individual initiative, deter self-effort, impair character, and which could ultimately enslave the individual.

What can we women do about these? How can we, the average women, the housewives on the farms and in the cities, impede or negate these adverse influences and promote that which has been proved good?

Let us first consider the problem of moral lassitude. Our greatest danger today, according to many thinking people, is from ourselves, from our growing disregard for principle and our reliance upon expediency.

The decline in national character is a serious danger to democracy because if we lose our standards, our liberties may also be lost through abuses, corruption, and chaos. Personal integrity, honesty, trustworthiness, honorable intent and action, and moral conduct in private and public life are the character fibers of democracy. These cannot be "taken on" as an individual grown to manhood or womanhood steps out into the affairs of the world. They must be inculcated in the individual in his infancy and youth. These are given root and most effectively nourished in the home. Through her training, example, and watch-care, a mother *can* implant moral principles in a child so that when his influence is extended into public life, there will be no winking at unscrupulous or dishonorable be-havior, but a steadfast adherence to right. In molding national character and creating public opinion that looks upon moral lassitude with a high degree of disfavor (and this, I believe, is the most effective way of dealing with this evil), no group has greater power than women.

This may seem a slow way of dealing with an urgent problem, but as we consider the quick pace of time between childhood and adult life, it isn't so slow; and, nonetheless, it is sure. There is no way, in my judgment, whereby women can make a better contribution to public life.

Next, let us consider the materialism that is exerting itself as never before. Materialism is threatening our rich, spiritual heritage. Spiritual strength, faith in God, and a reliance on his providences are essential to well being. Skepticism and unbelief are weapons of despotism. Tyranny and oppression do not thrive in an atmosphere of faith and religious devotion. Women have been regarded in the past as architects of spirituality. Today it would seem that the spiritual natures of many of us need an overhaul-ing. Material advantage all too often seems to motivate our actions. When the spiritual natures deeply embedded in women become dormant or choked out, we have real cause to fear. Women should make every effort to build and strengthen the spiritual qualities of life through faith in God, through participation in church activities, through developing well-defined religious concepts and beliefs and teaching them to their children, and through cultivating their innate spiritual natures. Not what we *have* but what we *are* should be the watchword of women. Relative to disregard for law and order, it is reasonable that woman as mother, householder, educator, spiritual anchor, and the living conscience of her contemporaries would discountenance any attitude or action that would not uphold the sovereignty of law. True, she would be sensitive to human needs and sympathetic toward correcting or improving conditions which influence this attitude; she would work toward bettering conditions, but she would do so in an orderly way. She would not lend herself to action that would in any way agitate militancy or public disturbance. Rather she would concern herself with acquiring an understanding of the causes of the condition; she would thoughtfully determine how best to deal with these causes; she would work toward creating an enlightened public opinion; and she would accomplish desired changes within the framework of law. All too often, I fear, women who are inclined to be moved by their emotions become so exercised over a problem that they lose sight of the proper approaches to its solution. Mormon women know that latter-day revelation requires of us strict allegiance to civil law. It is my belief that organized women upholding the sovereignty of civil law and working toward needed social reform through orderly processes can be a power for good.

With regard to the fourth adverse influence to which I referred, let us exercise our hard-won franchise. Let us sense our individual responsibility to see that persons elected to public office are competent and morally sound, that they will protect the policies and practices of democracy and not yield to new and enslaving ways of governing, that they will so govern that national character will remain strong. Generally speaking, I believe that people resent help that does not allow reciprocal effort.

Let us as women take measure of our own attitudes and wants. What do we expect of government? Would those things which we want serve the greatest good of the greatest number of people? What are we willing to contribute toward their attainment? Are we content to limit our contribution to complaints or do we sense our responsibility to improve conditions through the orderly and intelligent exercise of our franchise? Let us keep informed on the local, national, and international issues before us. This is not hard to do in this day of extensive communication. Let us listen to the viewpoints of those who seek election to public office and who may have to deal with these issues. Let us consider whether their viewpoints square with the principles that have traditionally contributed to worthy government and the well-being of the people. Let us as Mormon women weigh them against the principles which have been taught us by our leaders from the very beginning days of the Church. Let us listen to the prophets.

I have faith in the women of the Church. I have faith that the countless good women of the world will realize that they have influence and power in correcting ills and in promoting right, and that they will prove themselves effective in the orderly achievement of a better world.

THE INDIVIDUAL IN SOCIAL ACTION

THE statement in italicized type at the end of the printed copy of "A Code of Personal Commitment" embodies a principle to which I fully subscribe. May I read it:

> I will know that as I build, so is the world built
> And if I am indifferent, I abandon the world.

We are heirs to a progressive civilization. Looking back we see that many of the patterns of life which in their time seemed baffling have taken shape and meaning. We live in a better world today than at any time in history, regardless of the tensions, pressures, insecurities, and endless changes to which we must adjust. I believe none of us would want to go back to the past—to the coal stove and candle light; to the days of no wonder drugs or the old-fashioned methods of caring for the sick; to the narrow boundaries of our local neighborhoods where we were without the great systems of communication and transportation that make us conversant with life far beyond our own dooryards.

The richness, the hope and promise of life today have not been achieved through the efforts of one or two great leaders; they have not been achieved through the organized effort of any one or two separate segments of our population; they have not been achieved through one single institution, business, or political structure. Rather, the advanced state of life today has been brought about by an endless number of individuals making an endless chain of worthy contributions, some working alone, others joining an organized group, most of them doing both.

Wonderful as is our world today, we need stout hearts to meet the future, a future pregnant with unborn events, big with possibilities, and stupendous in its demands. But we know that persistent climbing levels the hills and gives added strength to travel on. We know that a good tomorrow is dependent upon the same human forces that have brought us so good a today—a sense of social responsibility on the part of individuals and a willingness to engage in activities which promote human well-being.

The word *responsibility* is an interesting one. Webster defines it as "moral accountability." A simple but meaningful definition came to my attention recently. I visited a Sunday School class of eight-year-olds. The teacher used the word "responsibility" a number of times. Then suddenly she paused and said to the children, "Do you know the meaning of the word 'responsibility'?" To my surprise almost every hand went up. "Robert," she said, to a bright-faced little boy, "you tell us." To which Robert readily replied, "It means you have to do something yourself. You can't expect somebody else like your mother to do it for you. It's up to you."

Social responsibility applied to the individual then means that each person looks to himself to see what he can do, both working alone and with the group, for the welfare of human society.

Social responsibility is motivated by the spirit of brotherhood. It is neighborliness in action. It answers to the following impressive creed:

My neighbor is every man who needs my help; and I should think no more of asking whether he belongs to *my* country, *my* family, *my* political party or *my* church than I would if he were calling from a burning building.

The good neighbor never asks, "What do I get in return?" He never considers the inconvenience or asks, "Is it my duty? If so, I will do it; if not, I will not do it." He does it because it needs to be done.

Individuals are differently endowed. Each has his own gift, each has his own characteristics, each has his own circumstances. All affect his social contribution. We cannot all be a George Washington, a Benjamin Franklin, an Abraham Lincoln; we can't all be an Elizabeth Fry, a Florence Nightingale, a Jane Addams. But each can make his contribution to the total symphony of life. The following poetic lines from the pen of President Hugh B. Brown beautifully convey what I would say with regard to differing individual contributions.

> As the violinist tunes each string until it responds with an individual tone capable of harmonious response to a Master's hand;
> As Handel and Mendelssohn placed symbols on paper, which when combined with poetic images, became oratorios;
> As Cicero and Demosthenes used words with such discriminating skill as to make each one do its best and express an exact meaning, and then wove them into great orations;
> As Milton and Shakespeare arranged individual incidents into immortal dramas and poetry;
> As Lincoln and Churchill held aloft ideals and inspired their countrymen to save their nations;
> So each individual should do his best and know that his particular contribution is required in the immortal symphony of life.

A homely illustration comes to my mind. The same performance cannot be expected from a plow horse as from a race horse (and some are born plow horses while others are born race horses), but the performance of each is necessary.

It is an irrefutable truth that the world calls for many sowers of many kinds of seeds.

Regardless of the social contribution which we have the potential to make, we owe it to society to make that contribution as excellent as we can. We hear much of the

importance of physical fitness. We show great concern
over mental, moral, and spiritual fitness. What, I ask, of
social fitness! Are we sufficiently concerned with this?
To be fit, I believe, is to be healthfully competent, capable,
prepared or ready. The socially fit who have achieved a
healthy and responsible attitude toward others, are willing
to participate in social action programs, and are prepared
to do a good job. I commend a little more consideration
for our social fitness.

Today an endless chain of worthy social action programs bid for support. To identify ourselves with all or
even with an excessive number of them is neither reasonable nor wise. To do so is to dissipate our energies, spread
ourselves too thin, weaken the strength of our contribution
at every point, and lose the joy of a fully satisfying endeavor. So we must make choices. A knowledge of the
decision-making processes which will enable us to choose
programs which seem to us most valuable and to which we
can make the most effective contribution is imperative.

Having chosen, we must move forward with faith, with
courage, and with dependability. As we work with others,
we must learn to be sympathetic and sensitive to their
points of view. We must respect the opinions of others
but be unafraid to dissent if our differences of opinion are
based on sound judgment and respect for facts. We must
be unafraid of new ideas for they have been truthfully
called "stepping stones to progress." Weiman, a great
social analyst, said, "We must always be ready to reinter-
pret our concepts when they fail to pass the test of new-
found facts."

We must dethrone our prejudices and dedicate ourselves intelligently to the causes which we have chosen.

We are living in a great democracy where the well-
being of the individual is of paramount importance and
where the state is important only as it serves the people.
In our democracy we recognize the rights of the individual.
But when we accept the doctrine of "individual rights,"

we must also accept its concomitant "individual responsibility." Living in an ominous, portentious, demanding, yet
glorious era of world history, every one of us should accept
its obligations, rise to its privileges, and enjoy its blessings, ever impressing upon ourselves the importance and
truthfulness of the code,

> . . . as I build, so is the world built
> And if I am indifferent, I abandon the world.

THE EFFECTIVE CHANNELING OF WOMEN'S ENERGIES

THIS spring I was walking east from Main Street on South Temple in Salt Lake City. I saw approaching me a woman with whom I had once been intimately associated and whom I had not seen for several years. I slowed my steps to speak to her, but she merely nodded and swept by me. In a moment, however, she turned and overtook me. Apologetically, she said, "It seems I'm always in such a hurry and have so much on my mind, I'm scarcely courteous any more." She then explained that she was employed and that this was her day off. She had just come from a funeral where she had been soloist. She said she loved to sing and tried to keep up with her music by taking a few lessons and singing as opportunity and circumstances permitted. She said that on her way from the funeral service, she had dropped into the library to pick up a book. Inasmuch as her ward Relief Society was now meeting in the evening, she felt I would be glad to know she had accepted the call to teach the literature lessons. She continued on by saying that she was now hurrying to pick up a few bread rolls, since a committee of the P.T.A., of which she was a member, was meeting at her home later in the afternoon, and she wished to serve light refreshments. She said that inasmuch as her children were now all in school, she and her husband felt she should do her part in the P.T.A.

I inquired about her children. She said that the three older children were fine but the little girl had mumps. I asked who was caring for the child during the mother's absence from home. She replied that the grandmother, although old, was able to sit with the child. "But," she continued, "Grandma is growing very frail. She is really becoming quite a serious problem." Then, in a spirit bordering almost on despair, she concluded, "At times I grow quite discouraged and weary of it all. Try as I may, I don't seem to be able to keep up with all I have to do."

As we parted, she spoke in a more cheerful vein, referring to a mutual friend who had received a special honor. I said I had not seen this friend for years. She responded, "I see her occasionally. We both belong to the same woman's service organization, but I don't have time to attend very often."

In not more than five minutes, this woman had told me that she was employed outside her home; that she had four children, a husband, and an aged mother-in-law living in the home, for whom she was responsible; that she was taking singing lessons and accepting invitations to sing; that she was a class leader in Relief Society; and that she was active in the P.T.A. and partially active in a service organization. In addition, she had told me that the strains and pressures of her life were almost more than she could bear and that they were robbing her of much of the joy of living.

Here was a smart, ambitious woman, sensitive to her duties, willing to serve, interested in what is going on in life and wanting to be a part of it, anxious to succeed in whatever she undertook, yet bogged down by too much to do.

I am led to ask, "Is she the exception? Is she one in a thousand or is she one among thousands?" It is my conviction that her counterpart may be found all too often. We are living in a high-powered, fast-moving time, a period characterized by changed conditions and new values. No change, perhaps, is greater than the change in the status of women and, coincidental with this, the change in home and family life. The woman of yesteryear was housewife, mother, churchgoer. She was interested in the school and social life of her family. Perhaps she participated to some extent in community activities as she felt needed, but her world was largely for home and family. The woman of today is housewife, mother, wage-earner, church and civic leader. The doors of industry, business, the professions, and politics are wide open and beckoning her to enter. New horizons are daily being created for her, rich in new interests and values. Almost unlimited are the areas bidding for her time and energies.

In her age-old role of mother, her job presents new challenges born of the highly geared era in which we are living: She must cope with the changing, complex social order in dealing with her children; she must skillfully handle new attitudes and influences which could adversely affect her children; she must see that her children are maintained, trained, and educated in conformity with present-day high standards so that they may successfully compete in a strongly competitive world; she must guide, direct, and steer them into socially acceptable as well as morally sound behavior.

The average woman today shares in the business and social interests of her husband as seldom before. She has a live, active interest in his business activities and often participates in them. She attends conventions with him. She meets his friends socially and shares in their entertainment.

As a wage earner, she is in demand. Many women are being enticed, if not forced, into the labor market. [According to the last figures available to me, approximately 28,000,000 women work in the course of a year. Three out of every ten married women are now working, and nearly two out of every five mothers whose children are of school age are in the labor force.] Visualize, if you can, what would happen to your place of business, or to business houses with which you have dealings, if suddenly all of the women retired from their jobs. Consider what the situation would be if all mothers retired to their homes. I wonder what it would mean in terms of our industrial, economic, and social lives.

Professional women today are affected by a theory that the trained, professional woman has not only a right but also a responsibility to contribute to society the service for which she has been trained, whether she be married or not. The view is taken that she has benefited from long years of costly training at the hands of professional people and in return owes service to the profession and to society.

At an International Council of Women meeting in Montreal, Canada, in 1958, a woman leader said that a woman must have the right of choice as to what she will do with her life. The professional woman, however, must recognize that she has been the recipient of long-time, painstaking discipline of mind, character and, often, of hand. Her skill is, in large measure, the bounty of other professionals—her teachers. For her to feel that her obligation to her teachers, to her profession, to society, terminates because she marries is scarcely to live up to the intelligent thinking we have a right to expect of her. While she has a right to marry, she also has a responsibility to continue to use the skill she has acquired for the purposes for which she gained it and, in addition, she has the responsibility to pass on to the new trainee as much as possible of the knowledge she has acquired from others and developed herself in order that the profession shall live and advance.

An example of what is actually happening in relation to this attitude is shown in a report of a study made by one of our leading universities among women graduated from medical school in the United States between 1925 and 1940. The report shows that 86% of those who married have continued with medical work.

Women are also active in political life. American women struggled hard for complete suffrage. By amendment to the United States Constitution in 1920, they won the right to vote and hold public office. The influence of the woman vote is growing, and increasing activity is being demanded of her. In the last presidential election, it was conceded by a number of political authorities that the woman's vote was an important factor. Also, more and more women are being drawn into positions of trust and responsibility in government.

Woman has not made the spectacular gains in science that she has made in other fields. There is presently, however, considerable agitation for a greater acceptance of her in this area.

What of women in business and finance? Speaking of women as a whole, I believe they have considerable business acumen. It has been my opportunity to observe women closely as they earn, spend, invest, and account for money. Relief Society ward and branch organizations must maintain themselves financially and make a strict accounting of financial operations. I find the women, generally speaking, to be astute, wise, and honest in money management and accurate in financial accounting.

Now let us look at another area of national life in which women are becoming increasingly involved. This is the area of women's organizations. I don't believe I know a single woman, unless it would be an aged or infirm one, who doesn't belong to one or more women's organizations. American women are perhaps the most highly organized of any women in the world today, with the possible exception of Communist women. Women's organizations range from small, intimate social groups or clubs to powerful groups with extraordinarily large memberships, groups whose activities are national and international. Their purposes and programs are centered in specialized causes ranging from some minor interest of a few women to great health and human-betterment programs of tremen-

dous national and international significance. Generally
speaking, this is good. However, many thinking women
leaders today are beginning to feel that we have gone
overboard in forming organizations, that duplication of
purpose exists, and that many women are becoming involved in so many organizations that they do not plow
a straight or deep enough furrow in any one field. Also,
it is felt by some leaders that too much organized energy
is being turned to unprofitable and unimportant account.
Let me read you an opinion of a woman who has considerable stature nationally as a leader of organized women.
I am not at liberty to give her name but am authorized
to quote her opinions written to me in a personal letter.
She says:

> As nowhere else in the world, the women of America are
> organization women. This, in my opinion, is one of their greatest
> troubles because in too many of these organizations, too much
> energy is scattered on non-entities. As individuals, the women in
> America allow themselves to be smothered by the herd instinct.
> There are really very few independent thinkers and real leaders
> among them. To be a leader, one must exhibit constant unadulter-
> ated personal initiative, rigid determination, and strict adherence
> to a cause in which she believes and to which she is dedicated.
> One must possess innate, never wavering courage, radiantly ex-
> pressed in the face of doubting, faltering multitudes. One must
> not be a follower ready to succumb to joining all kinds of non-
> descript organizations of little importance. It is my opinion that
> relatively few of the typical programs arranged by the women's
> organizations are much above the commonplace in interest, im-
> portance, or achievement. Too much of the time is aimed at
> entertainment rather than at vital, strong programs which favorably
> influence American life.

As we consider all of the areas of human endeavor
crowding in upon women, we are led to ask, "How has this
all come about? What has brought us to the situation in
which we find ourselves?" I suggest three circumstances:

1. Woman's own efforts for emancipation or liberation; her unquenchable thirst for expression; her innate
desire to throw off every shackle that binds her and to

assert herself as a free-thinking, free-acting individual; her own overt acts born of the strong feeling within her that she should be allowed to do the things she wants to do, which she feels capable of doing, and which she feels she has the right to do.

2. The circumstances of war when men by the tens of thousands left their daily labors and went into the armed services, leaving the gaps to be filled by women who not only had to maintain the production and service status quo but also had to meet the special demands incident to the war. Through these demands women gained new insight into their powers and abilities. They tasted the satisfactions of new endeavors and achievements. They felt the security of money earned by their own labors. Their success, too, altered traditional attitudes with regard to the place of women in national life and the types of work they may appropriately do.

3. Scientific advancements that have taken the time-consuming elements and the drudgery out of housekeeping, thus releasing time to the homemaker to engage in pursuits outside her home.

A story illustrates this point. A repairman was fixing an automatic washer. He could see nothing wrong with it, so he put into the washer a few pairs of socks and a couple of shirts and turned the switch. The washer soon washed the clothing and it was quickly transferred to the dryer. The dryer spun around for a few moments and then stopped, only to have a gadget appear which neatly folded the socks and the shirts and tossed them across the room into a neat pile in an open left-hand dresser drawer. "Now," said the repairman to the housewife, "what's wrong with that?" "Wrong?!" retorted the irate housewife. "That clothing belongs in the right-hand drawer."

I wonder if women have not now reached a point where they must stop and evaluate what they are doing. Do we not need to ask ourselves: "Whither are we going

and why?" Does not each one of us need to look at herself
objectively and say to herself: "Are you really getting the
most in sound values from the time and energies you are
expending? Are you channeling your powers and capabilities along the most productive and rewarding courses?
Or are you spreading yourself too thin?" Would we not
be wise to pause and contemplate for a moment the elements that constitute a calm, unharried, poised, satisfying,
and satisfactory life? Is it not mandatory upon us, particularly as Latter-day Saint women, to define our basic duties
and responsibilities as women, and then weigh in the balance the energy we are expending upon less fundamental
duties? Should we not pause and evaluate the appeals
which cause us to undertake more than we should? And
should we not develop within ourselves the courage and
the ability to say "no" when circumstances justify? Would
we be in the wrong to occasionally say to ourselves, "Am I
truly getting from life the best it has to offer, and am I
realizing, as a person, the fullest possible joy from my
labors?"

Let us look back a moment upon the busy woman
hurrying past me. What steps might she take to relieve
herself of pressures and tensions? How might she more
effectively channel her energies?

Would she not first consider her employment, since
this requires such a large portion of her time and energies
and places her in the dual role of a wage earner and a
homemaker? It would seem that she might appropriately
examine her reasons for working to see if they are justified
in light of the well-being of herself, her home, and her
family. This analysis would require clear thinking un-
clouded by personal preference, job satisfactions, and the
desire for material things which her income may provide.
Many women find it hard not to rationalize in making
a decision about working. Even though home and family
are her greater responsibility and their well-being dictates
that she should give up her employment, it is not easy for
some women to willingly give up the personal satisfactions

of getting up in the morning, dressing for business, driving off to work, being a part of the ongoing current of business or industry, and coming home with a pay check, in exchange for the routine duties of home and family.

If, after every shred of rationalization has been removed from her thinking, this woman is honestly convinced that the interests of all concerned are best served by her working, she may need to take a look at the type of work she is doing to see if it is suited to her abilities and circumstances. She may need to look at the requirements of her job and see whether she is meeting these happily and with minimum strain. A change of work is sometimes desirable if an overburdened woman must work.

What of days off? Is the woman to whom I referred using them wisely to relax and to enjoy herself and family? Or does she grab at them to do countless extra things in which she has involved herself, so that at the close of these days she is more tired than at the close of a normal work day?

What of the grandmother? This woman might profitably pause to see why Grandma is becoming an ever-increasing problem. What about Grandma's health? She may need health care. Does she have opportunity to be with her own friends? Or is she largely confined to the home while mother is working, with little opportunity for association with anyone but the children? Every aged person has social and recreational needs. Are these being adequately met for Grandma? Is Grandma taking upon herself responsibilities for the home and children which she is unfitted to assume and which overtax her and contribute to her irritability and general decline? Does the home need someone in it other than Grandma for a few hours each week to keep things in smooth running order, thus relieving Grandma's tensions as well as Mother's work load?

And the singing: Are the values to the woman from voice training and meeting singing engagements commensurate with the costs in time, energy, and money? She alone must decide.

The three organizations to which she belongs—the Relief Society, the P.T.A., and the service organization—demand evaluation. Could she perhaps discontinue one, and if so, which one? Which of these has greatest claim upon her? Which offers the most in permanent values to her and her family?

Let her look at herself and the degree of intensity with which she enters into her activities. Surely there must be some to which she could give less time and ability and still make an acceptable contribution.

It is my conviction that this woman could modify her life to her advantage and that of her family. What is your opinion?

In the Book of Mormon, we read the words of Lehi to his son, Jacob. Speaking of the creations and the goodness of God to his children, he says "All things have been done in the wisdom of him who knoweth all things." (2 Nephi 2:24.) Then he continues with this beautiful, heartwarming message: ". . . and men are that they might have joy." The joy spoken of by Lehi is the joy that comes through righteous, well-directed effort; through knowing and meeting with intelligence and composure our basic obligations, first to the Lord, second to our families, third to our fellowmen. This attainment entails preserving ourselves in righteousness, wisdom, health, and strength.

It was not intended that our lives should be a succession of confused, wearisome, frustrated days; rather, it was intended that our lives should be orderly, fruitful, and happy.

Today is indeed a new day, but it need not be a day of pressure and tension for women. The challenge before women today, as I see it, is to rise magnificently to the things of basic importance, ridding themselves of the nonessential and less important interests and activities that encumber them and destroy their peace.

Matthew Arnold in his sonnet "To a Friend" gives us a message we might well remember.

Be his

My special thanks, whose even-balanced soul,
From first youth tested up to extreme old age,
Business could not make dull, nor Passion wild:
Who saw life steadily and saw it whole.

I love the women of the Church. My prayer for them is that they may not dissipate their energies by chasing after baubles, but that they may preserve themselves in wisdom and strength for the genuinely important things of life so that they may know the full joy of composed and fruitful living.

THE INDIAN STUDENT PLACEMENT PROGRAM

T HE Indian student placement program germinated in
our pioneer heritage of acceptance and consideration
of the Indians. Kindness and helpfulness have characterized our attitudes toward them since pioneer days, as
indicated in the following teachings of Brigham Young:

Look out for them, but they should be protected in their
rights.

Don't make them presents until they become demanding to
the point of taking from you what you cannot afford to give; but
if they would be friendly, teach them to raise grain and show them
how to work for their own benefit and advancement.

Feed the Indians; don't fight them.

Our records reveal that the pioneer women were helpful. They sewed for the Indians, taught them how to care
for their babies, and otherwise served them. The minutes
of one of our ward Relief Society meetings held May 21,
1875, state: "We were called upon to help the Indians;
we should respond and do all we could. Spoke of the Indians being desirous of learning all we could teach them."

During more recent years, this attitude has asserted
itself in a desire to help the underprivileged Indian children. This desire is in line with a general national upsurge
of concern for the underprivileged Indians. Elder Spencer
W. Kimball at a general conference of the Church said:

There has perhaps been more constructive consideration given to the Indian people in the last decade than in the entire century before.

In 1947 the cry was raised: "The Navajos are freezing and starving." You remember, I am sure. Truckloads of food and clothing were gathered here in Utah and taken from our Church welfare storehouses for these distressed Indians. Simultaneously, the press took up the cry and the warm-hearted people of the Nation, and particularly of the West, answered the call with bedding, food, clothing, and money. The echoes resounded from ocean to ocean and a sleeping nation roused itself.

It is a choice privilege today to be identified with the Indian student placement program of the Church. I consider it a great program. I know that it is a program born through the inspiration of the Lord. I know that Relief Society has been greatly blessed in being identified with this program. We were brought into it because our organization was licensed to place children in foster homes during the school year.

As I look back over the history of the program from the time of its inception until the present, I am reminded of our struggles in the early years of its development. I am reminded of the problems which confronted us. I am reminded of the joys and satisfactions that came with each small degree of success. I often think of the way the program came into being as an organized program of the Church.

The Indian people I believe were beginning to desire better opportunities for their children. They were pushing out from the reservations to where the children might have better opportunities. Our Latter-day Saint people, with the love which they have for the Indian people and the knowledge which they have of the divine destiny of the Indian people, wanted to take these children into their homes. A number of them did take them into their homes. Soon, however, we received visits from the State Department of Public Welfare advising us that our Latter-day Saint people who were taking these children into their homes for foster care were in violation of state law unless the placements were made through a licensed agency of the state. It was pointed out to us that these children needed the protection of law, that they easily could be exploited. The state officials urged that the Church do something to protect the interests of the families who were willing to help the children and, at the same time, protect the interests of the children by having the services to the Indian children brought under the direction of the Relief Society, which was already licensed to place children in foster homes. So bit by bit, under the great and inspired guidance of Elder Kimball, this program began to take shape.

I know that in any important activity we sometimes get discouraged. I recall one day that I felt particularly discouraged over the Indian program. It was hard to find homes; it was hard to select children; it was hard to reach the reservations; it was hard to get proper releases from parents, and so on. I thought perhaps the best and greatest work for the Indian children could be done through the regular, organized missionary program of the Church on the reservations. At that time Elder LeGrand Richards, who is now identified with this program along with Elder Kimball, was presiding bishop. He was also an adviser to Relief Society. I went to him and said, "Brother Richards, I wonder about this Indian program. I wonder if it will really be successful. It seems to me we are using an awful lot of energy for the little we are accomplishing." I asked, "Do you yourself believe in it?"

Bishop Richards replied, "Sister Spafford, I'm glad you came. You came just at the right moment. Just a few minutes ago President George Albert Smith was in this office. I want to tell you what he said to me. He said, 'Elder Richards, I'm growing to be an old man, and I'll soon be on the other side. When I go on the other side I will meet Father Lehi. And if I don't meet him, I think I'll look him up. I want to be able to shake hands with him. I want to be able to look him in the eye and say,

"Father Lehi, we have made a fresh beginning for your children.",

"Now," said Brother Richards, "if President Smith feels that way, Sister Spafford, you and I ought to be perfectly willing to do our part as we are directed by our leaders."

I left Elder Richards' office that day determined that I would do whatever would be asked of me in this program, and I have tried to the best of my ability to do so. The joy, the satisfaction, the conversion, and the wonderful blessings that have come from being identified with this program are immeasurable.

I recall one day as I was walking by the Church offices hearing President Smith call to me. He said, "Sister Spafford, just a moment." I stopped, and he said, "I have a word of counsel for you. Don't rob Father Lehi of his children." I thought for a moment and then I said, "In other words, President Smith, you don't want an adoption program for the Indian children. You want a foster home care program that will give children opportunities in our Latter-day Saint homes but will allow them to return to their own homes and strengthen their own people." He said, "That is exactly what I mean." So that policy characterizes this great program.

We must remember that we are each doing our bit, as opportunity comes to us. I firmly believe that we are each contributing to the fulfillment of prophecy made by ancient prophets and in a way directed by modern prophets. We are dealing with the reclaiming of a mighty nation—a nation that had its beginning in this hemisphere 600 years before Christ, a nation founded in righteousness by Father Lehi, a nation that turned away from the Lord, a nation that returned to the Lord and again turned away. We remember also that we are dealing with a nation for whom great promises have been made. I firmly believe that this program is a program in the hands of the Lord to help reclaim that nation so that the prophecies of his servants may be fulfilled. I am sure that those who are supporting it will receive untold blessings for the part they play.

TRUE EDUCATION

For those of us who were on the B.Y.U. campus in years gone by, homecoming week is a time for renewal of past friendships, for recalling happy experiences. It is a time for reflecting upon the influences of the school upon our lives, and perhaps even a time when we appraise our indebtedness to the institution.

I recall the day when faculty and students alike felt it a needless extravagance for every student to have his own textbook. Sharing was the order of the day. College Hall provided ample room for the student body to attend assemblies. The ladies gym on the corner of University and 6th North was regarded as a spacious hall for the Junior Prom and other social functions. Yet, in spite of the limited facilities and rigidly circumscribed financial budget, the students learned. They went from the institution well equipped with knowledge and character to make a worthy contribution to life, and many of them reached positions of distinction in the Church and in national life. This was so largely, I feel, because the school had great teachers—dedicated, scholarly men and women concerned with the academic achievements of the students and also with their character and soul development. Let me mention a few great teachers of my day: President George H.

Brimhall, Franklin Harris, John Swenson, Thomas Martin, Carl Eyring, and Christian Jensen. A notebook kept in my days at Brigham Young University contains an interesting statement of President George H. Brimhall. "Books, apparatus, maps, charts, in short, all the materials used in the teaching process are but the scaffolding that the wise teacher uses to build an intelligent man and a human soul."

Emerson once wrote his daughter that he "cared little concerning the name of the school she attended. Big name universities were not his concern. He cared much, however, concerning the teachers with whom she studied." He referred to the school as "a living agency, a place where life touches life," and to teaching as "the conscious act of the trained mind and spirit of a teacher influencing the less trained mind and spirit of the pupil, to the end that the pupil might come into possession of all the knowledge, culture, training, and character development he was capable of receiving."

So in my day on the campus, what was lacking in facilities, was compensated for in great teachers.

Transportation and the easy means of communication are bringing people of the world close together. Only a comparatively few hours separate us even from countries farthest removed from us by miles. Yet in many instances, we are very far apart in culture, tradition, degree of development, standards of living, ideals, and philosophies of life. I recall attending an international congress of women not too long ago. The United States women were concerned with showing a film on the use of radioactive isotopes in the detection and arrest of cancer. Side by side with them were women from the so-called developing countries concerned with such matters as bride price, child marriages, and the extension of education to females. These wide differences must be bridged and true education must be looked to as the bridgehead.

THE WOMAN'S MOVEMENT

ISTORY records an interesting story of the beginning of the woman's movement a little more than a century ago. A world's anti-slavery conference was held in London in 1840. The United States sent delegates—among them Elizabeth Cady Stanton and Lucretia Mott, both untiring laborers in the anti-slavery cause. When the women tried to take their seats, the conference denied them recognition because they were women. Champions arose to protest. After a long and agitated discussion, the house compromised by deciding that the women might not take part in the proceedings but might sit behind a screen in the gallery and listen. Hurt, righteously indignant, the women walked down Queen Street in London that night discussing the burning injustice of the day's proceedings. They had gone to England to help emancipate the Negro, only to have forced upon their attention in clear focus the fact that they themselves were not free. They resolved to go back to America and begin education for what they termed "woman's rights."

It was eight years later when the first public demand was made by women for equal educational, industrial professional, and political rights.

To us, it seems almost incomprehensible that in these

pioneering days there were no women in the trades, none in the professions, none in public life, only a handful in teaching, a smattering in the arts, and any woman who considered business as a career opened herself to the charge of being unsexed. Even as late as the turn of the century, domestic service claimed more than one-half of all employed women.

Today, however, we have a world peculiarly marked by strong feminine hands. We have organized women, dedicated to the well-being of women in business and the professions, and also making an effective contribution to the type and quality of American business and professional life.

FREE TIME FOR THE AGING

F OR many years the organization over which I preside has published a monthly magazine which carries a column headed "Birthday Congratulations." This column recognizes birthdays, called to the attention of the editors, of older members of the Society. When I was editor of the Magazine, the birthdays of women 75 or older were recognized. The number grew so large, however, that the minimum age had to be lifted to 80; then, to 85; now it is 90, with consideration presently being given to lifting it to 95. This is an index of the growing life span. This growing life span, coupled with a soaring population, has brought about a new generation in our society for whom there appears to be inadequate preparation—economically, medically, or socially.

While everyone is talking about aging, no one, insofar as I know, can give a satisfying, all-encompassing definition of it. In years past, people seem to have had a stereotype of old age which was one of dependency and ill health coupled with infirmity and eccentricity. The mental image of the aging was the tottery gait, the shaky hand, the dimmed vision, the dulled hearing, forgetfulness, and similar infirmities. This condition began somewhat earlier in life than it does for most persons today, yet no exact chronological age was associated with it. Of recent years, the concept seems to have been that aging is something more or less undefinable and undesirable that sets in in varying degrees on everyone at the chronological age of 65. Yet great numbers of people who are over 65 are living self-directing, self-maintaining lives, are making a creditable contribution to life, and are in comparatively good health. So we are changing our opinion of the aging process.

We have learned also that later life is a widely diversified period and that there is cause to be hesitant in treating all persons 65 and over as a unit. For example, some persons over 65 are in excellent health, while others are not; some are working, while many are not; some have adequate income, while others do not; some have absorbing personal interests which engage their time and attention, as well as adequate social and recreational opportunities, while many do not; some live alone, some with their spouses, some with their children or relatives, while some are in institutions; some have hospital and surgical insurance, but most do not. Only a very few have comprehensive medical insurance. Thus, circumstances differ greatly among individuals. Marion B. Folsom, former secretary of the Federal Department of Health, Education, and Welfare, has said that those who would plan for the aging "must avoid efforts which tend to impose uniformity on older people—efforts which apply policies and programs alike to men and women who are not alike."

While there is no specified number or uniform kind of predicament, or even one single dilemma in which all persons are likely to find themselves, certain problems occur more often and with greater intensity among older persons. Among these, the following five appear to be foremost: (1) Maintenance income; (2) Work opportunities; (3) Health and medical care; (4) Living arrangements; (5) Free-time activities. These, of course, are large, general classifications; each may be divided into a number of smaller areas.

There are inter-relationships among these five areas of need which should not be overlooked. All too often a problem in one area creates problems in other areas. For example, the lack of work opportunities may cause serious income maintenance problems, as well as a need for help to the individual in providing suitable activities for his free time; or, lack of suitable free-time activities may create emotional and even physical health problems.

Intelligent planning for the aging, therefore, calls for a multiple approach to problems. This morning, however, we are concerned with one area of need only: recreation or free-time activities.

Certainly we are agreed that activity is necessary at any age. In the later years, when the activities incident to one's employment are removed, it demands special consideration. Without stimulating and creative activities, persons tend to vegetate and soon die spiritually and break up physically. Dr. Fredrick Schwartz, American Medical Association, has said, "As physicians, we know that retirement to inactivity can, for many people, be an impediment to health."

The average older person wishes to engage in some type of needed service or productive activity. He is not content with only make-work activities or hobbies. He wants meaningful activities along with his relaxing diversion.

In considering recreation, the Situation Paper on Free-time Activities, prepared by the planning committee for the White House Conference on Aging said:

It is important to understand what it (recreation) means today—what its broad range of opportunities offers. Unfortunately, recreation for the aging is often thought of only as bingo, square dancing, and birthday parties. This is a tragic misconception and must be corrected if we are to appreciate the really significant contribution recreation can make to the abundant leisure of the aging. Recreation in today's concept is any form of free-time activity engaged in voluntarily and for the enjoyment and satisfaction it brings to the participant. It may provide an opportunity for self-expression, creative activity, service to others, or the pure joy of living. . .

Recreation includes physical recreation activities, the creative arts, music, dancing, dramatics, social activities, travel, outings, camping, gardening, family group living activities, table games, enjoyment and appreciation of nature, photography and other hobbies, reading, conversation, listening to the radio, watching television, performing worthwhile services, participation in civic affairs, special events, and so on.

A broad range of activities meets the needs of the aging in diversional opportunities, volunteer service, citizen participation, adult education, and religion.

Volunteer service and citizen participation in community programs are the activity manna for the average retired worker. They "provide an outlet through which a person can demonstrate capacity and social responsibility to themselves and others." They give to a person a sense of being needed. This sense of usefulness comes from the reality that the volunteer worker is essential in our community life.

Volunteer work in abundance and many opportunities for citizen participation in community programs are already being offered to persons in middle and later life by the Red Cross, local hospitals, community health and public betterment organizations, civil defense units, civic improvement groups, churches, and others.

The church offers a peculiarly important type of volunteer service, one that is particularly valuable since it is motivated by religious beliefs and convictions and carries with it a dedication. Church service tends to keep the natural focus toward the future—the future life. This sustains the individual, ameliorates many of the difficult circumstances of old age, and gives to him a feeling of the eternal value of his service.

In the church to which I belong, the Mormon Church, limitless opportunities for volunteer service are afforded. The General Church Welfare Program, for example, has hundreds of welfare production projects, including dairies, poultry projects, cattle ranches, fruit orchards, wheat farms, clothing production and processing plants, and other projects through which commodities are provided for distribution to needy Church members. These production projects, as well as the distribution program, utilize large numbers of retired workers who serve on a volunteer basis and find satisfaction in so doing.

The Relief Society, the woman's auxiliary of the Church, makes thousands of visits to the sick and homebound every year on a volunteer basis; its members give many hours of bedside nursing care to the sick, and in addition, contribute thousands of hours of labor to the General Church Welfare production and distribution programs. Most of this service is given by women in middle and later life, some 85 or older.

From my own experience, I know the retired person can and does give reliable volunteer service and derives from it a zest for living. Furthermore, it is my conviction that even as much as voluntary service is now used, it is not yet fully utilized either from the point of view of its value to the retired worker or from the point of view of community need for the service. An educational job still needs to be done to help the community appreciate and make greater use of the talents of older persons.

The need for suitable free-time activities for the aging has given rise to many centers or club programs for the aging. There appears to be no accurate information available on the number of such programs in our country or the number of persons served by them. The opportunities afforded by these clubs and centers vary from a few social activities to a widely diversified range of recreation and service activities varying from reading and watching television to social and square dancing. Many of them have developed special interest groups working on a wide variety of projects and activities. Recently I visited one center in my own community where an advanced student from the university was conducting a remarkably good class in oil painting. At the same time another group was weaving Easter baskets into which would be placed hand painted novelty Easter eggs made for the children in the crippled children's hospital. This same center has developed a service program whereby they take occasional entertainment programs to some of the community nursing homes. This entertainment includes playing quiet bedside games with the patients, reading to them, and offering short musical programs. The woman's harmonica band is in demand.

Formal education programs on subjects ranging from nursing and first aid to a study of languages are included in some centers.

A feature of most centers and clubs is the active participation of the older people in the management leadership and the general operations of the club or center, as well as in the provision and care of its facilities. To many of the elderly, these places become homes away from home.

It is true that many social problems are brought into focus for the first time in these centers—for example, the cost of transportation in bringing the patrons to the center. These problems must be dealt with through the cooperation of family members, community leaders, and both private and public organizations. Personal problems of the aging are also often revealed. As the patrons grow to love and respect the director and feel his personal interest in them, their confidence in him grows and they tend to tell him their troubles. It would seem helpful if professional case work services were more readily available to the aging through the centers.

There appears to be a growing trend for business management to sponsor organizations for its retired employees, where they may fraternize, keep in touch with the ongoing affairs of the company. It is my understanding that a few such organized groups are used in an advisory capacity to management. I was recently told of one such group composed largely of former company officials and highly trained personnel now being used by management as a referral bureau for persons and business institutions seeking consultation and service from the company. I was told that members of the group are kept quite busy.

The extension divisions of our universities, as well as the vocational schools, are offering excellent training and retraining courses which are attracting increasing numbers of our aging citizens.

It is not necessary, or even desirable, that all of the free time of the aging be spent in organized activities. In fact, I can think of no more unnatural situation. From the Situation Paper on Free-time Activities to which I have already referred I quote:

It would appear probable that considerably more than half [of our retired citizens] will seek their outlets for activity in general community service and facilities and commercial opportunites; others will use both organized special services and unorganized facilities. Many enjoy our parks, zoological and botanical gardens, libraries, museums, special community events, concerts, plays, lectures, and local places of scenic or historic importance. Where income permits, many will travel for pleasure . . .

Informal social visiting, reading, listening to the radio, and watching television all appeal to the older person.

The older person, however, should not be left in a position where he becomes overly dependent upon the passive forms of recreation. He should be provided opportunities for active participation. Nonetheless, he should be given his freedom in selecting his recreational activities. He should have ample opportunity to keep active without compulsion. This means that programs must be made inviting and improved methods be developed of acquainting the aging with their availability. In the final analysis, what a person chooses to do with his free time will be determined in large measure by his ambitions, qualifications, skills, financial circumstances, personality traits, health, basic life patterns, social and educational interests, his established tastes, and similar factors. Most older people find satisfaction and help in adjusting to old age if the group associations they have enjoyed in the past are kept open to them and if they are made to feel welcome and comfortable in their continued participation in the group. There is need to guard against the attitude that the aging are a separate segment of the population. While older people enjoy activities with their contemporaries, most of them find enjoyment and value also in some mixed-age participation. Annually we combine a number of the small choruses of our local Societies into a large chorus of more than 400 voices to provide music for our annual conference. The large chorus usually proves to be a three generation chorus, and the older women love it. They sing well, too.

We must remember that the need to help today's older people is but one phase of a problem; the other is to prepare now for the aging population of the future. Patterns of self-resourcefulness must be developed, as well as patterns of service and interest in civic affairs. The wide variety of opportunities now available for free-time activities of both the organized and unorganized types must be extended and continually improved.

The ever-increasing life span should not be viewed with alarm as a tragic situation in which we are all apt to find ourselves. Rather, the gift of age should be viewed in its truer light as the fortunate destiny of an ever-increasing number of Americans who, rich in experience, mature in wisdom, resourceful in meeting the demands of life, can continue to contribute to national well-being and live happy, well-adjusted personal lives. It is the responsibility of both the individual and society to make it so.

May I close with a few lines from Robert Browning's "Rabbi Ben Ezra."

> Grow old along with me!
> The best is yet to be,
> The last of life, for which the first was made
> Our times are in His hand.

And from Tennyson's "Ulysses."

> We are not now that strength which in old days
> Moved earth and heaven, that which we are, we are,—
> One equal temper of heroic hearts,
> Made weak by time and fate, but strong in will
> To strive, to seek, to find, and not to yield.

VOLUNTEER HELP FOR THE AGED

S OME volunteers are trained and experienced in the areas wherein they give free service. Generally, however, they are persons seeking not a post of authority but a niche of usefulness in helping their fellowmen. The proper use of volunteers enables an agency to cut down costs and extend services. The proper use of volunteers involves implanting in them an understanding that volunteering is not a gesture made in a moment of enthusiasm at the cost of a few intermittent hours of time. It is a serious responsibility requiring a regular block of time and the exercise of intelligence and energy. The volunteer must be helped to undertsand that in aligning himself with an organization, he is committing himself to responsibility and work. There must be developed within him an allegiance to the cause and to the sponsoring group. To his enthusiasm and good will there must be added understanding and skill through some type of organizational training to which he must be amenable. Tasks must be wisely assigned, well directed, and the volunteer consistently supervised and tactfully dealt with, since his is a free service. The value of his contribution must be recognized and acknowledged. Under these circumstances, both quantitative and qualitative work is possible.

It is my conviction that with the vast work to be done with and for the aged, volunteer service must be more fully utilized. Volunteers represent a large reservoir of scarcely tapped energy which can be effectively used in serving the needs of the aging. In using volunteers, opportunity is being afforded for satisfying work to large numbers of persons whose time is not fully occupied and who are in need of something worthwhile to do.

The organization which I represent—The Relief Society of The Church of Jesus Christ of Latter-day Saints, and the Church itself—relies in large measure on volunteer help in meeting the welfare needs of its people.

The Church works on the premise that good welfare service consists of appraising each individual's possibilities and needs, regardless of age, and of helping him at the point of his needs after he has done all that he is able to do for himself. In other words, the Church has a general welfare program rather than a so-called program for the aging. It recognizes that with advancing years many needs characteristic of later life arise, and effort is made to prepare the individual through education and training so that his needs in later life shall not go unmet.

What are the Church programs to help the aged? In the welfare program of the Church, responsibility for the care of Latter-day Saints needing assistance rests with the bishop of the ward in which the needy person holds Church membership. Commodities necessary to meet the needs of persons being assisted are drawn from bishops' storehouses on bishops' orders. The larger storehouses resemble a supermarket. Bishops' storehouses are stocked, in large measure, with items produced by Church members on a volunteer basis under the direction of their bishops. Production activities are referred to as welfare projects; they include dairies, poultry projects, cattle ranches, fruit orchards, wheat farms, the operation of a flour mill, a coal mine, a blanket factory, a mattress factory, a soap factory, a milk processing plant, cotton production, and similar activities.

The cash needs of families are met through fast offerings. One day each month Latter-day Saints observe the law of the fast, contributing to the Church cash representing the cost of the meals from which they abstain. This money is reserved by the Church for welfare purposes.

The welfare production projects and the distribution centers provide not only essential commodities for persons in need, but also abundant work opportunities. No cash wage is paid to persons in need who work on these projects, but commodities are allowed according to need. The fact that the individual works within the limits of his capacities removes any element of charity. Many persons whose advancing years, diminishing skills, and limited work capacities make them unable to obtain remunerative work elsewhere, find interesting and profitable employment on the welfare projects or at the storehouses.

The significance which loss of work has for a person, particularly as he merges into old age, is familiar to all. Recently I read this pertinent statement: "Of all the influences that condition our outlook, none is perhaps more deep-seated than our regard for work as a symbol for active living." Loss of work means not only decline in or loss of income; for most persons, it means loss of interests and activities, radical adjustments in standards of living, with an accompanying loss of ego and, all too often, an impairment of character. Our Church program, therefore, places particular emphasis upon providing work opportunities.

In addition to its production projects, the Church operates Deseret Industries plants whose primary purpose is to provide useful work for which a wage is paid. Here handicapped and elderly persons collect, reprocess, and sell goods which would be otherwise wasted. Wages are paid in cash and commodities (about 80% cash and 20% commodities). In addition, some of the plants serve a hot meal to employees daily at a nominal cost. In order that the work opportunities will reach those most in need of them, persons employed must be referred by their bishops.

The Relief Society operates a non-profit Mormon Handicraft Gift Shop through which the handwork of women needing to supplement their incomes without leaving their homes may be marketed. Most of the contributing women are homebound through age or illness. Approximately 60% of them are over 65 and many are over 80.

Two other work opportunities connected with our religious beliefs help solve the problems of the aging. One of these is genealogical research. The other, closely associated with it, is vicarious work for the dead performed in temples of the Church located in continental United States, Hawaii, Canada, England, Switzerland, and New Zealand. Countless older people spend many satisfying hours in these activities so important to the program of the Church.

Loneliness is also one of the tragedies of old age. The physical presence of someone else in the home doesn't always dispel loneliness. Loneliness is the absence of a positive feeling of closeness, of companionship, of being important in the minds of others—being cut off from the currents of life about one. This loneliness is notably evident among the homebound aged. Relief Society members going in pairs, upon assignment of the local Relief Society presidents, make monthly visits to the homebound, the majority of whom are the aged, as well as to all other women in their wards. In addition, monthly visits are made by priesthood representatives to all Latter-day Saint homes. These programs have proved to be valuable antidotes for loneliness in the lives of the aging.

The programs of the auxiliary organizations and priesthood quorums of the Church are geared to varied age groups. Social and recreational activities, such as parties, outings, concerts, entertainment programs, and dinners are an integral part of the programs of each. The social and recreational needs of the aging, as well as all others within the Church, are thus met in harmony with their age, interests, and capacities.

I am sure you will agree that religious concepts give one an ability to weather loss of spouse and other vicissitudes of life. If we can keep the natural focus toward the future, we are rendering an invaluable service to the aged. Conviction with regard to a future life, characterized by association with loved ones and eternal progression, sustains our people and ameliorates many of the difficult circumstances of old age.

Experience has taught us that many factors enter into what is adequate and appropriate care for the needy, and particularly the aging. We must match facilities with needs. This is the challenge to both public and volunteer agencies. Our joint job must be approached with imagination and dedication.

CARE OF THE AGED

THERE is no way of defining old age nor can we set an arbitrary chronological age requirement for classifying a person as "old." There is no sharp division between middle age and old age, but rather a gradual change in the physical, mental, and emotional state of the individual as he merges from middle age into old age. Sometimes a person of 80 may be active and alert with a friendly, outgoing personality. In contrast, the attitudes and physical infirmities of another person much younger chronologically may force us to regard him as "aged." I recall a recent experience wherein a caseworker, herself over 65, was sent to work out the problems of a couple reported as "very old." She found the couple younger than she was.

In our minds, also, we too often think of the aged as the infirm, usually the dependent infirm, without realizing that the dependent infirm actually constitute a relatively small percentage of those who have reached later life. These things we try to keep in mind in our consideration of the so-called aged.

The problems of old age or later life are the problems of human need heightened by waning strength and less hope of improvement in the future. Native peculiarities appear more pronounced since waning strengths lessen the tendency to hold them in check. So in dealing with the so-called aged, as with all others, the Church aims to meet the basic needs, adjusting its services to the individual.

The Church subscribes to the belief that responsibility for the care of a person who cannot care for himself rests first with his family and then with the Church. This applies to the aged as well as to any other group. Family responsibility in caring for persons in need we believe to be consistent with our religious doctrine that the family unit is eternal, that family ties are sacred and that great effort should be made by family members to preserve them. The Church teaches that children have a responsibility toward their aging parents which they should accept willingly, within the limits of reasonableness, in such a way that parents will be properly cared for and feel secure. At times it becomes necessary to help a family plan and arrange for an aged member so as to preserve the best interests of both the family and the aged person. This responsibility rests with the bishop. By the word of the Lord the sole mandate to care for and the sole discretion in caring for the poor of the Church is lodged in the bishop. It is his duty and his only to determine to whom, when, and how much shall be given to any member of his ward from Church funds and as ward help. This is his high and solemn obligation, imposed by the Lord himself. Whomever and whatever the help he calls in to assist him perform his services, he is still responsible.

To be sound, over-all planning for the aged should contemplate the needs of those who can and wish to work. It is the belief of the Church that as long as a person has any productive capacities, opportunities should be afforded him to utilize these. He should have the chance to work within the limits of his capabilities. In our national economy, remunerative self-employment is open to relatively few and the opportunity to work for wages, the normal means of self-support, is too often unavailable to persons in later life.

One of the most common hazards to the health and the happiness and emotional well-being of people in later life, regardless of his financial circumstances, is that of having no useful work to do. Therefore it is important that those who assume to meet the need of people in later life provide useful work opportunities. This the Church welfare plan embraces.

One of the first and most important objectives of the Church Welfare program is to place in gainful employment those who are able to work. This, of course, includes the group 65 or over which is ordinarily regarded as retired.

In his temporal administrations the bishop looks at every able-bodied needy person as a purely temporary problem, caring for him until he can help himself. The priesthood quorums assist the bishop in establishing needy members of the quorum in work and try to see that each member becomes self-supporting and active in his priesthood duties. To accomplish the objective of placing women who are willing to work in gainful employment (only in extreme cases should women with young children be provided work outside the home) the Relief Society assists the bishop.

When for one reason or another a person cannot be placed in gainful employment in industry, the Church supplies him with the means of living in recognition of faithful service in the past and his present willingness to accept the program and labor in it to the extent of his ability.

In order to keep people reasonably happy and emotionally healthy, some recreational activities must be provided, particularly recreational opportunities of a so-called social nature. Such activities are an integral part of the program of the Church and most of them are open to all age groups. For women, the Relief Society provides such social opportunities as parties, luncheons, lectures, concerts. One meeting each month is characterized by its informality and social aspect. The older women of our Society enjoy these social activities along with the younger ones.

In one ward where a large percentage of Relief Society members were older women, a study showed that 60% of the members were entirely dependent upon Church for social and recreational activities other than an automobile ride, and the radio and television. Priesthood quorums offer social opportunities for men, including, of course, the aged. A high priests group in one ward where 60% of the members are over 65 with 8 men between 80 and 90 years of age had 6 socials last year planned especially to meet the needs and interests of these older members.

In a general consideration of the problems of the aged, of unquestionable value are our well-defined religious concepts. Few could question the contribution that our religious life and religious beliefs make to our older people. Having these, the vicissitudes of life coming to the aging are less defeating. Therefore great effort should be and is made by the Church to keep close to its infirm aged and to have them attend Church services wherever possible.

I have learned through experience that old people prefer familiar ways and familiar places and that when acceptable solutions are found for Salt Lake's old people, it will be in Salt Lake; for Provo's old people, it will be in Provo; for New York's old people, it will be in New York.

I am also convinced that through good planning and intelligent effort the later years of life can be made a time for satisfaction and rich development.

CAN I BE CURED?

IT was nearing the July 24th holiday. There was considerable excitement in the household because the little six-year-old was to be in the parade and the father was to drive one of the floats. The mother felt called upon to curb the excitement and to teach the little child the significance of the day in relation to the pioneers. Taking the child upon her lap she said, "James, I want you to listen carefully while I tell you something that you should know. You have ancestors." Whereupon, the little boy with frightened look and quivering chin, asked, "Can I be cured?"

The question, "Can I be cured?" is one that people have been asking with regard to real or imaginary ills since the beginning of time. In the alleviation and correction of these ills, nursing care, that sevice which assists doctors in medical and surgical treatment and which ministers to the physical, emotional, and spiritual well-being of those who are afflicted, has played a vital role. There has always been a need for nursing care, and there will continue to be as long as there are human beings with human ailments.

Nurses, regardless of their degree of training, must realize that full success calls for the exercise, not only of the head and the hand, but also of the heart. Nurses are working in the field of human relations. The sick require loving, understanding care coupled with skilled care. As you combine in your work your talents, skills, understanding of human nature and the affect upon it of illness, and add to this a tenderness and patience with the sufferer together with a sincere desire to help him, your nursing experience will be a satisfying and profitable one for both you and your patient.

May I quote from an editorial published in the *Woman's Exponent*, the official publication of Relief Society, in 1873:

As there is nothing more productive of happiness than good health, nothing more uncertain than its possession, there can be no study pursued to better advantage than that which teaches how best to preserve and increase its properties. There is no calling of greater importance or more becoming to a woman, old or young, than that of being a good nurse since accidents will happen and sickness must occur while mortality lasts. Nursing merits the interest and support of all of us.

VOLUNTEER SERVICE

S INCE the inception of Relief Society, it has been deeply concerned with the care of the sick and has believed implicitly that the volunteer worker has an important place in the care of the sick. With the growing trend toward hospitalization for the care of the sick, it would seem that the volunteer worker must now direct her services more toward care within the hospital.

These services must be, of necessity, of the highest order, well organized, fully coordinated with hospital activities and procedures, and wisely directed so as not to conflict in any way with hospital management, regularly established hospital procedures and services, and so as not to be in the slightest measure detrimental. Thus, an organization appears to be necessary in order that the volunteer worker may be effectively used in the care of the sick, within the hospital. This the hospital auxiliary is set up to do, and insofar as I am able to learn, is effectively doing in the Latter-day Saint hospitals.

I see in the program made available to patients and their relatives who visit the hospital certain services which could not be obtained for hire, services which are important and needed.

I see ever-widening areas within the hospital where

voluntary services of women can be used to advantage as workers become available and become qualified and as the hospital itself opens up new areas of service. I see a tremendously important job being done in public relations. The feelings of people are tender as they or their loved ones are ill in the hospital. How easy it is to misunderstand or misjudge the hospital, or for the patients to be hurt by some little unintentional act or some unavoidable lack of desired attention. How receptive one becomes to the slightest special attention or special kindness. Either a good or bad attitude is carried into the community with regard to the hospital, depending often on a very small something that has happened to the patient or his relative. The volunteer herself is brought into close contact with the wonderful facilities of the hospital and the magnificent service it is rendering. She carries understanding and appreciation of it into the community. Thus, public relations so important to the hospital are strengthened favorably.

Although Relief Society is not a recruiting agency for the hospital in the sense that it actively enlists women for the auxiliary as it does women for nurse training, and while it cannot give credit on the Relief Society roll for service given the sick in hospitals by a member of the hospital auxiliary since the auxiliary is an organization separate and apart from Relief Society, we still encourage suitable women to join.

I assure you the Relief Society regards the hospital auxiliary as a worthy program. It has my personal interest and support.

DELEGATING RESPONSIBILITY EFFECTIVELY

P ITY the organization whose newly elected head approaches her job with the attitude, "Well, I don't expect to do anything very outstanding. This organization has always been weak and I don't know that anything much can be done to improve it," or who depreciates herself, thinking failure, talking failure, always holding before herself and others her shortcomings and inabilities. Doubt in the ability of an organization to succeed, or in oneself as a leader, spreads like a contagion and is damning both to the organization and the administrator herself.

When I was a little girl, we used to sing a song in Sunday School which said: "If we fail, we fail with glory." How I loved that song, and how I sang out those words. It seemed so noble to fail with glory. Recently, however, I read a comment about this song by Elder Sterling W. Sill, in his book on leadership. "Ridiculous," he said. "There is no glory in failure . . . Leaders are not given their positions to anticipate failure. Their business is to succeed."

Sir Winston Churchill has furnished the world with perhaps one of its most graphic examples of a leader who would entertain no thought of failure, even in the face of what appeared to be almost insurmountable dificulties. England, unready for war, was faced with possible annihilation as a nation by a strong, ruthless enemy. Sir Winston Churchill was named Prime Minister. When he met the House of Commons for the first time, he said:

You ask, what is our policy. I will say: to wage war by sea, land, and air with all our might and with all the strength God has given us; to wage war against a monstrous tyranny . . . that is our policy. You ask, what is our aim. I can answer in one word—victory . . . victory, however long and hard the road may be.

It goes without saying that a leader must call upon others to help. In other words, she delegates responsibility. No leadership is good that attempts to do the entire job alone, nor is it of highest quality when it gives the willing worker three or four jobs and leaves the others sitting on the sidelines in idleness. Overloading some because the abilities of others have not been uncovered is injurious to those on both sides of the activity.

I have recently returned from England, where I learned the story of Samson:

Samson was a beautiful dapple-gray horse with a splendid physique and such height that he seemed to tower above all the other horses. But, though large, he was gentle and friendly and everyone was attracted to him.

Samson was a chain horse and stood daily at the foot of a steep hill waiting for the heavy loads that had to be pulled. Samson always pulled in front of the other horses. When the lorry with the load would come, he would prick up his ears and stamp his feet eagerly—it meant an opportunity to show his strength.

Samson was an exhibitionist. When his keeper led him to the load and attached his chains to the shaft, he did not wait for the other horses—he was a Samson. Head down, knees almost touching the ground, sparks flying from his hooves, he practically pulled the whole weight by himself. He would not allow the other horses to pull their share.

Samson's keeper was asked why Samson was not given a rest from his chain horse position, and put into the shafts like the other horses. He replied that Samson would not pull when back with the others; he couldn't show off there. He didn't seem to be able to cooperate, he had to be out in front doing everything by himself.

One day Samson wasn't standing at the bottom of the hill, but another horse was in his place. Samson was dead. He had died of overwork. He had pulled too hard alone.

Many leaders are like Samson, wanting all the work and glory for themselves and refusing to cooperate with others. The power of any good organization is a combined power, and it is wasted by those who try to pull the whole load alone.

There is no place for Samsons in any organization. Wise leaders share responsibility. (*Millennial Star*, March, 1959.)

During my visit to England I attended a training meeting for local officers of a woman's volunteer welfare organization. The group was discussing the delegation of responsibility. The instructor asked the question: "What do we mean by delegating work?" Promptly a hand went up and a woman, acknowledged, replied, "Getting someone else to do the work for you." "Oh, no," wisely responded the instructor, "that is shelving your work. Delegating is sharing, not unloading. It is sharing knowledge, understanding, ideals, aims, loyalty, work, satisfaction, and the glories of achievement."

Delegating responsibility has been called "coordinated decentralization" and must take place if any big job is to be done. The wise administrator shares his work with enough persons to get the job done right and on time without overburdening anyone.

In delegating responsibility, it is of first importance to pick the right person for the job. Success is more adequately served if persons are selected whose qualifications fit the desired accomplishments. The administrator should know the individual to whom she is giving responsibility and should be reasonably sure that the assignment comes within the individual's capacity and that he can and will devote the time and energy necessary to carrying out the assignment properly. The importance of his full acceptance of the assigned responsibility is a factor in his success in fulfilling it.

Second, the way in which a responsibility is delegated is extremely important to its successful fulfillment. The process of giving an assignment can be a thrilling experience. The job and its requirements are transferred; so are enthusiasm for the job, conviction of its importance, recognition of its relationship to the bigger job. The assignor can stimulate the mind and the feelings of the assignee and so direct them as to lead toward accomplishment.

Third, the person delegating a responsibility must guide, direct, keep herself informed on progress and adequately supervise, but at no time should she take over the job. Theodore Roosevelt is credited with saying that "The best executive is the one who has sense enough to pick good men and restraint enough to keep from meddling with them while they do the job." While the good administrator does not meddle, he is always on hand as a resource person, a consultant—the person who has a knowledge of the job and how it can be done and a willingness to share that knowledge. He is the lifeline, so to speak. A good administrator never slights nor ignores a person who is sharing his responsibilities, nor does he take credit unto himself which belongs to his associate.

As people see that they have a place in an enterprise, as they find their contribution is valued, small though it may be, as they see they are fairly treated and justly dealt with, as they see the organization with which they have affiliated functioning with integrity, there develops within them a love for the organization and a sense of loyalty to it, as well as to those who preside over it. Loyalty merely means faithful allegiance. It is not hard for people to give faithful allegiance to that which they love and respect and from which they are benefiting. As pride in the organization and confidence in the leaders grow, as loyal ties become firm and true, the members usually become a united body, willing to harmonize minds and efforts for the good of the whole. With this unity comes essential organization strength.

The building of an organization to a position of strength is a challenge with many factors involved. Success cannot be attained through the efforts of any one individual. Only through the combined efforts of many, wisely and well directed, is success attainable.

A dramatic part of the history of the organization which I represent is the effort put forth in the pioneering days of Utah to provide adequate nursing service. From comparatively non-critical ills such as poison ivy infection and chilblain, through childbirth and on to the more serious illnesses, such a ruptured appendix or heart ailments or contagious disease epidemics, the people were plagued with sickness. Medications and treatments were simple. I have heard my grandmother tell how they boiled the gum weed and made ointment to treat poison ivy infection. I have heard her tell how the feet were packed in snow for chilblain. Midwives cared for mothers at childbirth, and the few doctors, with limited facilities, were reserved to care for persons with more serious illnesses. All of this called for nursing care, and it became mandatory for Relief Society to recruit women and train them as nurses.

Accordingly, a nursing school was opened, offering a 12-month course of training. Our records declare that classes were open to "females possessed of nerve, energy, and ambition for a laudable life." Relief Society leaders went from door to door recruiting women to take these classes. The so-called creed was framed in these words:

"Our creed—Work, strict application to study during the training period, and dedication to duty upon graduation." The goal was stated as follows: "Conscientious, skilled, warm-hearted care of all who stand in need of nursing service."

The first graduating class did not wear uniforms and there was no thought of an arm insignia and a cap and pin to designate the graduate as a trained practical nurse. For those who could pay no tuition fee, an agreement to give a specified amount of charity nursing service was acceptable as tuition. Each student was required, as full or partial exchange for her training, to give a stipulated number of hours of free nursing service. Thus, nurses were prepared to meet the requirements of a pioneering community.

In each era of time training programs have been geared to meet the needs of the day and it has always been recognized that some type of training is a necessary requisite for competency in nursing service. Florence Nightingale, who in the days of the Crimean War laid the foundations for the whole modern system of nursing in the army, prepared herself as a nurse by "devouring the reports of medical commissions, the pamphlets of sanitary authorities, the histories of hospitals and homes. She spent time in ragged schools and work houses, administering to those who were ill. There was hardly a great hospital in Europe where she had not studied its procedures, and hardly a great city whose slums she had not passed through."

The times and trends seem to forecast for the licensed practical nurse constantly improved training standards, with new and better patterns of education, to help her meet growing opportunities. She must realize, however, that even though skill and technical training have come to occupy first place in the equipment of the modern nurse, she has not reached her fullest stature as a servant of the sick without developing within herself and fully exercising the same great humanitarian impulses which in earlier days were often the major qualification of the nurse. Still vital to the healing of the sick are human kindness, understanding, concern for creature comforts, a willingness to administer to phantom as well as genuine illnesses, a readiness to go the second mile should the good of the patient require it. No nurse can be truly great in her profession, nor entirely successful, who divorces herself from these qualifications, regardless of the quality of her technical training. This profession came up from humanitarian beginnings and humanitarian elements must never be discarded. In nursing, more than in most any other profession, there must be a spiritual quality. Technical skill and spiritual values must be put to work side by side in the sick room. Only the nurse who regards her work as a great humanitarian art, as well as a profession, will realize full stature as a nurse.

NURSING — A HIGH PROFESSION

NURSING is a high profession, a dignified, lifetime vocation. It is one of three service vocations traditionally associated with women, the other two being teaching and social work. Although modern life has wrought changes in nursing, as in many other things, we can be reasonably sure that nursing will remain a life-time vocation. The great field of human physical and mental suffering, which calls for tender, skilled, humanitarian nursing ministrations, is enduring and endless.

In this day of automation and change, the durability of one's chosen vocation is a matter for consideration. The replacement of human power by mechanical power, the technological innovations designed to eliminate manpower, the scientific advances that create new jobs and wipe out established ones, are cause for concern both among the skilled and the unskilled, the professional and the non-professional. For example, it was reported at an all-woman conference that 10 years ago highly trained flight engineers were required to accompany the pilots on all air flights. Years of intensive training were demanded to qualify man for this position. Within the past ten-year period, however, jet planes have been perfected which do not require flight engineers. Thus the vocation of flight engineer which ten short years ago was a desirable and an essential profession has now become almost obsolete.

Not so with nursing. As long as there are human beings with human ailments there will be need for skilled nursing care, administered by human hands, with human love and human understanding. I feel safe in predicting that bedside nursing care will not yield to automation or technological advancements and become obsolete. From the days of the Old Testament when nursing hands treated the infection which was destroying the life of King Hezekiah by placing figs upon the boils, to the present day of wonder drugs skillfully administered by injections and otherwise, history is a record of human effort in caring for the sick.

The rise of practical nursing as an established vocation has been phenomenal, as have been the advancements in training programs. A vivid picture of the practical nurse of twenty years ago was recently published in the magazine *Practical Nursing*:

> Except for those graduates of a handful of schools of practical nursing, the practical nurse of twenty odd years ago had acquired skills through personal experience, usually in her own home. Her skills were, therefore, personal and individual. In those days sick people, especially convalescents, were more often than not nursed in their own homes. When a new baby arrived, the practical nurse cared for the mother and the baby and quite often also looked after all other members of the household. She cooked, served the meals, cleaned the house. Her uniform? She wore housedresses and the comfortable shoes made indispensable by her twelve to fourteen hour day. Patients and their families relied on her, loved her, yet they did not think of her as a skilled worker. Her status was undefined, more like that of a family friend; her wage was low, and board and room while on the case were considered part of her pay. Her contacts with other practical nurses with whom she might have a chance to discuss standards, education, working conditions and wages were rare—if any.

About 20 years ago practical nursing began its upward climb. Today practical nurses may be found in large numbers in hospitals, nursing homes, doctors' offices, institutions, private homes, and elsewhere. Today practical nurse training is a highly organized, highly standardized, well-regulated procedure. This development is essential in view of the advance in medicine, surgery, and hospital procedures.

An illustration of the scientific advances in medicine alone is vividly portrayed in a statement made by Mrs. Marguerite Clark, author, editor, and medical writer, at a recent nurses convention:

Twenty years ago, when I first started to report medical news, the science writers (and there were just a few of them) were lucky if they found one new major medical discovery in six months. Now we get these stories at a rate of one every twenty-four hours, and often we are hard put to find space in which to record all of the advances reported to us.

ACHIEVEMENT THROUGH ORGANIZATION

M AY I relate three incidents which convey their own message.

First, a large city in one of our western states had a beautiful park which for years boasted a row of memorial trees planted in recognition of historical events in the life of the city. The city fathers decided these trees should be felled to make way for a tennis court. It was their opinion that recreation for the youth was more important than retaining the memorial trees. Many of the citizens took issue with this opinion, and individual protests were lodged. The city council, however, was uninfluenced by these protests. At times, the mayor even refused to see protesting individuals. The council remained adamant in its position. At length, as a last resort, the citizens got together and formed an organization which they called "The Citizens' Memorial Preservation Committee." One morning when the mayor reached his office, a large delegation representing the organization was on hand. The mayor did not refuse to discuss the matter with this delegation—it was an organized body with a purpose and an appointed spokesman. The outcome was that the trees remained standing. The tennis court was located elsewhere in the park even through a new road had to be cut to it.

A second incident: A license had been sought for the opening of a liquor store in a residential area where there were many teen-age children. The residents were concerned. They called a mass meeting to which they invited representatives of the licensing unit. Surprisingly, only comparatively few residents actually turned out for the meeting and it looked as if the license would be granted. Then, a group of women representing an organized society appeared. Speaking in behalf of 65 organized women of the area, they condemned the contemplated opening of the liquor store and demanded that the license be denied. The licensing agent said he could not stand against such an organized group of women. The liquor store was not opened in the area.

A third incident: A bill was before a certain state legislature, providing for the establishment by the state of a school for mentally retarded children. Many prominent citizens favored passage of the bill and worked hard for it as individuals. The bill, however, did not pass. At the next session of the legislature an almost identical bill was passed. In the meantime, three strong civic organizations had taken up the cause. The strength of the efforts of these organized groups was the determining factor in the passage of the bill.

It is an old analogy that it is easy to break a single stick, but bind enough of them together and it is almost impossible to break them.

SECTION FOUR

The Woman's Role In The Eternal Plan

"WE LIVED AFTER THE MANNER OF HAPPINESS"

IN the Book of Mormon Nephi spoke of his people who were living in the land of Nephi, saying ". . . we lived after the manner of happiness." (2 Nephi 5:27.)

None would deny that living in such a manner is highly desirable. As we contemplate conditions in this day, we might add that it is even enviable. We are living in a time characterized by crisis after crisis. New ideas, new philosophies, new issues assail us on every hand, causing grave concern and anxiety. We are harassed by an endless stream of reports of unrest, social upheavals, and tragic happenings. In addition, personal problems and worries come to torment us until, at times, we almost wonder if the world today is devoid of happiness. We thoughtfully consider the words of Nephi, asking, "What is the manner of happiness? Can it be achieved in today's world? Should we strive to seek after it?"

The achievement of a happy life is a universal goal of mankind and properly so. The Book of Mormon tells us, ". . . men are that they might have joy" (2 Nephi 2:25.) The Prophet Joseph Smith pointed out that we cannot escape trial, for earthlife is a probationary period wherein we prove ourselves by the mastery of trials. He taught that the law of heaven does not promise that the believer in every age should be exempt from the afflictions and troubles arising from different sources and in consequence of the acts of wicked men on earth. Nonetheless, the Prophet declared that happiness is the object and design of existence. The Declaration of Independence of the United States declares that all men are endowed with certain inalienable rights, among them the pursuit of happiness.

Men pursue happiness in many different ways and according to differing concepts of what brings happiness. To some, the source of happiness is material wealth; to others, it is power and dominion. Yet again it may be personal popularity and acclaim or personal pleasure; or, it may be overcoming the difficult, discovering the new, or conquering the unknown. To many of the Father's children, it is the peace that comes through obedience to his teachings. To most people, however, happiness at times seems abstract, transitory. Today it may be present in rich abundance, while tomorrow it may seem to have completely departed.

We must learn, therefore, what constitutes true happiness—the kind that brings a certain form of inner delight, peace, and contentment which is as enduring as life itself.

What, then, should be the pattern of our lives if we are to live after the manner of happiness?

Let us consider how the people of Nephi lived when he declared they "lived after the manner of happiness." Nephi and his followers had suffered all manner of persecution at the hands of the Lamanites, even to the point that the Lamanites sought to take the life of Nephi. The Lord warned him to separate from those people and flee with all who would go with him into the wilderness. The great exodus took place, accompanied by many hardships. At length, the group established itself at a place they called Nephi after their leader, and they designated themselves the people of Nephi. They appealed to Nephi to be their king, but he was desirous that they should have no king but should be a free people. He became their chosen leader and teacher.

Nephi states that they observed to keep the judgments and the statutes and the commandments of the Lord in all things. They raised flocks and herds of all kinds. They sowed seeds and harvested. They built buildings and worked in all manner of wood and of iron, and of copper and of brass and of steel, gold, silver, and of precious ores which were in great abundance. They constructed a temple after the manner of the Temple of Solomon wherein they might worship the Lord their God.

Then Nephi continues: "I . . . did cause my people to be industrious, and to labor with their hands . . . and the Lord was with us and we began to prosper exceedingly, and multiply in the land." (2 Nephi 5:17, 13.) This, then, might be called Nephi's code for living after the manner of happiness: Freedom to choose who should be their ruler, industry, willingness to work, the development of talents and skills, love of God and obedience to his commandments.

The blessings of growth, prosperity, and happiness follow. This has been true with any nation or people who follow the eternal principles upon which true happiness rests. One of the favorite expressions of President George Albert Smith was: "The pathway of righteousness is the highway of happiness."

It is not enough that we shall live after the manner of happiness for the benefit of the collective body only. The individual, too, must seek after his own personal happiness, knowing that this, too, is obtained through following the same basic patterns of living.

Sometimes our personal problems bear us down and heavily tax us. Because they are hard to bear they loom large and make deep impressions which remain with us, crowding out feelings of happiness, while the joys of life are so pleasant as to pass by swiftly. They seem to be so fleeting as almost to be non-existent.

The memory of one's trials and the seeming fleeting nature of one's hours of happiness often lead to the feeling that there is precious little happiness in life. Yet, if it were possible to weigh both in the scales of life, I believe almost everyone would find life affords us far more true pleasure than pain. Otherwise, why does almost everyone cling so fast to life?

I recall an aging sister whom I used to visit several years ago. She was physically infirm. Her financial income had been quite sufficient for her needs—then suddenly it became limited. Then her busy family, while kind to her, spent less time with her than she thought they should, and she felt neglected. Each time I called on her, I heard the same question: "Why do I live on? I'm growing so old and feeble; I'm so unhappy. I wish I could die!"

One day, feeling particularly sympathetic toward her plight, my husband and I took her for a ride into the canyon to see the beautiful fall mountain foliage. When we were well into the canyon, we came upon some road repair work. My husband had to back the car a short distance and turn in a very narrow space. Some distance below us at the back of the car was a noisy rushing creek. "Oh!" the sister screamed, "be careful! You'll back us off the road and into the creek! We'll all be killed!" Calmly I replied, "Sister Smith, I thought you wanted to die. You've told me this many times." She promptly replied, "Not today!" After we were safely on the road, she laughed and said, "You know, I'm really not as miserable as I like to make people think I am. Life has been good to me, and even now I'm quite happy."

True happiness is within the reach of every one of us. Perhaps what we need is a better understanding of the factors that contribute to it and how we may grasp these and make them a part of our lives. One wise philosopher has said:

Happiness consists of being, not having. It is not dependent upon wealth or even upon health. It does not rely on fame or so-called worldly success, but rather upon the conformity of our lives to those things which set at rest our minds and at peace our hearts.

Latter-day Saints know that its fountainhead is love of God and obedience to his laws, and that one of its greatest sources of nourishment is love of fellowmen.

Service to others is essential to joy in living. We cannot live selfishly and be happy. Some of the greatest joys and happiness-promoting experiences of our lives come to us when we do for another, lifting the load, buoying up the spirit; and, conversely, some of the most poignant and enduring torments of conscience come from failure to meet our responsibility to others. Happiness is an infallible by-product of service. We know, too, that while trial may bring pain and suffering, the ability to rise above it or master it brings compensatory inner satisfactions and joy as well as eternal rewards.

The development and expression of our creative abilities also result in good feeling. I am always impressed with this when I read in Genesis the story of the creation of the earth. It concludes: "And God saw everything that he had made, and, behold, it was very good." (Genesis 1:31.)

Sad, indeed, would be the life of any individual who did not live creatively and productively. To be a contributor to life, within the scope of our capabilities, rather than a drone, is expected of us. In so doing, we earn a cherished reward—the happiness that comes from being useful.

Thus, as individuals, we pursue happiness—through righteousness, through service, through creative expression, through social usefulness. These things do not spring up and flourish voluntarily. They are fostered through the labor of our minds, hearts and hands.

Relief Society offers limitless opportunities to the women of the Church to nourish the essential elements of a happy life and through the years sisters have testified that this, indeed, happens.

Let me read one typical testimony, taken from the minutes of the Kanab Relief Society, March, 1882:

Sister Morris put in over thirty years of Christian work in Relief Society. Her life, though continuously fraught with trials and hardships, has been to the outward observer like a placid river, flowing toward the Kingdom of God. When the summons comes for her to join the choir invisible and gather with that mighty throng of men and women whose garments have been washed in the blood of the Lamb and who have valiantly trodden the winepress of affliction, she will receive the Master's "well done, thou good and faithful servant; enter into the joy of the Lord." Happy, happy, happy has been her earthlife. Joyful will be her eternal life.

Another testimony, written in a letter received at the general board office within the past week, reads:

I felt I should write and tell you of the recent death of our beloved Mother, Sister Lydia Larson, at the age of 91 years. For 73 years, she has been a faithful member of Relief Society, joining when she had just turned 18. She loved the Society and all it stands for. She taught her five daughters never to underestimate its worth.

Mother lived a simple, beautiful life. I don't mean to say she had no hardships or sorrows; in fact, as we look back over the years, we think that perhaps she had more than her share of life's vicissitudes. But none of us remember her ever seeming to be defeated or unhappy. Her life seems to have been like a symphony of sweet thoughts, good deeds, inner strength and courage, peace and happiness. We girls all know that Relief Society brought to her the teachings, the opportunities, and the feelings of usefulness that gave her a saintly composure.

Today, there is much talk in our nation about a volunteer army to fight our military battles. May I suggest the need of the world for a volunteer army to fight the forces of evil that are impairing man's well-being and destroying his happiness. Within the Church there is such an army with its recruits stationed in many lands—men and women who carry on the works of righteousness; men and women with faith in God, who watches over his children; men and women of charity, of courage, of patience, of understanding insight; men and women who take the high path and who reach up and out and forward; men and women who stand by the ideals and patterns of life revealed by the Lord to his prophets—patterns of life for which the reward is inner peace and true happiness.

THE MISSION OF WOMANKIND

I F I were to ask almost any faithful Latter-day Saint mother what were the two dearest things on earth to her, I think she would unhesitatingly reply, "The restored gospel and my family." The gospel gives to Latter-day Saint mothers the loftiest concept of home and family life known to mankind.

Recently I visited a mother whose 40-year-old son had suddenly passed away. He had lived an unusually successful and exemplary life. His devotion to his mother and his watchcare over her had been of the highest order. Familiar with the deep affection of this mother for her son and knowing her reliance—yes, even her dependence—upon him, I expected to find her prostrate with grief and anguish of heart. Rather, I found a composed, albeit a sorrowing mother.

She said, "Had the Lord told me when he gave me this son that I might have him for 40 years, but at the end of that time I would have to part with him forever, I feel sure I would have gladly acceped him. But the Lord was good to me. He gave me a choice spirit, an exceptional son, with the knowledge that he would be mine eternally. While I now must part with him for a few years, the knowledge of our eternal relationship forbids me to be aught but grateful to the Lord." What a moving demonstration of the sustaining power of gospel truths!

The knowledge which the gospel gives us of the eternal organization of the family is precious to all true Latter-day Saint mothers and serves as a guide in all of their activities in relation to their families.

The gospel teaches that marriage is an eternal principle ordained before the foundation of the world. It teaches that in our existence here, through husband and wife, the spirits which God created shall be given tabernacles of flesh. It is here we prove ourselves and prepare ourselves and our children for the place we shall hold in our eternal home.

In explaining this doctrine, President Joseph F. Smith said:

> Our associations are not exclusively intended for this life, for time, as we distinguish it from eternity. We live for time and for eternity. We form associations and relations for time and all eternity. Our affections and our desires are found fitted and prepared to endure not only throughout the temporal or mortal life, but through all eternity. Who are there besides the Latter-day Saints who contemplate the thought that beyond the grave we will continue in the family organization? the father, the mother, the children recognizing each other in the relations which they owe to each other and in which they stand to each other? this family organization being a unit in the great and perfect organization of Gods work, and all destined to continue throughout time and eternity? (*Gospel Doctrine*, Ninth Edition, p. 277.)

Surely with such a concept, husbands and wives should love one another with a deep, a sacred, and an enduring love. Children should be cherished with the strongest bonds of affection; there should be the greatest solicitude of parents for children. No effort should be too much, no sacrifice too great to protect them from evil and preserve them in righteousness, that none shall be deprived of his eternal blessings. The love and the sanctity of the home should be zealously safeguarded.

Just as the knowledge which we have of the divine destiny of the family is a comfort, a strength, and a blessing to us, so it also places upon Latter-day Saint parents, and today I speak particularly to mothers, a greater responsibility, a more solemn obligation than that held by any others to make all else in life subservient to the well-being of our homes and families.

Church leaders have continually emphasized the importance of the doctrine of the eternity of the family unit, and they have guided us in applying this doctrine in our lives. Always in the Church, people have been admonished to marry in the House of the Lord, to establish homes and bear and rear children in righteousness. An appealing picture comes to us in the teachings of President Brigham Young:

> Young man, set you up a log cabin, if it is not more than ten feet square, and then get you a bird to put in your little cage. You will then work all day with satisfaction to yourself considering that you have a home to go to and a loving heart to welcome you . . . Strive to make your little home attractive. . . . Let your houses nestle beneath the cool shade of trees and be made fragrant with perfume of flowers (*Discourses of Brigham Young*, p. 301.)

To the young women he said:

> It is the calling of the wife and the mother to know what to do with everything that is brought into the house, laboring to make her home desirable to her husband and children, making herself an Eve in the midst of a Paradise of her own creating, securing her husband's love and confidence, and tying her offspring to herself with a love that is stronger than death, for an everlasting inheritance (*Ibid.*, p. 307.)

From such humble homes as are pictured in these words of President Brigham Young, lacking perhaps in the pretentious, material comforts of life but by no means impoverished, have come some of the Church's and the nation's most stalwart men and women.

President David O. McKay came from such a home. In writing of the ancestry of President McKay in the *Relief Society Magazine*, his sister, Jeanette McKay Morrell, describes the home of President McKay's childhood as follows:

Following their marriage, David [President McKay's Father] took his bride, Jennette to the log cabin in Huntsville, and they commenced life as young pioneers. . . . Two daughters . . . were born in the log cabin before the front part of the rock house, now known as "The Old Home," was completed. It was a happy day when this small family moved into the larger and more comfortable home, and it was in this house that President David O. McKay was born. (*Relief Society Magazine,* Sept. 1953, pp. 580-581.)

When President McKay was eight years old, his father was called on a mission to Scotland. Sister Morrell writes: "The hopes and plans that had been in their minds for so long, regarding the enlargement of the house and furnishing it, seemed almost within their grasp, and now because of this call everything must be postponed." But the mother of President McKay was equal to the sacrifice. Her great goal was the eternal well-being of her family.

Today we are not called upon to live in log cabins, and the physical make-up of our homes has greatly improved. But the past has proved that pretentious houses with fine furnishings are not essential to happiness nor to the development of children of strong and righteous character.

Not only does the physical make-up of our homes differ from the past, but homes as we have traditionally known them are undergoing other basic changes. Many functions formerly performed in the home are now performed outside the home. Scientific advances have provided labor-saving equipment; so-called "built-in maid service" comes to the homemaker in such things as frozen, canned, and packaged foods, relieving mothers of much drudgery formerly required of them.

Perhaps the most basic change affecting homes today, and the one fraught with the greatest uncertainty insofar as the ultimate well-being of the home and children is concerned, is the growing trend of mothers to enter the labor market. Leaving their homes, mothers are going to work each day, the same as are fathers, returning home at the close of the work day to their duties as mothers and homemakers.

There are varied views among so-called authorities as to the effect upon homes and children of mothers entering the labor market. At a conference of the International Council of Women, a delegate from Great Britain, declaring her opinions to be based on survey and study, said that "when the mother was in employment, the home was not less well-kept nor were meals neglected, nor the children less clean. When the mother was a capable woman and able to make satisfactory arrangements for the care of her children when she was not at home, the children did not appear to suffer." It was apparent, she said, that "The condition of the home, the happiness of the marriage, and the care of the children depended more on the character and competency of the mother than on the fact that she went to work." She claimed that, "There was an overwhelming consensus of opinion that there had been no increase in juvenile delinquency due to mothers taking up employment."

At the same International Council of Women conference, another authority, a Canadian woman, gave a counter view. She declared that undoubtedly some of the problems of child waywardness and adolescent upheaval are related to the weakened discipline and influence of the homes, resulting from mothers being away from home at business and being too occupied with household tasks during the hours they are in the home to give proper attention to the emotional, spiritual, and disciplinary needs of their children. She warned, "If the mother who embarks on home and marriage underemphasizes the home, it is inevitable that the husband, the children, and the community in the end will follow her lead and all will suffer proportionately."

The Manpower Council summarized the situation by saying, "What all this means to the home and family has not been validly appraised. Research, study, and time are all needed."

Certainly women are facing a curious combination of certainty and uncertainty. The choice between their homes to the exclusion of a career outside the home and their homes *plus* a career outside the home is one of the most pressing questions before women today.

Latter-day Saint women are not immune to present-day trends, attitudes, opinions, influences, and practices in these matters. I say this, my sisters, by way of warning. However, there are no sisters in all the world so well positioned to make wise decisions. They have the doctrine and teachings of the Church to guide them. They know the essential elements of good home and family life. They know the factors that are important in the well-being of children. They also know where to place their values. They must be concerned with long-range consequences, eternal values, not with short-run gains.

To bear and rear children, to feel the dependence of husband and family, to know that upon her rests, in large measure, the health, character, and happiness of human beings whom she has brought into the world and for whom she is responsible, to see herself laying and preserving the foundations of so basic and necessary a structure as a family, to build so that this family will be of service to the Church, society and country, is a responsibility of greatest magnitude.

The Latter-day Saint mother knows that no other work to which she might set her hand could be so broad and inspiring, so filled with interest, so demanding of intelligence and capability, so rewarding.

Moreover, the Latter-day Saint mother knows that hers is a divine calling, that she was created and placed on earth to be the mother of spirits created by our Heavenly Father to come to this earth and prove whether they would obey the commandments which the Lord their God should give them. She knows that this is her great and all-important mission. Everything else is subordinate to it. Blessed are women in this day who have this knowledge.

May the Lord bless Latter-day Saint mothers that all of their decisions in relation to their homes and their families may be made in the full light of the knowledge which they possess. And may they fulfill their divine calling to the eternal joy and well-being of themselves and their families.

THE WISDOM OF THE AGES

"THE wisdom of the ages" is a phrase frequently used, implying that the experiences of eons of time have proved certain statements to be true and certain actions to be judicious, prudent, sensible, and good. In the history of the world, perhaps none other, save the Master himself, is so well known for his wisdom as is King Solomon who reigned over ancient Israel. Scripture records that in Gibeon the Lord appeared in a dream by night to Solomon, who had succeeded King David as ruler of Israel, and God said, "Ask what I shall give thee?" and Solomon replied, "Give thy servant therefore an understanding heart to judge thy people, that I may discern between good and bad . . . And the speech pleased the Lord that Solomon had asked this thing. And God said unto him, Because thou hast asked this thing and not asked for thyself long life; neither asked riches for thyself, nor asked the life of thine enemies; but hath asked for thyself understanding to discern judgment; Behold I have done according to thy word: lo, I have given thee a wise and understanding heart; so that there hath been none like thee before thee, neither after thee shall any arise like unto thee." (1 Kings 3:5, 9-12.)

The importance of an understanding heart for those

who would govern others, and the wise sayings of King Solomon, are an important part of the wisdom of the ages. Among the words of Solomon worthy of contemplation by mothers of the Church today are these: "Train up a child in the way he should go: and when he is old, he will not depart from it." (Proverbs 22:6.)

Today, social life has become complex and social ills pronounced. Mothers sometimes wonder if indeed it is possible to rear the child so as to assure the righteousness of the mature man.

Ever before us are unsettling, frightening accounts of temptations and evils which beset the path of boys and girls. All too many children are being caught in the web of destruction.

Because of conditions, social studies and social welfare programs are rapidly increasing, with emphasis on remedial measures and social case work techniques to deal with problems. These remedial programs must be administered, in large measure, by social welfare institutions. Valuable as these may be in the treatment process when a child has fallen by the wayside, is not the better approach the preventive measure through early training in the home by wise and righteous parents?

Church leaders have long taught us that the character of our homes and the training we give our little ones play a determining role in the character and behavior of the adolescent child and later in manhood or womanhood. From time to time we hear an echo of this truth from those whom the world regards as authorities. In the *Deseret News* of August 19 was a report of a paper presented at the First International Congress of Social Psychiatry in which Dr. Eleanor Glueck of Harvard Law School, an eminent criminologist, said the mother plays a determining role in whether a child is to become a delinquent and later perhaps a criminal. Dr. Glueck declared that the three vital factors which determine the mother's influence on the child are the amount of supervision given, the amount of discipline she is able to infuse, and the amount of cohesion she is able to bring into the family.

The Church gives us a broader view, a greater concept of our reponsibility to our children. It gives to us first an understanding of what was meant by Solomon when he said, "Bring up a child in the way he should go." The "way he should go" is made unmistakably clear. The Church further gives us specific counsel as to how to guide him along the way. In addition, this Church undergirds us with marvelous priesthood and auxiliary programs.

Although through unfortunate circumstances or perhaps unjudicious action on the part of parents, a child may fail to receive the firm and wise direction required to avoid the pitfalls of life, I believe the Church has a vast majority of competent mothers; and our young people generally merit our confidence. At times even one who strays from sound parental teachings returns in later life, repentant. Only recently a son, now 84 years of age, who had been taught by righteous parents told me a fascinating story of his repentance. Said he, "During the days of my recalcitrant youth and young manhood, my parental teachings remained with me as a restraining influence and held the line to some extent. I could never entirely rid myself of them, and finally they led me back to right living and happiness."

It seems human nature to talk of the one who goes astray and call little attention to the countless numbers who follow the right path.

President McKay referred to this tendency and expressed his confidence in youth:

So while we solicitously call attention to the tragedies in the stream of human life, let us not be unmindful of the much greater group who move steadily and successfully along, avoiding the sandbars and rapids of sinful indulgence and spiritual decay, whose noble lives confirm and increase confidence in the growing generation. As we seek the lost sheep, let us be appreciative of the "ninety and nine" that are safe in the fold. (*Motherhood—a Partnership With God,* Compiled by Harold Lundstrom, pp. 4-5.)

I attended a dinner not long ago with a group of non-L.D.S. women who were active in civic and social welfare programs. Considerable concern over the growing anti-social behavior of youth was expressed. The group seemed in general agreement as to the need to strengthen the American home. At length a woman seated next to me directed two pertinent questions to me. She inquired, (1) "Do you have any juvenile delinquency among the youth of your church, and if so, do you have any statistics comparing the percentage of delinquents among you with the national percentage?" (2) "Also, you have extremely high standards of home and family life as well as a rigid set of behavior disciplines. How effective are these as controls in the lives of your young people?"

I had no figures I could give her. I could not in honesty say we had no delinquency. But I felt confident in saying that our standards and teachings brought forth good fruit. Without hesitancy I said I felt they produced an abundant harvest of upright, law-abiding men and women.

I was mindful of the thousands of young missionaries now serving the Lord. I thought of the tens of thousands in years past. There came to my mind an impressive sight I had just witnessed of thousands of young men and women crowding into the tabernacle for MIA conference—young people chosen to be leaders in this marvelous youth program because of their worthiness. I thought of the many young men who are in bishoprics and stake presidencies. I thought of one young man, the excellence of whose home training I knew so well. Recently he had been chosen of the Lord through his prophet to be an apostle—a witness for Christ to the world. I thought of others similarly taught and similarly called who are today a power for righteousness among the nations. I thought of the endless number of intelligent young women of faith and testimony presiding over Relief Societies. A visit to a campus Relief Society is a heartening and inspiring experience.

Yes, I thought of a conversation I had had in one of the large eastern cities with a little 12-year-old Scout who had been carefully trained by a righteous and beautiful mother who had just passed away. The boy had been on a weekend Scout outing. With face aglow he told me the group to which he belonged had been singled out by a national leader for special recognition and privilege. The national leader had said, "How is it that so many fine boys belong to this one group?" With certainty that he knew the answer, the child had said to me, "We were all Mormons." A seemingly endless chain of evidence of the fruitfulness of Church teachings, inculcated in children largely by righteous parents in the home passed before my mind. I felt the effectiveness of our standards and disciplines is best measured by the Lord's statement: "Wherefore, by their fruits ye shall know them." (Matt. 7:20.)

What I like to regard as a great body of scripture, words spoken by the Lord and by our Latter-day prophets through inspiration of the Lord, and recorded for our study and use, fortify us in our struggle to train our children in the way they should go. May I present a brief sampling: The admonition of the Lord recorded in the Doctrine and Covenants 68:25-28 is familiar enough that I feel it is not necessary to read it. To those unfamiliar with this scripture, I commend it.

Latter-day Saints have always been taught that marriage is divinely instituted and that temple marriage is the surest foundation upon which to build an eternal home. The Prophet Joseph Smith declared that "marriage was an institution of heaven, instituted in the garden of Eden; that it was necessary that it should be solemnized by the authority of the everlasting Priesthood." (*Joseph Smith's Teachings*, 1912 ed., page 103.)

President McKay made this fervent plea:

Oh may our youth throughout the land realize that they have within their grasp the possibility of that form of marriage which will contribute more to their happiness in this world and their eternal union and happiness in the world to come than can be obtained anywhere else in the world. (*Motherhood—A Partnership With God*, p. 119.)

President J. Reuben Clark reminded us of the fundamental and eternal relationships of the family:

The family looked at broadly, is as nearly basic to the principles and plan of the Restored Gospel as any principle of which I know. We have a Heavenly Father and Mother, the eternal parents of the spirits of us who are here. And those spirits were created that they might come to this earth and receive mortal tabernacles so that in the due time of the Lord we may lay away the mortal tabernacle; then in due time we shall resume it, and become the perfect soul, the body and the spirit reunited . . . the family relationship is fundamental, because without it we cannot reach out to the destiny our Heavenly Father has provided for us. (*Ibid.*, pp. 10-11.)

President Joseph Fielding Smith sets forth our duty in rearing our children:

It is the duty of parents to teach children the saving principles of the gospel of Jesus Christ so that they will know why they are to be baptized and that they may be impressed in their hearts with a desire to continue to keep the commandments of God after they are baptized, that they may come back into his presence. (*Ibid.*, p. 148.)

Discipline is embodied in the gospel of Christ. It is fundamental to good child rearing but must be wisely exercised.

President Brigham Young early taught Latter-day Saint parents wise principles of child government: "Bring up your children in love," said President Young, ". . . study their dispositions and their temperaments, and deal with them accordingly, never allowing yourself to correct them in the heat of passion." (*Ibid.*, p. 23.)

Elder Orson Pratt enlarges upon this counsel, which unfortunately is still needed among us:

Do not correct your children in anger. Be deliberate and calm in your counsels and reproofs, but at the same time use earnestness and decision. . . . Do not find fault with every trifling error you may see, for this will discourage your family, and they will begin to think it is impossible to please you; and after a while they will

become indifferent as to whether they please you or not . . . Do
not be so stern in your family government as to render yourself
an object of fear and dread. (*Ibid.,* p. 29.)

Elder Harold B. Lee emphasizes the need for the
spiritual touch: "The maintenance of spiritual contacts, the
exercise of family prayers, the constant attention to Church
duties, have all been some of the things that have helped
these [our L.D.S.] homes to be successful." (*Ibid.,* p. 159.)

President John Taylor spoke of the need to educate
our children, to afford them opportunities for instruction
and learning, as follows:

We do not want a posterity to grow up that will be ignorant
. . . but one that will be intelligent and wise, possessing literary
and scientific attainments, and a knowledge of everything that is
good, praiseworthy, intellectual and beneficial to the world . . .
(*Ibid.,* p. 26.)

It is noteworthy that today, when individual liberty
is threatened in so many ways, President McKay has placed
upon the home responsibility for teaching this divine principle. Said President McKay: "The home is the best place
in the world to teach the highest ideal in the social and
political life of man; namely, perfect liberty of action so
long as you do not trespass upon the rights and privileges
of another." (*Ibid.,* p. 6.)

A host of our leaders have given the same counsel as
to the most effective means of teaching our children. Elder
Howard W. Hunter puts it in these simple words: "We
should be good examples to our children, for the greatest
teaching is done by way of example. . . . This is the great
challenge of parenthood." (*Ibid.,* p. 51.)

Latter-day Saints have often referred to themselves as
a peculiar people, accepting the definition of peculiar not
as queer but as distinctive. Elder Richard L. Evans declared:

The word peculiar is not peculiar to us; it is peculiar to scripture. It is a word by which the Lord describes a generation that he
will have, peculiar in purity, in honor, in righteousness as indicated
in both Old and New Testament texts. (*Ibid.,* p. 45.)

In our homemaking and child rearing then, as in other things, we must be a peculiar people. In a day when views and patterns with regard to homemaking and the role of woman are marked by change from the traditional, we do not follow that which is heralded as modern and progressive and which is popularly acclaimed as new and exciting, unless it squares with the teachings of the Church. It is true that in today's world eternal vigilance is required to keep children in the path of virtue and truth. But we may take comfort in the fact that this achievement is not only possible but is generally accomplished among Latter-day Saints who adhere to the teachings of the Church.

I commend our Relief Society mothers. I am particularly grateful for the lives of our young mothers, many of whom have a number of young children. Their courage, their love of truth, their desire to know and to follow counsel, their faithful Church attendance, bids well for the next generation. It is an inspiration to see them gather for their Relief Society meetings with their little ones clustered about them, seeking to learn the way they should go.

May the Lord ever bless our mothers with understanding hearts and the wisdom to train their children in righteousness so that when they are old they will not depart from it. May the fears of our mothers with regard to rearing their children in today's changing and troubled world be supplanted by the peace of heart which comes through adherence to Church counsel.

WHAT DO YOUR CHILDREN REMEMBER?

A MONG the choice experiences that have been mine was the privilege of an occasional interview with President Stephen L Richards. Regardless of the purpose for which the interview was called, our conversation usually ended with President Richards referring to the importance of Latter-day Saint mothers maintaining good homes and the role of Relief Society in helping them to understand the eternal significance of this task and of being proficient homemakers.

As many of you will remember President Richards was a great advocate of the Latter-day Saint home in all its superior aspects. He frequently spoke on this subject at general and quarterly conferences. He regarded the Latter-day Saint doctrine of the eternity of the family unit as sublime. He further took the position that there was nothing in society so important and so contributive to the well-being of the individual and the nation as well-ordered homes, that heaven itself was little more than a projection of a Latter-day Saint home into eternity.

These are sweeping statements. Nonetheless they are, I believe, irrefutable.

Latter-day Saints have a rich homemaking heritage, more precious than all the material luxuries that money can buy. This heritage results from our concept of the eternity of the family unit and the teachings of the Church with regard to our homes and family life.

We know that the family unit is eternal, that family ties are sacred and are to be safeguarded at all costs. We are taught that the home is a holy place that has its pattern in the heavens. We are further taught that we came from a celestial home and that we shall return to a celestial home. We know that our earthly home is expected to provide for the spirits which come to it an environment that shall meet the strictest requirements of righteousness and enable these spirits to return unscathed to the presence of the Father.

At one of our Relief Society general conferences President David O. McKay said:

> I urge that increased attention be given and more intensive effort put forth by the women of the Church to structure their homes so as to make them an unshakable foundation upon which righteous character may be established in the children and a truly civilized Christian society be developed.

What constitutes a good home? It is not based upon material possessions. These may or may not contribute to a good home, depending upon their use and the value placed upon them. Rather I would say a good home is a clean, orderly place where family members are well-fed and well-taught, but this alone does not make a good home. The good home must possess spiritual qualities—love, understanding, security, and peace. Family companionship must abide therein. A good Latter-day Saint home reflects the teachings and standards of the Church in its practices and procedures. In a good home children are genuinely happy and the patterns of life are so favorably impressed upon them as they contribute to their happiness and well-being that these patterns remain unforgotten and are generally carried over into the homes which the children themselves establish. Memories of the patterns and practices of the parental home, its traditions and ideals, become sweet and treasured possessions which children consciously or unconsciously perpetuate in their own households.

Every detail of the parental home and family life does not stand out in memory with equal prominence. Rather, family patterns are remembered more as in a bas-relief and it is often surprising to parents to discover those which stand out with the highest degree of projection. Sister Sharp drew an interesting analogy a few years ago. She had taken her first cross-continent airplane ride. It was a clear, beautiful day. She watched the passing terrain with great interest. Upon the return home she made this observation in a *Relief Society Magazine* editorial entitled "Family Patterns":

The earth patches of different colors, each one denoting a particular situation and condition, merged into a composite pattern. Viewed from the perspective of the plane small individual plots of land became a part of a picture which could be classified generally as fertile or barren, wooded, or desert, thickly settled, or sparsely populated.

So it is with families. The individual characteristics and differences become merged to form a definite family pattern . . . hour by hour, day by day, and year by year, it is formed, made by the individual thoughts, hopes and beliefs, transmuted into family behavior, standards, and actions. Families come to be noted either favorably or unfavorably for their attitudes, convictions, and patterns, and a certain response may be expected when a family pattern is known.

Children remember and are influenced by those patterns which bring them the greatest satisfaction. Have you ever considered what you remember of your parental home? Have you young parents with growing children ever asked, "What will my children remember of this home?" Have you parents with grown or married children ever asked them what they remember? Would it be the family gathering in prayer? Would it be the busy preparations for the Sabbath? Would it be father and the boys going together to priesthood meeting? Would it be the entire family going together to sacrament meeting? Would it be the family hour to which each child made his contributions? Would it be the family joining in holiday fun? Or on the other hand, would it be never finding mother at home when returning from school? Would it be the memory of some trifling irritation born of the excitement of a holiday—an unwarranted display of temper on the part of father or mother, which took the joy out of all that had been done to make the occasion happy?

I asked a mother of five growing children the other day what she remembered about her parental home. Promptly she replied, "Every holiday we had a freezer of home-made ice cream. Mother would cook a thin custard and we children would wait what seemed to be an interminable length of time for the custard to cool. Then Dad and the older boys would turn by hand the big two-gallon freezer. Usually in winter the boys gathered icicles from the eaves of the house with which to freeze the ice cream. We little ones gathered about and watched and waited to 'lick the dasher.' Then the ice cream was firmly packed until our party or outing in the afternoon. Our holidays were great fun."

I said, "Do you make ice cream for your children?"

"Oh, no," she laughed, "we don't own a freezer; we buy what we want. Things are different today. It's cheaper to buy ice cream than to make it." Then after a moment's pause she said, "But we do what the freezer of ice cream symbolized. We maintain the pattern of a family project every holiday in which every member of the family takes part. Our holidays are our family days, just as were mother's and father's."

Family patterns and traditions are sacred. However, regardless of how well-established and beloved they may be, they are not indestructible. Often selfishness, an unkind word, an altered circumstance can cause them to collapse, never to be rebuilt or reclaimed. So we aim not only to build, but to preserve.

Mothers, in large measure, set the family patterns.

They create the tone and spirit of the home. They establish the traditions that have meaning in the lives of their children. Theirs is the most potent influence in determining whether the home is a good home which will influence aright the homes of future generations and favorably affect children for time and eternity.

Relief Society can and does help mothers to maintain good homes, not only homes that reflect good housekeeping and wise home management, but homes which nourish the spiritual nature of family members and help them live by the standards and teachings of the Church. Relief Society keeps before mothers the eternal rewards of their homemaking labors.

Mothers are not sufficient unto themselves in dealing with the varied and endless ramifications of homemaking. They need the supporting influence and guidance of Relief Society in order that our Latter-day Saint homes may reflect the teachings of the Church and fit into the everlasting celestial pattern designed by our Heavenly Father.

THE PLACE OF WOMEN IN THE CHURCH TODAY

F ROM the vantage point of the one hundredth anniversary of the founding of the Young Women's Mutual
Improvement Association, those who guide its desti-
nies today must look back with unshakable conviction that
only through divine inspiration could such an organization
for young women have been established.

There must be a deep sense of gratitude for the great
women leaders who through the years have presided over
this institution. There must be a thankful recognition for
the inspired priesthood direction that has been continuously
available to the organization; there must be an almost
overwhelming sense of joy and satisfaction in accomplishment.

Through the past century the YWMIA has touched
the lives of hundreds of thousands of young women, holding before them the ideals of the Church, influencing for
right their thinking, shaping their standards, and training
them in a mastery of their conduct. It has developed their
characters and provided opportunity for the enlargement
and well-directed exercise of their talents. It has given
them abundant and varied social experiences. None need
to have remained on the outside looking in because of lack
of activities for which her talents were suited. The YWMIA

has been a potent influence in bringing young women of the Church to maturity in thought and action and helping them acquire strong testimonies of the gospel.

President Heber J. Grant gave this impressive promise to the YWMIA:

As you shall inspire the young girls with the love of God, with the love of home, the love of the gospel of Jesus Christ, with a desire to seek to do that which will be pleasing to our Heavenly Father, you will grow in ability, strength, and in the power of God. (*Gospel Standards*, p. 151.)

This promise has truly been fulfilled.

Not only have the young women of the Church been fortunate beneficiaries of the work of the YWMIA, but immeasurable strength has accrued to the Church itself through the activities of this great organization.

Relief Society, designed for the mature women of the Church, recognizes its debt to the YWMIA. As the young woman is brought by the natural processes of life to shift her interests and activities from those of her young womanhood to those of her mature years, she naturally seeks avenues whereby these changing interests and needs may be served. Countless thousands of young women who have been trained by the YWMIA move naturally into the program of Relief Society with purpose and dedication. They bring with them stability of character, developed talents, leadership skills, and a devotion to the Church that become a bulwark of strength to Relief Society in meeting the responsibilities assigned to it as a companion organization to the priesthood.

The Latter-day Saint woman has a significant role in the affairs of the Church. It is expected of her that she will lend her full strength, according to the nature of woman, and as directed by priesthood authority, to the building of God's kingdom on earth.

The Mormon woman actively participates in the work of the Church. She serves as a proselyting missionary; she inspires sons and daughters to do likewise, and, in countless instances, she provides the necessary financial support. She serves in the auxiliaries of the Church. She renders untold hours of compassionate service in the name of the Church and loyally supports other types of Church welfare service. She devotes herself to genealogical research and vicarious work for the dead in the temples of the Church. Such services increase as the Church grows.

President Heber J. Grant generously praised the women when he said: "Without the wonderful work of the women I realize that the Church would have been a failure." (*Ibid.*, p. 150.)

From the beginning days of the Church, women have been given voice in the affairs of the Church. They have voted side by side with men on all questions submitted to the Church membership for vote. The will of the Lord in this matter was made clear in a revelation given to the Prophet Joseph Smith, Oliver Cowdery, and John Whitmer at Harmony, Pennsylvania, July 1830, three months after the Church was organized. The Lord said: "And all things shall be done by common consent in the church. . . ." (D&C 26:2.)

This recognition was an advanced concept in 1830, when no women had political franchise.

It was the desire to increase woman's usefulness to the Church that led the sisters of Nauvoo to approach the Prophet and seek to be organized. They had been zealous in their service as individuals, but they felt greatly limited in working as such. It must have been comforting to them when Eliza R. Snow, having represented them before the Prophet in their request for an organization, conveyed to them these meaningful words of the Prophet: "Tell the sisters their offering is accepted of the Lord. . . . I will organize them under the priesthood after a pattern of the priesthood."

With the growth and expansion of the Church, the contribution of the women has been multiplied a thousand-fold over that of the sisters of Nauvoo. As we contemplate

the blessings enjoyed by Latter-day Saint women today—
greater perhaps than those enjoyed by any other single
body of women—may we not feel the contribution of the
women of this day is accepted of the Lord?

The doctrines of the Church accord to women a position of dignity, respect, and responsibility in God's eternal
plan for his children. The gospel teaches that salvation
and exaltation in the Father's kingdom are for all honest
in heart in all the world, men and women alike, through
individual obedience to the laws and ordinances upon
which these blessings are predicated.

While the priesthood is given only to men in the
Church, its benefits and blessings are shared by the wives
and every member of the family. Elder John A. Widtsoe
said:

> In the ordinances of the Priesthood man and woman share
> alike. The temple doors are open to every faithful member of the
> Church. And, it is to be noted that the highest blessings therein
> available are only conferred upon a man and woman . . . jointly.
> Neither can receive them alone. In the Church of Christ woman
> is not an adjunct to, but an equal partner with man." (*Relief Society
> Magazine,* June-July 1943, p. 373.)

Elder Bruce R. McConkie, in discussing the doctrine
recorded in Doctrine and Covenants 131:1-4, makes this
significant statement:

> . . . he [man] cannot attain a fulness of joy here or of eternal
> reward hereafter alone. Woman stands at his side a joint-inheritor
> with him in the fulness of all things. Exaltation and eternal increase
> is her lot as well as his. (*Mormon Doctrine,* 1966, p. 844.)

Among the great doctrines of the Church, none is
perhaps more sublime or more comforting to women than
the doctrine of the eternity of the family. According to
the late President J. Reuben Clark, Jr., the Latter-day Saint
family, in a Latter-day Saint home, has three great functions:

> First—it must bring to its members such lives as will enable
> them to return to the inner circles of that celestial home from

which they came—a dwelling with the Heavenly Father and Mother throughout eternities.

Second—it must so carry out its duties, rights, and functions as to enable it, in turn, to found a celestial home that shall in some eternity hereafter be equal in power, opportunity, and dignity with the celestial home from which we came and to which we shall return.

Third—it must so live its life as to provide for the spirits yet waiting to come to this earth for their fleshly tabernacles, both bodies and minds that shall be healthy, for the spirits coming through them are the choice spirits, which have earned the right by their lives in their first estate, to come for their second estate, to the righteous homes—to the families of greatest worth, promise, and opportunity; and this family must provide for this spirit which it invites to come to its hearthstone, an environment that shall meet the strictest requirements of righteousness. (*Relief Society Magazine,* Dec. 1940, p. 808.)

As we contemplate the Latter-day Saint family, we are impressed with the orderliness of its organization. President Grant has told us:

The blessings and promises that come from beginning life together, for time and eternity, in a temple of the Lord cannot be obtained in any other way and worthy young Latter-day Saint men and women who so begin life together find that their eternal partnership under the everlasting covenant becomes the foundation upon which are built peace, happiness, virtue, love, and all of the other eternal verities of life, here and hereafter. (*The Improvement Era,* April 1936, p. 199.)

The man is by divine decree the head or the presiding officer: he is the family provider. Woman is his companion and helpmate; she is the child bearer and child rearer. In this role, woman finds not only her divine mission but also her greatest life-fulfillment. This divinely ordained division of labor for forming, maintaining, and protecting the family unit makes one parent no less important than the other; and when respected in their individual roles, they lay the surest foundation for family well-being.

The place of woman in the Church, having been defined by divine decree, does not change from time to time. It remains constant. It is the same today as yesterday;

it will be the same tomorrow. As woman understands her place and functions as God intends, there come to her the richest possible life fulfillment and the greatest eternal rewards. Blessed above all women of the world are the women of the Church who have this knowledge.

HOME—THE PLACE OF PEACE; THE SHELTER

THE great poets impart wisdom, beautifully expressed, with a minimum of words. Wordsworth has said, "Poetry is the breath and finer spirit of all knowledge." So we find ourselves turning to the poets and using their words to express our own convictions.

I would like to draw upon the writings of one of the great poets of Scotland, Robert Burns. In his "Cotter's Saturday Night." he conveys with depth of feeling the peace and rest and rejuvenation, the contentment and happiness that abide within a well-ordered home. A few selected lines will serve to show you the characteristics of such a home as portrayed by the poet.

November chill blaws loud wi' angry sugh;
The short'ning winter day is near a close;
The miry beasts retreating frae the plough;
The black'ning trains o' craws to their repose;
The toil-worn cotter frae his labour goes;—
This night his weekly moil is at an end—
Collects his spades, his mattacks, and his hoes,
Hoping the morn in ease and rest to spend,
And weary, o'er the moor, his course does homeward bend.

At length his lonely cot appears in view
Beneath the shelter of an aged tree. . . .

His clean hearth-stone, his thrifty wifie's smile,
The lisping infant, prattling on his knee,
Does a' his weary kiaugh and care beguile,
And makes him quite forget his labour and his toil. . . .

Their eldest hope, their Jenny, woman-grown,
In youth fu'bloom—love sparkling in her e'e—
Comes hame, perhaps to shew a braw new gown,
Or deposit her sair-won penny-fee,
To help her parents dear—if they in hardship be.
With joy unfeigned, brothers and sisters meet,
And each for others weelfare kindly speirs;
The social hours, swift-wing'd, unnotic'd fleet.
Each tells the uncos that he sees and hears. . . .

Their master's and their mistress's command
The younkers a' are warned to obey. . . .

"And mind your duty, duly, morn and night;
Lest in temptation's path ye gang astray,
Implore His counsel and assisting might;
They never sought in vain that sought the Lord aright. . . ."

But now the supper crowns their simple board,
The halesome parritch, chief of Scotia's food. . . .
The cheerful supper done, wi' serious face,
They round the ingle (fireplace), form a circle wide.
The sire turns o'er with patriarchal grace,
The big ha'-Bible, ance his father's pride. . . .

The priest-like father reads the sacred page,
How Abram was the friend of God on high;
Or Moses bade eternal warfare wage
With Amalek's ungracious progeny. . . .

Then, kneeling down to Heaven's Eternal King,
The saint, the father, and the husband prays. . . .

Then . . . all take off their sev'ral way;
The youngling cottagers retire to rest.
The parent-pair their secret homage pay,
And proffer up to Heaven the warm request,
That He who stills the raven's clam'rous nest,
And decks the lily fair in flow'ry pride,
Would, in the way His wisdom sees the best,
For them and for their little ones provide;
But chiefly, in their hearts with grace divine preside.

When I was a little girl, my mother often read this poem to me. I felt as if I knew the cotter and his children, and often wished that I might live in their home.

Certainly these lines present an inviting picture of a contented home. One feels the glow of warmth that rests over it and an assurance of the well-being of the family. We are led to say, "Would that all of our homes could possess its virtues and enjoy the attendant blessings." But we are reminded that this is a description of a Scottish peasant home in 1783—a home located on the bleak Scottish moors more than 185 years ago. This was a time when the simple virtues characterized most homes, and when the acquisition of material things beyond the ordinary needs of life did not engross the family members as it does today.

Tremendous changes have taken place in the world during these past 185 years. Their impact upon our homes has greatly modified our lives. Much that was sacred and traditional seems to have gone out, and new standards, different patterns of living, and expanding interests of family members have taken over.

Effort is being made to analyze the changes and their effect upon the homes, and to develop ways of meeting them that will leave the home unimpaired in its ability to fulfill its obligations to family members and to society.

This past summer I served as moderator of a panel attempting to define some of the major changes that are taking place throughout the world. The discussion aimed at a better understanding of the significance of these changes upon family life with a view to helping toward a more intelligent approach to meeting the challenge presented.

Panel members were distinguished members of the faculty of a university, men of high standing in their respective fields and well qualified to deal with the subject at hand.

The panel presentations and the discussions established the fact that the fast trend toward industrialization and urbanization, advances in science and education, the change in the status of women, the increasingly high standards of living, the new roles being assumed by government, and other factors are affecting our homes. It was pointed out that the home is becoming a consuming rather than a producing unit. Young people are reaching out as never before for more general education, as well as more specialized training, placing new demands upon the family. It was declared that we are losing sight of the fact that education is the function of the family as well as the school.

The physical aspects of the home are demanding more and more attention, we were told. The traditional roles of the mother as the homemaker and the father as the breadwinner have been greatly modified. In many homes today both the father and mother are wage earners and housekeepers.

Children are being called upon to assume new responsibilities. All too many children now have too much unsupervised time devoid of careful parental planning and firm, wise guidance.

Recreational and social activities within the home have largely been transferred to the outside.

It was recognized that new patterns of family life difficult for many of us to understand are emerging. Nonetheless, it was felt that the effect on the home and family of our changing world has not all been bad. Rather it has been mostly good. It was the opinion that few of us would want to go back to the patterns of the past.

The conclusions of the discussion were that the challenge before us is to be aware of the changes that are taking place, to recognize their impact upon our homes, then gain a knowledge of the decision-making processes and choose those values which are constant and which will preserve family solidarity and enable the home to fulfill it two primary functions. These were defined as follows:

1. To provide a place of refuge and security for family members.

2. To develop responsible citizens capable of taking their places in a rapidly changing world.

It was interesting that no one so much as implied that the basic functions of the home had been altered by changing times and conditions, nor had the factors which contribute to family solidarity.

Sound as are the functions as defined, to Latter-day Saints they are not all-encompassing. In fact, they fail to take into account the greatest purpose, which is so to influence the lives of family members as to fit them for place in God's household, in God's family, in our heavenly and eternal home.

The fulfillment of our divine purposes is not dependent upon things within our homes which yield to change, but rather to the exercise of the simple, constant virtues which brook no alteration because they are founded upon eternal truths.

May I enumerate a few of the more important of these virtues, recognizing of course that for Latter-day Saints the happiness of the home and its eternal well-being are most assured when the home is founded upon eternal marriage—eternal marriage that is understood, respected and safeguarded.

Within a good home there must be parental authority, righteously exercised. In the Latter-day Saint home the father, holding the Holy Priesthood, is by divine decree the head, or presiding officer. The mother is the homemaker, the teacher, the faithful, patient, daily guardian against evil and detrimental influences. In these positions of responsibility and trust, parents are to be respected.

Love must abide in a well-ordered home, fostered from the very beginning by joyous preparations and a happy welcome for each new life sent by the Father. The home protects love against destructive influences such as quarreling, bickering, fault-finding, selfishness. Love is nourished by happy, harmonious family relationships, by understanding and an appreciation of one for another, by unselfish consideration of one another, by thoughtful kindness and, at times of special need, by open, affectionate tenderness. President McKay has told us that in every good home there must be "fidelity" to love.

Discipline must characterize a home if it is to fulfill divine destiny—discipline founded upon righteous principles which become so rooted in family members as to bring out a willing self-discipline. No home devoid of discipline can be a truly good home.

There must be loyalty, unity, and a willingness to share in the home responsibilities. President McKay has said: "The first contributing factor to a happy home is the sublime virtue of loyalty, one of the noblest attributes of the human soul." And I am sure that we would all agree that unity is one of the foundation stones of strength. We know also that there are few things which enhance family life more than a willingness to share.

A love of the Lord, daily communion with him through individual and family prayer, and obedience to his commandments are the great controlling safeguards. President McKay has told us that: "The Gospel of Peace should find its most fruitful effects in the homes of Church members."

Now these virtues which I have enumerated were found, in large measure, in the cotter's home over a century ago. They were good then; they are equally good today; they will continue to be good. They will always contribute to the well-being of family members and to the stability of the home, enabling it, when disturbed from its equilibrium, to master the forces which restore it to its original condition of strength, resolution of purpose, and constancy.

Ruskin wrote impressively of the home and of the place of the wife in it:

This is the true nature of home—it is the place of peace; the shelter, not only from all injury, but from all terror, doubt, and division. In so far as it is not this, it is not home: so far as the anxieties of the outer life penetrate into it, and the inconsistently-minded, unknown, unloved, or hostile society of the outer world is allowed by either husband or wife to cross the threshold, it ceases to be home; it is then only a part of that outer world which you have roofed over, and lighted fire in. But so far as it is a sacred place, a vestal temple of the hearth watched over by Household Gods, before whose faces none may come but those whom they can receive with love,—so far as it is this, and roof and fire are types only of a nobler shade and light,—shade as of the rock in a weary land, and light as of the Pharos in the stormy sea,—so far it vindicates the name, and fulfills the praise, of home.

And wherever a true wife comes, this home is always round her. The stars only may be over her head; the glow-worm in the night-cold grass may be the only fire at her foot; but home is yet wherever she is; and for a noble woman it stretches far round her, better than ceiled with cedar, or painted with vermilion, shedding its quiet light far, for those who else were homeless. . . .

So far as she rules, all must be right, or nothing is. She must be enduringly, incorruptibly good; instinctively, infallibly wise. (Except from Lecture II—"Lilies: of Queens' Gardens," from *Sesame and Lilies*, by John Ruskin—1819-1900.)

The women of the Church will find wisdom and treasures of knowledge, they will develop an innate goodness to help them in their divine calling as mothers and homemakers through active affiliation with Relief Society. Women who become active in Relief Society grow to love it. Their knowledge and skills increase, their testimonies of the gospel become firmly rooted. There develops within them a desire to help in the building of the kingdom of God on earth. This influence they carry into their homes and disseminate among the family members. The home then becomes enriched, a place where the Spirit of God may dwell, a home prepared to fulfill its divine destiny.

The primary concern of Latter-day Saint women should not be with the impact of the changes that are taking place, except as we need to understand them to cope with them wisely. One poet has said, "To see clearly is poetry, prophecy and religion, all in one." So we must see clearly. Our primary concern, however, is that we shall firmly position ourselves in preserving the enduring, spiritual values which time and the prophets have taught us are unchangeable, and which are the guarantee of the stability of our homes, and the eternal well-being of our children.

WOMAN ENNOBLED

IN March 1840, Elder Parley P. Pratt, exuberant with joy and gratitude over the truths revealed through the restored gospel, released his feelings in poetic words which were published on the first page of the initial number of the *Millennial Star*, and later set to music. As we, too, have rejoiced in the knowledge and the blessings which have come to us through modern revelation, we have sung the words penned by Elder Pratt with depth of feeling:

> The morning breaks, the shadows flee,
> Lo, Zion's standard is unfurled.
> The dawning of a brighter day
> Majestic rises on the world.

Truly women *should* rejoice in the brighter day which dawned for womankind with the restoration. As the rays of the gospel shed their light upon the earth, the lofty position accorded woman in the gospel plan and the importance of her divinely ordained earthly mission were made clearly visible, and new vistas for development and purposeful living, under the guidance of the priesthood, were opened to her view.

In the early part of the nineteenth century, there appears to have been little consideration given to the divine nature and destiny of woman, and life for her encompassed but few of the opportunities and advantages contemplated in the gospel plan. Let us briefly review her position and circumstances. True, it is hard to arrive at a precisely clear picture which might apply to every woman of that day. The differing economic and social circumstances, the varied conditions and cultures of her area of residence, the western movement in America which demanded unusual adaptations in order to meet the requirements of survival—all had bearing on the life of a woman. This we know, however; her world was in large measure her home, her church, and her neighborhood. Life for the average woman was hard, and many shackles bound her in the development of her talents and in the exercise of her abilities, as well as in the exercise of her God-ordained free agency.

There were rigid barriers of law against property holding and guardianship of children. Most industries refused to employ her and those which did offered her only routine labor with long hours and low pay. The taboos of society on education and public expression, along with the prevalent superstition which held "the weak, feminine brain, incapable of serious thinking . . ." shackled her personal development. The advantages of education were extremely limited. Colleges of higher learning did not admit her. True, women had served as teachers of a sort, but they were primary teachers instructing only in the three "Rs." They received miserable pay, usually living in the home of a student with board and room as the teaching wage. When education ventured beyond the primary level, it was for the benefit of the male, and teaching became work for the schoolmaster, not the schoolmistress.

In the field of religion she had the privilege of organizing ladies aid societies, though after a timid and limited fashion. Most churches seem to have maintained their female society, with the women being allowed to decorate and tend the altars, meet for prayer and religious discussion, sew for the church, and administer to the poor through the earnings acquired through the sale of their own products. They were forbidden, however, to vote in the affairs of the church.

The political privileges of women were nil. There had been sporadic women's clubs of a sort—neighbors meeting together for sociability and the exercise of their minds—with some groups working in a haphazard fashion for the public good. These clubs were poorly organized, however, and affairs were largely controlled by husbands of the members.

In 1833, a few bold women formed the first woman's club with a political purpose—the Philadelphia Female Anti-Slavery Society. The furor aroused is described in the book, *Angels and Amazons,* issued by the National Council of Women of the United States. It states that the woman who identified herself with this group was regarded as bold and unwise indeed, for a respectable woman did not speak in public, nor did she organize in behalf of any political cause. At the first convention held by this group, a mob roared outside the meeting place, and following the meeting, the building was burned.

With such conditions for woman extant, came the light of the gospel, dispelling darkness, injustice, and bigotry, and glorifying woman as a beloved daughter of our Heavenly Father with a divinely ordained mission in earth life. It illumined the paths that led to the development of her divine mission. It opened for her endless doors of opportunity.

The doctrines and teachings of the restored Church were explicit with regard to woman and removed for all time the age-old controversy of woman's rights versus man's rights.

The late Dr. John A. Widtsoe, in an article published in the *Relief Society Magazine,* clearly sets forth some of these doctrines and teachings as follows:

. . . she (woman) bears joint responsibility with man in establishing the kingdom of God . . . full equality has been provided in the Church between man and woman. They are equal in opportunity, privilege, and rights. They have a common destiny, which as free agents they may attain or lose through their own actions. . . .

It [the Church] has given her full rights of suffrage and property ownership. It recognizes her equal mental powers with those of man and the right to use her inborn talents to the full. . . .

This equality does not ignore the natural differences between man and woman. Woman is the child-bearer and child-rearer. . . . Man is provider of the necessities and comforts of the family. This does not reduce woman to a dependent. . . . It [family life] is . . . a cooperative enterprise based upon a divinely ordained division of labor for forming, maintaining, and protecting the unit of society known as the family. . . .

The family must have organization. The man . . . is by divine decree the head or presiding officer. . . . To him is committed the Priesthood . . . but the benefits and blessings of the Priesthood thus conferred are shared by the wife and, as needed, by every member of the family. . . . The highest blessings [available in the temple] are only conferred upon a man and woman . . . jointly. Neither can receive them alone.

If she [woman] accepts gladly the glorious gift of motherhood, she may use whatever time and strength remain in the exercise of her talents.

. . . The privilege of self-expression belongs to her. . . . She may enter industry, education, the professions—every worthwhile pursuit with the good will of all.

Dr. Widtsoe continues, "Divinely commissioned, in her keeping are the choice spirits who have come to earth to win an earthly body. . . . In her hands lies the future of the race." (*Relief Society Magazine,* June-July, 1943, pp. 372-375).

This was new doctrine, greatly at variance with prevailing beliefs in the early part of the nineteenth century.

In 1830 when the Church was organized, there came a startling innovation for woman when she was granted by the Church the religious vote. Through revelation, the Lord directed the Prophet, Oliver Cowdery, and John Whitmer: "And all things shall be done by common consent in the church. . . ." (D&C 26:2.)

We remind ourselves that, in 1830, no woman and few men voted in any church body, and no woman had political franchise.

In 1842, the work of the women in building the kingdom having been accepted of the Lord as testified by the Prophet when he said, "your offerings are accepted of the Lord," the women were given by the Lord through the Prophet an organization established according to the laws of heaven—The Female Relief Society of Nauvoo, now known as the Relief Society of The Church of Jesus Christ of Latter-day Saints. This organization was the medium through which women might express themselves, find opportunity for personal development and service, and more effectively do the women's part in building the kingdom.

According to Elder Bruce R. McConkie in an article published in the *Relief Society Magazine*:

> By turning the key [in behalf of women] the Prophet delegated to the duly appointed officers of the new organization a portion of the keys of the kingdom. Under the Priesthood they were now authorized to direct, control, and govern the affairs of the society. . . . Under this appointment their lawful acts would be recognized by the Lord and he would work with them in the rolling forth of the kingdom in the sphere assigned to them. (*Relief Society Magazine*, March, 1950, p. 151.)

The significant statement by the Prophet with regard to turning the key in behalf of women is the foundation upon which an extensive educational program for women has been established and carried forward by Relief Society. The program includes, as expressed by President Lorenzo Snow, "a study of those subjects which tend toward the elevation and advancement of women along all lines of thought and action." This statement is also the basis for the Society's benevolent activities.

That our pioneer women caught the vision and the implications of all the privileges outlined for woman in the gospel plan is abundantly evident. That they sensed their responsibility to disseminate these truths is also apparent. Their pioneer publication bore the title, *Woman's Exponent* —exponent meaning expounder, interpreter, champion, representative. On the front page of the publication, directly under the name, was the caption, "The Rights of the Women of Zion, and the Rights of the Women of All Nations."

The organization of Relief Society with the significant pronouncement of turning the key in behalf of woman preceded, by six years, the first public declaration made by women demanding equal social, industrial, educational, and political rights—a declaration issued at the Seneca Falls Convention called by a small but determined body of women known as the National Woman's Suffrage Association.

This declaration is generally regarded in the United States as the beginning of the so-called women's movement —a movement that has gained momentum with each passing year until, today, women may be found in almost every field of human endeavor, and in most nations they are a power to be recognized in national life.

In the struggle of woman for emancipation, woman suffrage and the right to hold public office have been prime goals. Utah women were early granted suffrage. Even in the territorial days they enjoyed the elective franchise. They played a conspicuous part in the national woman's suffrage movement in the United States which culminated in the adoption of the nineteenth amendment to the Constitution in 1920, granting women of this nation full suffrage.

The struggle for suffrage still goes on in a number of countries; a few have recently won these rights.

Recently Sister Florence Jacobsen, President of the Young Women's Mutual Improvement Association, and I attended a conference of the International Council of Women as voting delegates from the National Council of Women of the United States. The conference was held in Teheran, Iran, at the invitation of the Princess Ashraf, twin sister of the Shah and President of the High Council of Women of Iran. The conference was held in Iran in recognition of Iranian women having been granted suffrage in 1963. It was in 1936 that these women were unveiled.

We were given to understand that the Shah regards the liberation of women as one of his major programs designed to advance and modernize this ancient nation and to promote the well-being of its people.

An interesting experience was mine during this conference. An Iranian woman who was a member of the parliament of that country sought me out. She told me of her long, arduous efforts in behalf of liberation for the Iranian women. She explained that, in the beginning, she had little knowledge of how to proceed in working toward suffrage, so she made extensive studies of the movement in other countries. In so doing, she learned of the leadership Utah women had given to this cause. She had written a book, she said, in which she made reference to their work. Then handing me her card, she invited me to correspond with her, "for," said she, "women who were so forward looking in gaining suffrage as were Utah women must have something to offer by way of its proper use. Liberation calls for responsible action."

How right she is! It is not easy properly to use freedom. Righteous principles and sound guidelines must be followed.

While woman's emancipation has brought endless opportunities and advantages, it has not left her devoid of problems. In her zeal for expression and freedom, we find her all too often developing attitudes, expressing opinions, engaging in activities, and seeking goals that are not in the interest of her ultimate best good nor in harmony with her feminine nature or her earthly mission. Rather than striving for the realization of her full potential as a woman, we see her all too often in competition with man, aping his behavior, his habits, even his dress and general appearance. We see her somewhat insensitive to her primary role as his companion and helpmeet, the guardian of his home, the guide and protector of the spirits entrusted to the home. We see her disregarding his role as head of the household in righteousness.

The demands of modern life entice, if not force, many women to engage in activities outside their homes, particularly in the labor market. To engage capably in these activities and at the same time competently meet the requirements of the home and family and to maintain a poised balance in dealing with the responsibilities of life, test the greatest powers of judgment and organizational ability, home management, and physical, spiritual, and mental health. These women must continually ask themselves which of all our multitudinous responsibilities have first claim upon us?

An article in a national magazine recently reminded women that human beings have remained human because there were women whose duty it was to provide continuity in their lives—to be there when they went to sleep and when they woke up, to ease pain, to sympathize with failure and rejoice in success, to listen to tales of broken hearts, to soothe and support and sustain and stimulate husbands and sons as they faced the vicissitudes of a hard outside world. Throughout history, the article says, children have needed mothers, men have needed wives, the young, the sick, the old, the unhappy, the triumphantly victorious, have needed special individuals to share with them and care for them. They have needed women who see this as their primary work.

It is troublesome to note that, at times, attributes, opinions, and actions of women today are inconsistent or at variance with their earnestly desired and worthy goals. For example, at the Iranian conference, speakers spoke feelingly of the need to build a stronger, more useful, and happier society. In order to accomplish this, they advocated more intensified effort toward community development which would allow better opportunities for women and children, who, in turn, would be able to make more significant contributions to a good society. At the same time, they advocated programs for community development that would take women more and more into com-

munity life and more and more away from their homes
and their children, thus weakening the basic foundation
of a good society and of useful, happy citizenship.

Also, may we not question opinions such as that expressed by a conference delegate, "Women must learn to
regard the period of child bearing and child rearing as
temporary retirement from life"?

I suggest that the time has come when woman might
with profit evaluate the direction emancipation is taking
her, assess the values which motivate her views and actions,
and endeavor more earnestly to seek out truth as it relates
to the proper uses of her God-given freedom.

To stem the tide of error, to alter confused thinking
and modify improper action on the part of women will require strong and intelligent leadership. Upon whom rests
the burden of this responsibility? Certainly upon those to
whom the Lord has revealed his plan and purposes for
womankind. In my opinion, it rests upon the shoulders of
Latter-day Saint women.

Can Latter-day Saint women meet this responsibility?
Of course they can! They have the truth, the daily guidance
of the prophets, the Relief Society as the medium through
which to work. They may do it by the example of their
lives, by refusing to succumb to the pressures and fashions
of the day. They may do it by their teachings. It is not
usually necessary nor advisable to crash head-on with op-
posing forces, but by clear and measured thinking, by
courageous and patient teaching, by example and per-
suasion, they may point the way.

The world is full of good women seeking the right way,
ready to accept truth when it is presented to them with
clarity and conviction, devoid of criticism, and when one's
own actions give credence to the words.

May the Lord give to the women of the Church today
the vision to see themselves as the woman's exponent,
dedicated to the use of their freedoms according to divine
mandate.

WOMAN'S ROLE AS HOMEMAKER

R ECENTLY I read on the woman's page of a newspaper, in a column reserved for advice on personal matters, the following interesting problem presented by a woman: "I am the mother of eight children. Ever since my marriage I have devoted almost my entire time to my home and to rearing my children. I long to do something worthwhile with my life. What would you suggest?"

Wisely the columnist answered: "I know of nothing more worthwhile."

To match this is the attitude of a married woman with five grown, educated, likable children, who is often heard to say: "After all, what have I accomplished? I have sacrificed my own life for my children."

Women today point with pride, and justly so, to their accomplishments in the professions, the arts, commerce, industry, education, and politics. We are grateful for all that modern progress has done for woman—her liberation, her education, her opportunities. We view with pride all that she has achieved. But with a more complete understanding of her mission comes the realization that, although she may wish to combine another role with homemaking, it is in her age-old role of mother and homemaker that she makes her supreme contribution to the world.

The work of homemaking offers to woman her greatest opportunities and her deepest satisfactions. Here her creative urges may find fullest expression, her administrative ability develop most naturally. Here her talents may be put to the most practical uses and her skills function most freely. Here continuous claim may be laid upon her resourcefulness and ingenuity, and her intelligence find a constant challenge. Here her spiritual nature may flower fully and her character grow to its greatest stature. Here her influence may be most potent and her contribution to society most effective.

It is a matter of deep concern that social and economic conditions today are effecting far-reaching changes in our homes and exerting a pulling power away from the home. They are enticing, if not forcing, many women out of the sphere in which they can find the most happiness and do the greatest good. There are many influences in contemporary life which impinge upon the family and make it difficult for parents to maintain stable homes and direct their children aright.

On every hand we read of the concern that is felt for our homes. This rather disconsolate picture of the American home was published in *Family Life*, the official organ of the National Family Life Association:

> As the machine age spreads its patterns ever more widely, we have taken out of the home everything that has to do with living. You can't be born there, die there, be buried from there. You can't be taught there, be sick there. You can't work there, nor learn a skill. And entertainment must certainly be found elsewhere. What is there left but a lifeless dormitory where one changes one's clothes and where food, prepared elsewhere, is served?

Our Church leaders have always taught us that "the home and family are sacred institutions. They are not manmade, but have been established by a kind Providence for the blessing of his children."

President Smith has admonished us, "You fathers and mothers who are rearing sons and daughters, don't put off the opportunity that is yours to win them to a righteous life . . . ."

President J. Reuben Clark, Jr., has told us that "to the Latter-day Saint the home is a holy place. It has its pattern in the heavens." He has further told us:

Each family unit here that is created by and under the authority of the Priesthood in the House of the Lord, is potentially another celestial family, another Heavenly Home, like to the one of which we are members,—a family unit that may ultimately do for other intelligences what God did for ours. . . .

President Clark has placed upon the mothers of the Church first responsibility for maintaining our homes according to the teachings of the Church. In addressing the Relief Society sisters in a general Relief Society conference, he said:

Need I point out to you Relief Society sisters where your high duty lies in all this;—your duty not only, but your lofty destiny as well? . . . the great work [that of homemaking] is yours, yours by your very natures, which means by divine design and appointment. You shall fail in your mission if you do not do it, and the world will be lost.

The positive concern of our leaders for our homes is evidenced in the "Message from the General Authorities Endorsing and Instituting the Family Hour Program." "The need for them [Family Hour programs] was never greater in the history of the Church."

With this feeling existing with regard to homes in general, we are led to ask, "Now, what of our individual homes—yours and mine?" This is a time when it might be well for every sister to make an honest and fearless appraisal of her home and of herself as a mother and homemaker. Well might we ask ourselves:

"Is my home a place of refuge to which family members may return from a confused and troubled world and find peace, security, and rest?"

"Do love and comradeship exist therein, with quarreling and bickering finding no lodging place?"

"Are pride in our choice lineage, family traditions, and ideals transmuting family members into a close-knit family unit which will continue eternally?"

"Does my home bespeak culture and refinement or do profanity, vulgar stories, and cheap literature find harbor there?"

"Is my home a place of industry and thrift?"

"Is my home rich, not necessarily in income, but in what President McKay has termed 'The great imponderables of life, such as serenity, faith, warm emotions, protectiveness, charity, affirmation, yes, and even common sense?'"

"Am I meeting my heaven-imposed responsibilities?"

The Lord has given to Latter-day Saint parents this exacting counsel:

And again, inasmuch as parents have children in Zion, or in any of her stakes which are organized, that teach them not to understand the doctrine of repentance, faith in Christ the Son of the living God, and of baptism and the gift of the Holy Ghost by the laying on of the hands, when eight years old, the sin be upon the heads of the parents.

For this shall be a law unto the inhabitants of Zion, or in any of her stakes which are organized.

And their children shall be baptized for the remission of their sins when eight years old, and receive the laying on of the hands.

And they shall also teach their children to pray, and to walk uprightly before the Lord. (D&C 68:25-28.)

Only as we do this will our homes fulfill their divine destiny.

And what of those other aspects of homemaking—also vital, part and parcel of the business of good homemaking? What of the physical care of our children? What of our housekeeping?

Do we make of housekeeping a fetish to the point of destroying ease and comfort within our homes? Or, on the other hand, are we careless, neglecting to sense the importance of order, cleanliness, and attractiveness?

Family Life, the publication to which I have already referred, recently published a rather startling article entitled "Good Housekeepers Are Scarce." The article opened by saying:

Really, first-class housekeepers are few and far between, if the results of a survey . . . are an indication. The average man would have only one chance in twenty to marry such a housekeeper. In fact, he has only about a 50-50 chance to get one who is even good.

Time will not permit me to give the details of this survey, but the results are worthy of mention. Of 351 homes rated, in only five per cent the housekeeping was classified as excellent, in 40 per cent as good, in 43 per cent as fair, and in 12 per cent as poor. The report comments that the 12 per cent classified as poor were definitely bad, and it adds that these figures correspond rather closely with previous findings. It further states that the population of the homes studied was drawn from many parts of the United States and represented people of varied economic status. It concludes by saying:

If the findings from this sample are representative of any considerable section of the nation's homes, they suggest that the standards of attainment in house-keeping are not favorable to sound family life. They reflect little credit on either parents or public schools who should have taught young people *how to live.*

The questions I have suggested, and many more, might be asked as we appraise our homes. And having appraised them and ourselves as homemakers, have we the courage, the will-power, and the intelligence to correct bad practices and patiently and wisely establish new and better patterns?

The Relief Society, since its inception, has accepted as one of its major responsibilities the task of guiding, directing, and training its members in their role of mother and homemaker. In fact, to develop within the members a firm and abiding testimony of the gospel and to make of them good mothers and homemakers are two of Relief Society's first concerns.

YOUNG WOMEN NEED RELIEF SOCIETY

I T is my opinion that today the Relief Society membership is predominantly mothers with growing children.
Last evening I spoke in a ward that was created a short
time ago by a division of an established ward. The ward Relief Society now has a membership of 55 sisters. At last
week's Relief Society meeting there were 48 women in attendance with 70 children in the nursery. The president, in
telling me this, said, "Our children are well behaved because
our nursery program is equal to their interests and needs." A
singing mothers chorus composed of 32 sisters provided
music for the meeting. The bishop announced that these
mothers had a total of 105 children. The president, herself,
had six lovely children. She is a charming, capable leader.
Every one of her children was in attendance at the sacrament meeting. Their pride in their mother was evident.

This situation is duplicated in countless ward and
branch Relief Societies throughout the Church. Last night
I thought how important it was that these young mothers
should have the influence and training of Relief Society, as
they rear their children in this complex world.

THE WOMAN IN TODAY'S WORLD

ALTHOUGH a few women hold positions of power today, it is my opinion that in world and national affairs, women rule, in the main, by influence; men rule by power. I recall that when I first served in a Relief Society presidency, the ward had built a new meetinghouse and had to raise a few thousand dollars more in order to dedicate it on the date scheduled. Relief Society was called upon to prepare and serve a turkey dinner to a large group. It was the first dinner in the new meetinghouse. We found the kitchen to be insufferably small. The women were in each other's way, slowing service. One woman fainted with the heat. The next day, in distress over the circumstance, I went to the bishop, explained the situation, and requested that they knock out one wall and extend the kitchen to include adjoining space which had been allocated to a classroom. He responded with sharpness: "Certainly not," he said. "We aren't going to start remodeling before the building is dedicated."

On my way home, discouraged and feeling somewhat reprimanded, I called at the home of one of the older sisters. I poured forth my troubles, concluding with, "In this Church men have all the power; women are helpless." She replied, "No, women are not helpless." Then she added,

"If someone came to you, Sister Spafford, and had a good but different gift in each hand and one was power and the other influence and you were given a choice, which gift would you choose?" I thought a moment, and then said, "I think I would choose influence." "That," she replied, "is God's gift to women. Appreciate it and use it aright. Do not covet that which has been given to the brethren." A great lesson I have not forgotten! I commend it to you young women in your companionships, in your homes, and in your church and community life.

I have just returned from attending a two-week's conference of the International Council of Women, held in Bangkok, Thailand. Approximately 400 women representing National Councils of 64 free nations attended. Three new Councils were admitted to membership during the conference: Nepal, Madagascar, and Turkey. So important did Nepal regard this conference that the one representative from this country walked 35 miles carrying her bag from her place of residence to the airport, where she took a plane to attend. Two Russian women were admitted to the conference as observers. The Russian women have an organization comparable in structure to the International Council of Women, known as the W.I.D.F. (Woman's International Democratic Federation). The two Councils are the only woman's organizations with consultative status at the U.N. I am told the influence of each is immeasurable.

It was my privilege as President of the National Council of Women of the United States to serve as chairman of its 20-woman delegation. Since voting is done by unit rule, it was my responsibility to cast all votes for the United States' Council. This was a rich experience but an exacting and difficult duty. One thing I learned from the experience was the value of patience and restraint in leadership.

The delegates to the International Council of Women Conference were on the whole women of stature—members of the parliaments of their respective countries, university presidents, other prominent educators, scientists, doctors, lawyers, and women with other types of professional training. They were informed women with intense feelings, vocal and courageous in their viewpoints.

The theme of the conference was "Living Amid Change." The conference called upon the women to look backward and to accurately assess the present as they moved forward. Discussion centered around such important issues as patterns for peace and the avoidance of conflict. This discussion was perhaps the most discouraging of all because it dealt not only with Vietnam but also with the Middle East, disarmament, the United States' and Russian positions on the A.B.M. (anti-ballistic missile) and the M.I.R.V. (Multiple Individually Targetable Re-Entry Vehicle). The final draft of the resolution on peace, in my judgment, was almost meaningless. It was without teeth. I couldn't see how the women could be brought to a common mind, so varied were their national interests.

Discussions also included the improvement of international relations; the status of woman in law and its improvement in practice; strengthening the stabilizing influences of the family as the foremost social institution; and education—the need for drastic revisions at the elementary, secondary, and college levels to meet present-day living. (Since returning home, I have been advised by letter that a special task force under the aegis of Robert Finch, Secretary of U.S. Department of Health, Education, and Welfare, has been charged with developing proposals for new structures in U.S. higher education. Mrs. Audrey C. Cohen, the only woman on the task force, is president. She says it is the intention to put forward some new and radical ideas regarding the education of women. She has requested that I contribute my thinking on the matter.) The section of the International Council of Women Conference on education dealt also with literacy in the developing countries and the urgency of writing for the newly-literate. Environmental problems received considerable attention: air and water pollution—their sources and control, waste removal, the conservation of natural and man-made resources, the dangers in overuse of pesticides. Health, food production, nutrition, and population growth were also considered. The Council's responsibility to modern mobility of people from rural to urban life and across frontiers demanded attention, as did causes and plans for treatment of urban problems. Communication media—the press, radio, television, and films—was an engaging subject as values and evils were debated along with what women must stand for in enlarging their values and reducing their evils. Leadership for the future—youth actvities and training—held an important place. And running throughout it all was the role of the Council in national development and international good will—the Council as Catalyst.

The discussion of these subjects led into a consideration of such delicate and controversial matters as divorce laws, birth control, sex education in the schools, sexual promiscuity and its effect on the home and society, unrestricted abortions, the working mother, income tax exemption for the working mother, the establishment of free nurseries for pre-school age children; better control of crime and delinquency with more effective law enforcement, legislation to insure the legal rights of children born out of wedlock; drugs—their use and control, together with treatment of the addict; the false image of today's woman as created by advertising through all media; the curbing of pornographic publications, scenes of violence, nudity, and sex in films. Freedom of the press was debated. What does it mean, and what is its responsibility toward self-imposed restraints?

In these matters, I found myself deeply grateful for the teachings and guidance of the Church. We have light on these controversial matters not vouchsafed to others. As the conference progressed, I realized that this is indeed a troubled world. As I listened to viewpoints and opinions, I felt there was a need to have come ringing down through the ages the echoing voice of Moses from Mt. Sinai when he declared the Lord's Ten Commandments—commandments that have never been recinded:

> Thou shalt have no other Gods before me
> Thou shalt not kill
> Thou shalt not commit adultery
> Thou shalt not steal
> Thou shalt not bear false witness against thy neighbour
> Thou shalt not covet . . . anything that is thy neighbour's
> (Exod. 20:3, 13-17.)

The conference impressed me with the fact that human needs and aspirations are the same the world over. Differences lie in the traditions of the respective countries, in their cultures, their degree of development, and their national political interests. National political interests are particularly strong.

Personally, I was disillusioned at times to see brilliant, purposeful women resort to action which I regarded as a sacrifice of principle to expediency, national advantage, or personal ambition and power. To me, integrity is not a marketable commodity. It should neither be sold, bartered, nor sacrificed. I saw more clearly the problems faced by our own national leaders in their international relationships.

To young women and men alike, I say we are living in a troubled world. Its problems will not all be resolved by today's leadership, for they are too many and too deep-seated, and viewpoints are too beclouded with false concepts and erroneous standards. Problems will yield to some extent, but they will not all be overcome. To you we turn with hope—the trained, straight-thinking leaders of tomorrow. The best advice I can give you is to take full advantage of your educational and leadership opportunities and cling fast to the Church and its teachings. In the restored gospel is found truth and the correct plan for good living and the only sure road to peace, prosperity, and happiness.

I᠆T has been my experience to mingle with many non-Latter-day Saint women—smart women of good conscience with a desire to do right by their families and their fellow men. I am frequently impressed, however, with the baffling shadows which obscure the vision of women when there is no priesthood guidance. They grasp first at one cause and then another with no sure base for judgment in making choices. All too often, they have no sure foundation on which to build a discriminating sense of the true and enduring values of life in the rearing of their children.

No Latter-day Saint mother need be so handicapped. Latter-day Saint mothers know that the home, ordered according to the teachings and standards of the Church, is the anchor spot for the development of character. It is the launching platform for the eternal happiness and well-being of children. The Latter-day Saint mother knows that her home should be a place of refuge to which family members may return from a confused and competitive world and find peace, security, relaxation, and rejuvenation.

We need have no misgivings as to how our homes shall be governed. They are priesthood governed. That is, the father honoring his priesthood is the head of the household, governing in a spirit of righteousness and love.

The Doctrine and Covenants, Section 31:9, gives us light on this subject: "Govern your house in meekness, and be steadfast."

It is expected that the Latter-day Saint mother will be literally a pillar of stability in her home and in her dealings with her family. Through her intimate associations with her children, she is in a position to profoundly influence their lives.

"Are today's mothers spending enough time in the home with their children?" It is recognized that some mothers, due to economic necessity, are away from home each day in gainful employment—working mothers we call them. Where there is economic need to meet the necessities of life, this situation may be understandable.

It is not always economic need, however, which takes mothers into the labor market. It came as somewhat of a shock to me at a manpower conference to learn that economic necessity was tenth down on the list of reasons for mothers working.

Mothers who work, whether of necessity or otherwise, impose upon themselves a heavy responsibility in making the hours with their children doubly productive in terms of companionship, guidance, and character development.

I am reminded also that it is not always employment that takes mothers from their homes. Social interests, the desire to be in the swim, the inability to say no to the endless requests and invitations which come to them and which take them away from the home, a lack of regard for homemaking and child rearing as the highest calling for a woman—all of these factors enter in. Recently, a young woman said to me, "I can hardly wait for the holiday season. My husband and I have invitations out almost every night beginning with the week before Christmas and continuing until after the New Year." She spoke with pride in their social popularity. I could not but wonder, "What of the children during the long winter evenings of the holiday season, particularly the eldest, a 16-year-old boy, while the parents pleasured.

Discipline is a part of every good Latter-day Saint home, discipline of both parents and children. Dr. Ariel Ballif refers to discipline in a Relief Society lesson as follows: "Parents must accept responsibility for the degree of order and discipline in the home, both for the group and each individual member, including themselves . . . Every child should learn to respect the rights of others, to respect leadership . . . Parents in turn should respect the rights of children . . . A firm hand and steady, at the proper time, will build character instead of trouble in the life of the child."

The Lord gave us the key to successful homemaking and child rearing when he imposed upon fathers and mothers responsibility for teaching the gospel in the home. We teach by precept and example. Brother Ballif tells us, "Every day parents are setting the pattern of living that will automatically become the pattern of their children."

Further, I remind the sisters of the Church that Relief Society is the organization designed by our Heavenly Father to help mothers in these vital matters. It gives instruction and guidance in knowing the things of first importance as well as practice in obeying them. We are continually learning the truths of the gospel in Relief Society. We study the will of the Lord. We discuss it. We learn. Thus we build a firm base for ordering our homes and influencing and directing our children.

Through this great medium of Relief Society, we are not only helped to meet our first responsibility as women but we are enabled also to meet in an orderly manner the assignment declared by President McKay to be of second importance to us as women—that of rendering helpful service. The compassionate and welfare services rendered by Relief Society are monumental. Through these services, assigned and directed by Relief Society, the poor and the suffering among us are made to rejoice and endless blessings have flowed unto Relief Society and to those who have served in its name.

We are all striving for happiness in life. It doesn't come to us because we wish it, nor does it stay because we appeal to it to do so. It must be earned and retained by continually putting first in our lives those things which our prophets have declared to be of first importance.

STRENGTHENING COMMUNITY VIRTUES

A T the recent General Relief Society Conference, Elder Mark E. Petersen of the Council of the Twelve impressively called to the attention of Relief Society officers and members one of the original assignments given to Relief Society by the Prophet Joseph Smith, namely, "to assist in correcting the morals and strengthening the virtues of the community." Elder Petersen declared that in his opinion the need for this service was greater at the present time than at any other time within his recollection. He said we are passing through the worst moral breakdown of our generation, and he admonished the sisters to be alert to evil conditions within their communities and to meet their responsibilities toward the important assignment given them by the Prophet.

It is of interest that at the time the Prophet gave to the sisters of Relief Society the injunction to correct the morals and strengthen the virtues of the community, there was no particular wave of crime or delinquency in Nauvoo, such as we have in many communities today, to evoke such mandate. Nauvoo was a beautiful, prosperous city that had been reclaimed from the wilderness by an industrious people led by a Prophet of God. While, undoubtedly, some of the people's conduct was at variance with the teachings of the Church, the community as a whole was one of highest moral rectitude. Nauvoo was a city of brotherly love, a righteous city, a city of the saints.

It is of interest, also, that, at that same time, women were not generally identified with community life. Why, then, would the Prophet give such an assignment to the Relief Society? Certainly he knew the ways of men. He had prophetic insight into the evils that would thrust themselves upon the world. He had a divinely inspired comprehension of the influence of women and the place of Relief Society in helping them to make a better world.

Now, with world problems creating tensions and insecurity, with crime and delinquency on the rise, with the general breakdown of moral integrity in public, as well as in private life, it is well that Relief Society shall be reminded of its responsibilities in these matters. It is time that serious consideration be given to how best we are to meet our responsibilities.

To achieve a virtuous community we must first develop virtuous citizens, for the community is but a body of individuals living together in one place. No community can be any stronger morally than the combined moral strength of the individuals who comprise it. Therefore, there is no sounder approach for Relief Society in meeting its responsibilities toward good community life, than vigorously to function in the building of citizens of strong moral character.

The place where good character is most effectively built is the home. This has always been true; it is true today. If attention is not conscientiously and continuously given to this important matter in the home, it is not to be expected that it will be accomplished elsewhere.

Good character is developed through love, acceptance, and feelings of security. It is engendered in children through wise teachings and through discipline that leads toward self-discipline. It is tremendously influenced through parental attitudes and examples. A lack of restraint and self-discipline on the part of the parents can outweigh all their good precepts and adversely affect children throughout their entire lives.

As Relief Society helps its members toward proper attitudes, as it guides them in their homemaking, as it teaches them the doctrines of the Church particularly with regard to home and family life, as it awakens in them a sense of responsibility to maintain their homes and guide their children in harmony with Church teachings, as it helps them to see the relationship of what they do to what their children are most apt to do—to this extent the Society will help them to be individuals of strong moral character themselves, and it will also be an effective agent in helping them to rear children of strong moral character. Thus, Relief Society best meets its responsibilities to assist in correcting the morals and strengthening the virtues of the community. Ours is not necessarily the role of the campaigner against one or another of the existing community evils; ours is the role of the steady, consistent builder of men and women of integrity and moral fortitude who will uphold and promote virtuous community life.

MOTHER'S DAY

A BIT of old Dutch wisdom comes to us in the quotation, "He that remembers God and his mother is shielded against all evil." The second Sunday in May has been set apart for loving remembrance of mother, for a glance through the pages of time and a recollection of the lessons she has taught and the principles she has endeavored to inculcate in us. It is a day in which our appreciation for her loving service and our thankfulness for her life are expressed in word and deed. It is a day dedicated to the most powerful force for good the world has ever known—mother love.

That a special day is necessary to induce one to recall mother and to stimulate expressions of appreciation for her is difficult to understand. She who has shared our troubles, rejoiced in our successes; she who has largely charted the course of our lives and has been our best friend should continuously receive expressions of appreciation stimulated by a constant awareness of her sacrifices, her strength, her love, and her influence for good. Perhaps a reminder is necessary merely because we are careless and so engrossed in our own affairs that we neglect to do the thing we know we should do and would really like to do. But all too often children magnify their own powers and minimize the influences that have contributed most to their strength; they become so accustomed to the strengthening influence of mother that they lose sight of it; they forget their obligations of love and gratitude to her. William George Jordan says, "Ingratitude is a crime more despicable than revenge, which is only returning evil for evil, while ingratitude returns evil for good."

The tasks confronting a mother are not easy. Though they bring their compensations, their satisfactions and joys, she who fills this position in life experiences moments of sorrow, days of anxiety, great sacrifices, and responsibilities which cannot be evaded. The mother of yesterday, presiding over the home where she was the central figure in a closely-knit family, living in a world of rather even tempo, had a sufficiently difficult time; but today's mother finds herself living in a world of confusion. She faces a streamlined, speeded-up world, and stands dismayed. The life patterns of her youth are not the patterns of her children's day. Her pleasures were to be found around the piano in the family parlor while her daughter seeks hers in a high-powered car. Mingling with girls who smoked or used alcoholic beverages in mother's youth would have made her a social outcast; daughter lives in a world where such things are socially acceptable to many people. Understanding between youth and maturity seems to be a constantly widening gap. Economic problems today are pronounced. Living standards are growing increasingly high, and human wants are multitudinous. The simple things that brought joy to mother's heart would scarcely thrill the girl of today.

The problem of bridging the gap between mother and children, the task of meeting economic needs, the difficulties involved in rearing a family in an atmosphere of kindness and affection, of allowing freedom without license, of maintaining daily intimate relationships with children, of earning their respect, of establishing mutual interests and understanding in today's world are overwhelming.

The mother of today must realize that "instinct doesn't

furnish all the equipment necessary to meet her child-rearing problems, and mother love is not an adequate substitute for knowledge and efficiency." She must make a scientific approach to her task of child guidance. She must recognize that divine wisdom must be constantly applied in solving her problems. She must wisely appraise her situation and earnestly strive to preserve fundamental values. Every effort must be exerted to wisely direct and adequately supervise children, that they may be fortified to live well in a topsy-turvy world.

Surely, such mothers will be successful mothers, mothers who not only merit the praise of a nation on Mother's Day but the deep-seated, everyday gratitude of those whose lives they mold—that gratitude which is "thankfulness expressed in daily action—the heart's recognition of kindness that lips cannot repay."

REVERENCE FOR MOTHER

IN 1914 the second Sunday in May was first set aside for honoring mothers by official proclamation of the President of the United States. Since that time, each succeeding President has proclaimed this day National Mother's Day.

Reverence for mothers, however, did not begin in 1914, nor did observances in honor of mothers. Reverence for mothers is universal and ageless. Recently I read that mothers as a group were first officially feated in Rome about 250 B.C. The Romans called their Mothers' Day, the "Feast of Hilaria." It was celebrated during the Ides of March, and the people brought offerings to a giant temple erected for the purpose. Through the ages every race and creed have honored their mothers.

This is right, for by divine command we are told to honor our father and mother. God, speaking to a fallen and sinful ancient Israel, reminded them that he was the Lord their God who had brought them out of Egypt, out of the house of bondage. Then he gave to them ten commandments that have never been superseded in importance for man's well-being. "Honor thy father and thy mother" (Exod. 20:12.) was the fifth of these commandments and has been called, "the first commandment with promise."

I have always felt this commandment meant we should honor our parents not only with words and other expressions of esteem, but by the proper conduct of our lives.

A sweet story from Roman history comes to my mind. Cornelia, a Roman matron, had three sons whom history refers to as the Grachi. (Grachus was the family name.) These sons so distinguished themselves as soldiers, reformers, and statesman that a great statue was erected in recognition of their service, but the statue was not erected to the sons themselves; rather it was erected to the mother who bore and reared them. On it were inscribed these words; "To Cornelia, mother of the Grachi."

It is my conviction that the blessing "that thy days shall be long upon the land which the Lord thy God giveth thee" which was promised for obedience to the commandment, "honor thy father and thy mother," is not necessarily a promise of long life to the individual, as such; rather, it is a promise to the generations of the family—a promise that the family shall be perpetuated in honor upon the earth through the generations of time. Sons and daughters conscious of their sonship and daughterhood, mothers and fathers conscious of their responsibility toward a long continuance of a righteous posterity are the filial threads that bind the generations together and perpetuate the family in honor.

Every mother's job is to transmit the ideals and dreams of life to her children, and to influence them righteously. Regardless of the greatness of our religious, educational, and social institutions, the most important lessons of life are still learned at the mother's knee. The influence of the mother upon her child has been recognized through the ages. A classic example comes to us from the Book of Mormon story of the sons of Helaman. Scripture tells us:

They were all young men, and they were exceedingly valiant for courage and also for strength and activity, but behold this was not all, they were men who were true at all times in whatsoever thing they were entrusted, yea, they were men in truth and soberness for they had been taught to keep the commandments of God, and to walk uprightly before Him.

Now they had never fought, yet they did not fear death; and they did think more upon the liberty of their fathers than they did upon their lives; yea, they had been taught by their mothers that if they did not doubt, God would deliver them.

And they rehearsed unto me the words of their mothers saying, we do not doubt, our mothers knew it. (Alma 56:47-48.)

An example of the influence of a mother's teachings through her personal example comes to my mind. It was my privilege to be a guest in the home of a distinguished couple in New York City recently. Among the guests was a playwright whose play was having an extremely popular run on Broadway. I noticed with interest during the evening's conversation his great familiarity with the Bible and his ability to use it with adroitness in the discussions. I was led to comment to him, privately of course, about this. He told me this story. He said he came from a humble home consisting of a number of brothers and sisters and a widowed but religious mother who read the Bible. He said she tried to get the children to read it but that like most children they were indifferent. Later in life he served in World War II. One night when his company was slated for the front lines, a terrible fear gripped him. He said it was so consuming that he entertained thoughts of desertion or even suicide rather than face enemy fire or be taken captive. Suddenly the memory of his mother flooded his mind. He recalled that when great worries or fears assailed her, she would take her Bible, go into their little parlor, close the door, and remain there for some time. Always she would come out of the room composed and master of herself. Always she would say, "God's word is comfort and strength." Remembering this, he said he almost instinctively reached for the Bible she had given him when he left for the service. By the light of a flashlight he read the book far into the night, until he finally dropped off to sleep, his fears at rest. From that time on, he said he had read and loved the Bible. He spoke of its influence in helping him to live decently in the midst of temptations. He referred to its inspiration in his play-writing. He spoke of it as being like a flint. "Once one has struck against it," he said, "it gives spark to his life." He concluded his story by saying, "Mother's words had little effect in leading me to study or love the Bible; her example in turning to it in time of stress made a profound influence upon my life that could not be obliterated."

Children, too, are kept so busy they scarcely have time for home, father, and mother. Only today I received a letter from my nine-year-old grandson. Let me read a few lines from it.

Dear Grandmother:

I'm sorry I haven't wrote to you for so long, but I couldn't find time to. I've had so many things to do that I'm almost over loaded.

And overloaded is the child. He goes to school, takes violin lessons, plays in the school orchestra, is a Scout, and goes to Sunday School and Primary.

What is happening to the quiet, intimate, unhurried moments we should be spending with our children, helping them to dream great dreams, to aspire to noble living; leading them to open their hearts to us, revealing their hopes and fears, their desires and ambitions, so that we may guide and direct them aright and build within them feelings of security through an assurance of our understanding and love.

In 1954 I attended a conference of the International Council of Women at Helsinki, Finland. There were in attendance approximately 500 of the world's leading and most distinguished women representing 34 free nations. In addressing the conference at its opening session, the President, Dr. Jean Eder—a Swiss woman—said, "Today's generations are fated to stand on the frontiers of new developments, gazing with awe into a future destined to be very different from the past. . . ." But she pointed out, "Woman must continue to carry her world old duties of mother, householder, educator, and the living conscience of her contemporary if the world is to be safe."

In a Relief Society literature lesson wherein we studied the works of Ibsen a few years ago, we read these words of the great literary genius and social annalist: "Women can solve the problems of mankind, but they will do it only as mothers."

INTELLIGENT MOTHERING

INTELLIGENT mothering is certainly more than highly emotionalized mothering which showers love and adoration upon the child to the point of overindulgence, mothering which is blind to the weakness of the child and justifies and upholds him when he errs, mothering which so sacrifices itself to the child that he never learns the meaning of co-operation and unselfishness. Intelligent mothering realizes that the child's future to a large extent is measured in the mother's ability to influence and direct wisely. It establishes in the home worthy ideals and standards; it teaches faith; it trains the child to conquer self; it teaches the gospel of work; it develops honesty and loyalty. It provides opportunity for the best development of the child physically, mentally, morally and spiritually. It constantly holds the child up to his best efforts.

The genuine mother reaches beyond her own, sensing her responsibility to all children. Wherever a child is found cold, hungry, in need of attention or care of any kind she renders loving and intelligent service.

THE WOMAN'S ROLE AT HOME

THE WOMAN'S ROLE IN THE ETERNAL PLAN

T HE impact of change on our homes, the shifting emphasis on what constitutes woman's primary role in life, together with prevailing faulty attitudes as to how desirable home and family life may be achieved, are giving us considerable concern, particularly as we see the dangers of their influence upon the thinking and the aspirations of some of our young mothers and the young women who within a few years will be mothers and homemakers. To curb the birthrate is commonly advocated. On a recent broadcast, it was reported that a law was introduced in Congress that would allow tax exemptions for no more than two children as a means of controlling population growth. It is not uncommon to hear, "better an abortion than an unwanted child." Also, we know that great effort is being made to encourage the general establishment of free nurseries for pre-school children of working mothers. Tax exemption for working mothers is also receiving support. All too many women are saying, "Let the schools take over more responsibility in moral and ethical training and in sex education."

The value of the homemaking skills of our mothers and grandmothers are now under question. A recent co-educational survey made by one of our Utah universities revealed the changing aspirations of 300 women students, 90% of whom were residents of Utah. They rated the development of homemaking skills as their least important goal in college. The highest priority was assigned to intellectual growth, and second was preparation for a career. The survey indicated that 42% of the girls planned to continue working after marriage.

I recently heard the dean of the college of home economics and family management of one of the great universities of the nation insist that this college must change its curricula in the light of the homemaking needs of the average woman today or fade out entirely. She said the day is past when there is need to spend time teaching nutritive values of food, food preservation, and preparation. Packaged, pre-cooked and frozen foods are the order of the day, and essential nutrients are commercially added, she declared. She also questioned the need of teaching sewing skills, saying a woman's time is too valuable to sit and sew when mass production makes stylish clothing so readily available to her. A study of fabrics, included in most home economics courses, seems no longer essential since law now requires labeling of fabrics.

In view of all this, the General Presidency feels that the most important and perhaps most difficult task before Relief Society today is to help the mothers of the Church to maintain their homes in strictest harmony with Latter-day Saint teachings and standards, and to fortify the sisters against the destructive influences that are abroad by giving pronounced emphasis through the lessons and homemaking teachings to gospel truths that have bearing on home and family life. In this important work, we would enlist the full cooperation and continued guidance of the priesthood.

FAMILY HOME EVENING

Generally speaking, I believe Latter-day Saint parents have always been concerned over the well-being of their homes and families. I also believe that as a general rule, Latter-day Saint children respect their parents' teachings, as well as the standards of the home.

Today, however, the circumstances of life heighten parental concern and in all too many instances, seem to be impinging upon desirable parent-child and child-home relationships.

This has given rise to intensified effort on the part of the Church to be helpful by a re-emphasis of Church teaching in relation to the home, the family, and its divine destiny. New programs have been introduced to assist families. Among them, the family home evening program.

There is a story which epitomizes the beauty and significance of a properly conducted family home evening and clearly depicts the role of the mother. The story is historically true.

The family was a farm family. It had had reverses due to drought and unproductive soil that had forced it to move into a neighboring state. The father, a hard-working, righteous man who loved his family, was nonetheless undiscouraged. He counseled with mother and children on major family decisions. They had had voice in the move. The mother was of a deeply spiritual nature, wise and with an understanding heart. Her love for her children led her to endure without complaint bitter hardships and even physical suffering.

Eight children made up this family. The children worked together for the good of all in a spirit of loyalty and affection for one another. So deep was the affection of the eldest brother for a younger brother that it endured through endless persecution, unspeakable suffering, even unto martyrdom. The relationship of these two brothers has been compared to that of David and Jonathan.

One day his younger brother, the third son in the family, a fourteen-year-old boy, had a tremendous spiritual experience which, according to his mother, left him "overwhelmed and astonished." This was followed by other spiritual experiences in which an angel talked to the boy. Upon the second visitation of the angel, the boy was directed by the angel to tell his father all that he had seen and heard. Childlike, the boy was afraid to do so for fear the father would not believe him, so unusual were these experiences. The angel, however, assured him the father would believe every word he had to say for the angel knew the remarkable tenderness and sympathy of the father for his children.

The father did listen to the boy's story with credulity. He evidently discussed it with mother. Subsequently father and mother gathered the family together in the peace of the evening when the day's work was done, so that all might listen while young Joseph related particulars of the visitation of God the Father and the Son, Jesus Christ and of the subsequent visits of the Angel Moroni, and of the work which Joseph had been appointed by the Lord to do. With the passing of time, many such evening gatherings were held as new experiences came to the boy. The mother's account of these family evenings follows:

I presume our family presented an aspect as singular as any that ever lived upon the face of the earth—all seated in a circle, father, mother, sons and daughters—and giving the most profound attention to a boy . . . who had never read the Bible through in his life; he seemed much less inclined to the perusal of books than any of the rest of our children, but far more given to meditation and deep study.

We were now confirmed in the opinion that God was about to bring to light something upon which we could stay our minds or that would give us a more perfect knowledge of the plan of salvation and redemption of the human family . . . the sweetest union and happiness pervaded our house and tranquility reigned in our midst. (*History of Joseph Smith by His Mother, Lucy Smith, 1958 Edition, p. 82.*)

To me, this is a unique account of an impressive family home evening.

How many of us could make a more determined effort to be assured that "the sweetest union and happiness would pervade our house and tranquility reign in our midst"?

And now may I pose one or two questions for your consideration.

Did the evening family gatherings significantly help Joseph to accept and devote himself to his divine calling?

Did they have any direct bearing on the great work of Hyrum in support of the Prophet and in his conviction of the truthfulness of the restored gospel and his dedication to the work?

Could the family loyalty to the cause of the restored gospel have been rallied to greater advantage in some other way than in bringing family members together?

Why would the angel direct the boy to tell his father? Why not his mother, his brother, an intimate friend, or even someone from a church? On whom in this life does the Lord place primary responsibility for a child?

What was the mother's role in bringing the family together? Did she have any part in influencing the receptive attitude of the children to her son's miraculous story?

Conversely, suppose the father, busy and tired with his farm labors, had brushed aside the boy or even discredited his story.

Suppose mother had felt outside interests and activities would not allow time to bring her family together. Suppose mother had said to father, "Let us deal with this matter ourselves. We work hard all day. I'm just too tired at night to get the children together for what is nothing more than another meeting. We go to enough meetings already." Even suppose the mother had not been at home to aid in arrangements and to participate in these family gatherings.

Suppose father and mother had not created the right listening and believing atmosphere and had allowed the children to be disorderly, to have laughed or had even ridiculed the fourteen-year-old boy's story. Would this have added a burden to an already overwhelmed and astonished soul?

All too often parents do not know what is in the minds and hearts of their children. All too often they allow the unimportant to crowd out the important. All too often they are too busy to gather the family together and to sit down and listen.

Furthermore, only upon the rarest occasions are parents given to know the divine mission of a child. We are given to know, however, that these great men in the presiding councils of the Church are chosen of the Lord to guide and direct this people. We are given to know that they do so through revelation and inspiration. We know that they know and understand the doctrine of the eternity of the family unit. They know how to bring to our people the guidelines that will bind families together eternally. Our role is to listen and to obey.

The Lord has said, "For if you will that I give unto you a place in the celestial world, you must prepare yourselves by doing the things I have commanded of you and required of you." (D&C 78:7.)

We remember always that the Lord speaks to us through the voice and the writings of the presiding priesthood of his Church. May we follow the counsel of these brethren not only with regard to conducting Family Home Evening, but in all matters related to our lives so that we may enjoy the attendant eternal blessings.

SECTION FIVE

Relief Society In A Priesthood-Governed Church

"IF IT'S RIGHT, WE CAN DO IT!"

I T has been said that "we look back in order that we may
go better forward." Today I would like to turn back
the pages of history to the year 1842—12 years after
the organization of the Church—the year in which Relief
Society was founded in Nauvoo, Illinois, through revelation
by the Lord to the Prophet Joseph Smith.

The Honorable John Tyler, an able and independent
Whig from Virginia, was President of the United States. It
was the day of Stephen A. Douglas, a fiery orator and
leading political figure and, at that time, a friend of the
Mormons. It was the day when Abraham Lincoln, a
promising young lawyer from Illinois and a rising politician,
was looking forward to his marriage to the charming and
ambitious Mary Todd. It was the year of the establishment of the boundary line between the United States and
Canada, a line that has defined territory but never restricted neighborliness.

Nauvoo was a western frontier town, a part of a vast
new America reaching ever farther out to the West. Oregon
and California were exciting words, although as yet no
wagon train had passed beyond the Rockies.

The city of Nauvoo was only three years old, but it
was a thriving city with sturdy two-story houses of brick

and frame, with churches and stores, and a university. The rising structure of a temple enlisted with rare dedication the interest and the labors of the populace. At the busy harbor of the river's bend, boats from down the river came to anchor, bringing hundreds of converts from the Old World.

It was at this growing, happy period of time for the Saints that the Prophet Joseph Smith, on March 17, in a meeting assembled with Elders John Taylor and Willard Richards and 18 sisters uttered these "long to be remembered words" that initiated a new day for Latter-day Saint women and, indeed, for all womankind:

I now declare this Society organized with president and counselors, etc., according to parliamentary usages—and all who shall hereafter be admitted to this Society must be free from censure and be received by vote. (A Centenary of Relief Society, p. 15.)

Elder John Taylor addressed the assembly on that memorable occasion, saying that he "rejoiced to see the institution organized according to the law of Heaven." The law of heaven is divine law. Thus, Relief Society differs from all other women's organizations of the world.

On the eventful day of the Society's founding, an open Bible lay on the pulpit of the historic room. The following words were found written on a scrap of paper lying on the open Bible: "Oh, Lord, help our widows and fatherless children! So mote it be, Amen. With the sword and the words of truth defend thou them, so mote it be! Amen."

With gratitude and dedication, the members of the newly formed Society moved into the work defined for it and as guided by the Prophet, defending the widows and fatherless children, nursing the sick, finding employment for those with such need, feeding the hungry, comforting the sorrowing, clothing the naked.

At the same time, the young organization looked to the righteousness of the individual lives of the sisters, and the Prophet admonished the sisters with regard to their duties to their husbands. Counselor Whitney cautioned the sisters "to avoid all evil, even the appearance of evil." She urged them to "pray for one another that they might succeed in the work before them and have wisdom given them in all their pursuits." (A Centenary of Relief Society, p. 16.)

The Prophet instructed them:

Let this Society teach women how to behave towards their husbands, to treat them with mildness and affection. When a man is borne down with trouble, when he is perplexed with care and difficulty, if he can meet a smile instead of an argument or a murmur—if he can meet with mildness, it will calm down his soul and soothe his feelings; when the mind is going to despair, it needs a solace of affection and kindness. (A Centenary of Relief Society, p. 16.)

The prayers of the sisters were answered and their efforts were blessed. The Prophet, meeting with them in the summer of 1842, said, "I have come here to bless you. The Society have done well: their principles are to practice holiness. God loves you and your prayers in my behalf shall avail much. . . ." (A Centenary of Relief Society, p. 17.)

Following the Nauvoo period, the sisters in true companionship with the priesthood entered upon the path of religious empire-founding in the heart of the Rocky Mountains, and they were vigorous in the promotion of righteousness according to revealed truth.

As we look back over their labors, even to the present time, a divinely guided drama of selfless service unfolds, revealing the strength of the sisters born of faith and testimony and the power of the organization as it functions according to the law of heaven.

A small sampling of activities will serve to illustrate the obedience, the intensity of devotion, the spirit of love and service that characterized efforts and led to almost unbelievable accomplishment.

In September 1876, President Brigham Young gave to Sister Emmeline B. Wells the mission of leading the sisters in grain saving. Sister Wells, in a report to the members in 1915 said: "We began that very year, and though we were laughed at, we did buy grain,—the Relief Society did; I did not do it myself—the Relief Society gave money and grain was bought that year. . ." (*Relief Society Magazine,* 1915, p. 48.)

The sisters garnered in the fields, sold Sunday eggs, quilts, rag carpeting and other products of their hands to acquire the grain, disposed to do so because the spirit of the gospel bade them accept the mission in loving obedience to their great prophet, President Brigham Young.

In February 1915 when Sister Wells was 87 years old, prophetic tribute was paid to her by Sister Annie Wells Cannon: ". . . no doubt, she [Sister Wells] will be able to see clearly through the devastating wars that are now raging in Europe, that the mission that was given her so many years ago, was not in vain. Many starving mothers will be rescued, no doubt, through the faithful integrity of President Emmeline B. Wells and her associated sisters in the Society, in saving grain for famine's need." (*Relief Society Magazine,* 1915, p. 50.)

During World War I, President Clarissa Smith Williams, writing in the *Relief Society Magazine,* gave evidence of the fulfillment of this prediction:

> The Relief Society has turned over to the United States Government [at a price set by it] over 200,000 bushels of wheat . . . how proud we are to perform this service for our suffering and glorious cause. Our hearts and prayers go with the gifts which we have laid upon the altar of our country. (*A Centenary of Relief Society,* p. 72.)

Today as a praiseworthy symbol of the continuing blessing of the wheat program, there rises toward the heavens on Welfare Square a great grain elevator filled with Relief Society wheat stored against a day of need— wheat obtained through the investment in wheat of money paid the Society by the Government during the war.

Another impressive demonstration of the unselfish spirit of sisterhood within the Society comes to us in the action of the sisters at the end of World War II. A letter from a president of one of the European missions to the Church Welfare Committee graphically described the urgent need of the people of Europe for soap. A strong appeal was made for help. The Welfare Program had but one soap plant and in no measure could it meet the request. Soap at the commercial markets was rationed and only available through the use of coupons issued by Government to individuals. The sisters were notified of the need through the General Presidency, with the approval of the First Presidency, and compassion touched their hearts. They rallied to the call for help. In ninety selected stakes of the Church in Zion, the sisters drew from their home supplies precious bars of soap. (Only bar soap could be shipped abroad.) Within one week after the local Relief Societies had been notified of the need, the soap was collected and over 50,000 bars were on their way to Europe —almost unbelievable willingness to share had been demonstrated. Individual women were generous to be sure, but how helpless each would have been without the power of the Society to notify of need, to inspire, to organize and direct the activity.

At the same period more than a carload of beautiful new quilts, on hand in the local Relief Societies, was donated to the suffering people of Europe. These, too, were collected and shipped in a period of a little over one week. In a report I made to the National Council of Women in New York City at that time on the war services of Relief Society, I mentioned the number of quilts that Relief Society had sent to Europe. Following my report, the President of the Free Czechoslovakian Women, an escapee to United States from that invaded country and a former Deputy-Mayor of Prague, rose and said: "Mrs. Spafford's report is overly modest and has dealt only with figures." Then she explained that as deputy-mayor she had been assigned by her Government to oversee the distribution of commodities from the United States. The quilts were not to be reserved exclusively for the Mormons.

She concluded by saying: "They [the quilts] were new and beautiful. They not only warmed cold bodies, but brought sunshine to wintered spirits. They were gifts of understanding love."

There is one other story I wish to tell. A president of a small Mexican branch of Relief Society in Salt Lake City sat in this historic tabernacle and heard a plan proposed whereby the sisters were to raise one-half million dollars for a Relief Society headquarters building. Each local Society was to be responsible for seeing that every one of its members was represented by a $5.00 contribution. That dutiful Mexican president had great feelings of trepidation because of the magnitude of the undertaking. But strong in testimony her response came: "I don't know how we can do it. My sisters are poor. Yet, President McKay is listening. The First Presidency has authorized it. If these Brethren authorize it, it is right. If it is right, we can do it!" And do it, they did. This Mexican Branch was the first to submit its money, soon to be followed by full contributions from the other sisters of Relief Soicety. More than one-half million dollars was contributed in one year. The Relief Society Building stands today a monument to the faith and labors of the sisters.

Recorded in the minutes of the general board is an address given March 17, 1914, in the Assembly Hall by President Joseph F. Smith. I quote:

> When rightly wielded, governed, and directed, I think the influence of this great organization in the Church is, without doubt, the most cogent and the most powerful of any other single organization of the Church, for this reason, it is not confined to three nor to twelve, nor to seven nor any other definite small number of people, but it extends to the outermost borders of the Church and in every part of the Church. In every live branch of the Church the Relief Society is found, and it is found there for good. . . . Its work is good, and its power for up-lifting, for comforting, and for sustaining the cause of Zion, I think, is most potent. . . . Where on earth should we look for good, for the spirit of truth, for sincerity, for divine love, for patience and long suffering and forgiveness and endurance and charity for teaching the ways of righteousness and every other

blessed thing, if we do not look for it in the organizations that develop the mothers and daughters of Zion. What power you possess, my beloved sisters, . . . powers . . . that you may wield among the people of God and among any people among whom you may be permitted to associate! . . . What a mighty, what a great and powerful organization is the organization of the Relief Society of The Church of Jesus Christ of Latter-day Saints, and what responsibilities rest upon it! Not only the responsibility of being capable yourselves of sustaining the spirit of the organization to which you belong and of maintaining its rights, and of performing your duties in it in a temporal way; you have also the responsibility resting upon you to impart . . . knowledge, wisdom and understanding to all others with whom you may come in contact.

Today is not an easy, comfortable period of time. More changes and scientific advancements have taken place in the last fifty years than in any comparable period in history. Change and scientific advancement call for continuous adjustments in our way of life. These adjustments must be made with wisdom and in a way that will preserve the enduring and eternal values of life. Relief Society must rise in power in helping mothers to do this.

Today we stand fortified in meeting the requirements of this troubled time by the size, the greatness, and the power of our organization, and by the glorious accomplishments of the past. Also today we have unusually choice women. I have met with Relief Society sisters in many parts of the world. I have felt the power of their faith. I have seen striking evidence of their testimonies. I have noted the zeal and dedication with which they work. I have watched, almost in amazement, the quality of their leadership. I have partaken of the sweetness and humility of their spirits. I have rejoiced in the beauty and refinement of their lives.

Three hundred twenty-five thousand such women, working through the Relief Society under priesthood direction and fortified by the glorious accomplishments of the past, are indeed favorably positioned successfully to meet the special needs of today. Strength is ours, greater perhaps than any of us comprehend.

Relief Society's task is not only worthily to meet the special humanitarian needs of today as did our sisters of the past in their day, but it also must be constant in its efforts to strengthen the moral and spiritual values of our homes. They are in jeopardy. It must train mothers to maintain well-managed, peaceful homes that draw family members to them even against the most appealing and glittering community enticements. It must create in mothers a recognition of the fundamental values of close companionship with their children, and it must guide them in the firm and wise direction of young lives; it must help women to maintain the God-ordained relationships with their husbands. It must strengthen community virtues, as directed by the Prophet Joseph Smith, through fortifying the sisters against degenerating influences such as declining moral standards and relaxed attitudes toward sexual purity. It must safeguard mothers against the taint of some of the present-day so-called religious attitudes through effectively teaching the beauties and truths of the gospel.

The task before us is great, but it is not beyond success. The Lord is mindful of his Relief Society. I am sure he loves the sisters of today even as he loved the sisters of Nauvoo, and he will bless and make fruitful our efforts. I bear testimony to the divine mission of the Prophet Joseph Smith, to the divine birth of Relief Society and to the inspired guidance that comes to it from God's prophets. I am humbly grateful for my membership in the Church and for my membership in Relief Society. When all else is gone in life, the blessings of this membership will remain for they are eternal.

ACCORDING TO THE LAW OF HEAVEN

T HE *Documentary History of the Church* under date of Jan. 6, 1842, records the rejoicing of the Prophet Joseph Smith over this period of time in the history of the Church as follows:

The new year has been ushered in and continued thus far under the most favourable auspices, and the Saints seem to be influenced by a kind and indulgent providence in their dispositions and [blessed with] means to rear the Temple of the Most High God, anxiously looking forth to the completion thereof as an event of the greatest importance to the Church and the world, making the Saints in Zion to rejoice . . . Truly this is a day long to be remembered by the Saints of the Last Days . . . a day in which all things are concurring to bring about the completion of the fullness of the Gospel— a fullness of the dispensation of dispensations, even the fullness of times.

Among the events of great significance to the sisters of the Church during the early part of 1842 was the founding of "the Female Relief Society" on March 17. It seems that this was a propitious time for the Lord to give to his daughters, through his prophet, an organization whereby they might more fully perfect themselves and more effectively serve the Church and its people.

The sisters had evidenced a readiness for this blessing. They had studied the scriptures. They had listened to their

Prophet and been obedient to this teachings; they had helped in the work of the Church; particularly had they endeavored to do the women's part toward the erection of the Nauvoo Temple. So eager were they more fully to do their part that they sought an organization at the hands of the Prophet for which Sister Eliza R. Snow had drawn up a proposed constitution and by-laws to be considered by him.

We may be sure that it was with eagerness and rejoicing that the sisters—18 in number—met on Thursday, March 17, at an hour and place appointed by the Prophet. With grateful hearts they heard their beloved and revered leader utter words "long to be remembered" by the sisters of the Church:

> I now declare this Society organized with president and counselors according to parliamentary usages. [*Relief Society Magazine,* March 1942, p. 151.]

Elder John Taylor, who with Elder Willard Richards accompanied the Prophet on this momentous occasion, addressed the sisters, saying that he "rejoiced to see this institution organized according to the law of Heaven." (*Relief Society Magazine,* March 1942, p. 151.) The law of heaven is divine law. Relief Society, therefore, according to Elder John Taylor, was organized according to divine law.

The First Presidency at the time of the centennial of Relief Society reminded us:

> We ask our sisters of the Relief Society never to forget that they are a unique organization in the whole world, for they were organized under the inspiration of the Lord bestowed upon that great Prophet who was divinely called, by a visitation of the Father and Son, in person, to open up this, the last dispensation—the dispensation of the fullness of times. No other woman's organization in all the earth has had such a birth. (*Centenary of Relief Society,* p. 7.)

During the Society's existence, tremendous changes have taken place in the world and among the world's people. Few changes, perhaps, have been greater than the change in the status of woman and her readiness to speak and act through organized groups. During the early part of the 19th Century the number of women's organizations was extremely limited, as was woman's influence in public life. Today women are highly organized and their views are sought and respected.

I recently attended a meeting where I was one among 300 presidents of women's organizations, none of which had a membership of less than 100,000. These 300 presidents represented a total of 50 million organized women. They had been called together to ascertain their views on a matter of great public concern. The group represented only a fraction, however, of the organized women of the world. It is a marvel that in the face of all the growth and changes which have taken place, the basic organization structure of Relief Society, its governing regulations and original purposes as set by the Prophet Joseph Smith when the membership consisted of only 18 women, residing in what was then a little western frontier town of the United States, have been able to remain constant; also that the Society under the pattern established a century and a quarter ago has been able to function effectively, meeting the interests and needs of women of many lands during each succeeding and changing era of time. This achievement alone would attest that Relief Society was founded according to the law of heaven and not according to man-made law.

Relief Society was continuously under the watchcare of the Prophet during the days of Nauvoo, receiving his counsel and instruction, just as it has been under the watchcare of God's chosen prophets who have succeeded him. In his instructions to the sisters, the Prophet told them, "You will receive instructions through the medium of those appointed to lead, guide, and direct the affairs of the Church in this dispensation." He taught the sisters, "if any officers are wanted to carry out the design of the institution, let them be appointed and set apart." He later said, "Those ordained to preside over and lead you, are authorized to appoint the different officers, as the circumstances shall require." The Prophet made membership of this organization a privilege; yet he opened its doors to all women who were "free from censure," making clear that they were to be received by a vote.

Insofar as a constitution and by-laws were concerned, which the sisters had submitted to him in the beginning, he said, "Let this Presidency serve as a constitution—all their decisions be considered law and acted upon as such . . . The minutes of your meetings will be precedence for you to act upon—your constitution and law." (*Centenary of Relief Society*, p. 15.)

The Prophet Joseph Smith turned the key in behalf of women in this dispensation. His words are impressive and treasured:

I now turn the key in your behalf . . . and knowledge and intelligence shall flow down from this time henceforth; this is the beginning of better days to the poor and needy who shall be made to rejoice and pour forth blessings on your heads. (*DHC* IV, p. 607.)

According to Elder Bruce R. McConkie:

By turning the key [in behalf of women] the Prophet delegated to the duly appointed officers of the new organization a portion of the keys of the kingdom. Under the Priesthood they were now authorized to direct, control, and goven the affairs of the Society . . . Under this appointment their lawful acts would be organized by the Lord and he would work with them in the rolling forth of the Kingdom in the sphere assigned to them. (*Relief Society Magazine*, March 1950, p. 151.)

The significant statement by the Prophet with regard to turning the key in behalf of women is the foundation upon which an extensive educational program for women has been carried forward by Relief Society. The program includes, as expressed by President Lorenzo Snow, "a study of those subjects which tend toward the elevation and advancement of women along all lines of thought and action." This statement is also the basis for the Society's benevolent activities.

Just as Relief Society was founded according to the law of heaven and just as it has been regulated by divine inspiration, so it has a divinely appointed mission. Listed simply, I would say its mission is: (1) to save souls; (2) to strengthen testimonies of the divinity of the restored gospel; (3) to succor the distressed; (4) to help Relief Society members realize their full potential as women; (5) to strengthen home and family life; (6) to serve as a handmaid to the priesthood in building the kingdom of our Heavenly Father on earth.

President David O. McKay had made reference to the mission of Relief Society in these impressive words: "By divine decree the women of the Church are assigned the noble mission of being exemplars and leaders to mankind in the two most worthwhile accomplishments in mortal life. First the development of character—that is done in the home principally; second, willingness and ability to render helpful service—that through the organized Relief Society. These two accomplishments, by the way, are all that we shall take with us when at the end of our earthly career, we pass through the portals of death into the realm of the eternal—character and service." (*Relief Society Magazine*, Dec. 1956, p. 807.)

Accepting its divine mission, unscathed by time or change, Relief Society, working under the direction of the priesthood, has a great responsibility to extend its influences to every Latter-day Saint woman. Indeed we may say to extend its influence to all women—for did the Prophet not say, ". . . As far as knowledge is concerned, it may extend to all the world; but your administering should be confined to the circle of your immediate acquaintance, and more especially to the members of the Relief Society." As for our own Latter-day Saint women, it is my conviction that membership in Relief Society, while it is a privilege, is also an obligation which none can afford to disregard.

I would like to conclude by reading a statement by Elizabeth Ann Whitney, the wife of Bishop Newell K. Whitney and counselor to Emma Smith in the first Relief Society presidency. This statement was expressed in an article by Sister Whitney which appeared in the *Woman's Exponent* November 15, 1878. Speaking of her Relief Society activities in Nauvoo, she writes:

We afterward moved upstairs over the brick store as it was designated. It was during our residence in the brick store, March 17, 1842, that the Relief Society was organized and I was chosen as a counselor to the president of this Society. In this work I took the greatest interest for I realized in some degree, at least, its importance and the need for such an organization. . . . The Relief Society then was small compared to its numbers now, but the Prophet foretold great things concerning the future of this organization, many of which I have lived to see fulfilled, but there are many things which remain yet to be fulfilled in the future of which he prophesied that are great and glorious, and I rejoice in the contemplation of these things daily, feeling that the promises are sure to be verified in the future as they have been in the past. I trust that the sisters who are now laboring and who will in the future labor in the interest of the Relief Societies in Zion will realize the importance attached to the work and comprehend that upon them a great responsibility rests. President Joseph Smith had great faith in the sisters' labors and ever sought to encourage them in the performance of the duties which pertain to the Society.

I, too, have faith in the sisters of Relief Society. I, too, feel assured that great and glorious things yet lie ahead for this organization. Relief Society belongs to the past; it belongs to the present; it will belong to the future; it belongs to good women of all nations. Its work is the Lord's work for his daughters. I, too, trust, as did Sister Whitney, that the conviction of the divinity within the Relief Society will ever be strong in the hearts of the sisters of the Church. Just as the Prophet had great faith in the sisters' labors and ever sought to encourage them in the performance of the duties which pertained to the Society, so does our great present-day prophet.

THE REWARDS OF SERVICE IN RELIEF SOCIETY

W HEN the Saints were in Nauvoo, the sisters, imbued with a testimony of the gospel, recognizing the great import of the doctrine of salvation for the dead as taught by their Prophet, earnestly desired to do their part in the erection of the temple. As individuals, they rendered such services as they could; as individuals, the women had earlier made an appreciable contribution to the erection of the temple at Kirtland.

The spirit with which their service was rendered in Kirtland has been graphically described in the writings of Heber C. Kimball. The same spirit characterized their efforts in Nauvoo. Says Brother Kimball:

This time the brethren were laboring night and day building the house of the Lord. Our women were engaged in spinning and knitting, in order to clothe those who were laboring at the building, and the Lord only knows the scenes of poverty, tribulation, and stress which we passed through in order to accomplish this thing. My wife toiled all summer in lending her aid toward its accomplishment. She had a hundred pounds of wool which, with the assistance of the girls, she spun in order to furnish clothing for those engaged in the building of the temple, and although she had the privilege of keeping half the quantity of wool for herself as a recompense for her labor, she did not reserve even so much as would make her a pair of stockings, but gave it to those who were laboring at the House of the Lord. She spun and wove and got the cloth pressed, and cut and made up into garments and gave them to those who labored on the temple. Almost all the sisters in Kirtland labored in knitting, sewing, spinning, etc. for the purpose of forwarding the work of the Lord. (*Temples of the Most High*, N. B. Lundwall, p. 14.)

The desire to forward the work of the Lord became so strong in the hearts of the women as the Nauvoo Temple progressed that they felt to increase and make more effective their individual efforts by organizing themselves. With this intent they sought their Prophet for counsel and direction. His response to their petition and the story of the birth of Relief Society are familiar to all of us.

The labors of the sisters in Nauvoo were characterized not only by service for the temple but also by care of the poor. The members brought to the Society provisions, clothing, thread, yarn, household commodities, even treasured pieces of jewelry to help provide for those less fortunate than themselves.

But their days in the beautiful city of Nauvoo soon came to an end, and life in a western wilderness became their lot. Regardless of circumstances, however, the spirit of benevolence, solicitude for the well-being of one another, unselfish sharing, and effective service in forwarding the work of the Lord lived on in the hearts and actions of the westward women as they built their homes and established their Relief Societies.

It is a stimulating and moving experience to read the minutes of some of the early-day Relief Societies in the West. They reveal well that the ideals and the spirit of service and devotion to the Church exemplified in the sisters in Nauvoo remained strong in the women transplanted to a desert land. To illustrate, let me read from minutes of the St. George Relief Society, April 20, 1869:

President Erastus Snow asked for 25 yards of carpet for a prayer circle room for the brethren, (visiting) teachers went out and got enough rags to make 50 yards. There were present at our meeting 90 women, sewing the rags in answer to President Snow's call. It was one of the most pleasant meetings ever held, though the sisters worked until their bodies were tired and their fingers ached from winding the balls, a happier group would be hard to find.

Relief Society, however, was not designed for the early days alone, nor was it designed only for women of eras that are past. It calls to women today who wish to develop themselves, to serve their fellows, and forward the work of the Lord. It is heartwarming to contemplate the faithfulness and devotion of Relief Society women today the world over and to review the records of their accomplishments. The sisters are devotedly contributing toward the erection of temples and meeting houses, toward welfare projects and other Church programs. They are ministering to the sick and homebound. They are teaching one another the precepts and doctrines of the Church. The sisters are training one another to walk in the paths of righteousness— all to the end that they may build for themselves and for others beautiful, useful, purposeful lives and that they may do woman's part in building the kingdom of God.

The spirit with which the work is carried forward today does not differ from the spirit of the past. The increased numbers of Relief Society members make their contribution to the work of the Church a sizeable one. Let me read you a typical statement from an annual report of a small ward Relief Society with an average attendance of 20 women.

I am happy to give this report of our Relief Society. We are fully organized. We have had a very good year in all of our activities and meetings.

On March 17 we held our birthday party in the form of a luncheon. . . . In April we served a dinner for the ward. In May during a Sunday night program we presented the bishop with a check for $500 for the stake building fund. In July we had a social and luncheon. In August we had a stake dinner lawn party. On August 13 and 14 we held a rummage sale. The clothes that were left were carefully repaired and given to the bishop for welfare. On August 16 we gave the bishop a check for $100 to be applied to the ward building fund. This makes a total of $900 given from our Society besides the $900 earned by us at the stake dinner we served for the stake building fund.

In October we had our opening social with 52 persons attending. On November 7 the Relief Society conference was held.

Our class leaders are some of the best, and they give wonderful lessons. We have very good attendance at the sewing meetings and have had some very good homemaking demonstrations. We have done much compassionate service, far more in comparison to other years. The Relief Society sisters of our ward are a congenial group and we have plans for a busy 1955. We hope and pray that we will have the blessings of our Heavenly Father to help us all and to work together in forwarding the work of the Lord.

We wish to thank the stake board and our bishopric for the help that they have given us.

There are times when special assignments make heavy demands upon the time and energy of our already busy mothers, but rarely, if ever, does the work become dull or so uninteresting as to become drudgery. "Work becomes drudgery only so long as what is done is done only because of the letter of the law and without the spirit." Service performed in the spirit of conversion to and love for the Master's cause and in obedience to eternal and righteous principles brings to one a fullness of *joy*—the joy referred to by the great prophet Nephi when he wrote: "Men are that they might have joy." Such joy is not the reward of superficial, spare-time, begrudgingly given performance; such a joy is reserved for those who enter into the work with full purpose of heart.

A testimony of the worth of service in Relief Society finds echo in the hearts of tens of thousands of members and in the hearts of their husbands and children. Countless numbers of children of Relief Society mothers have grown strong in the faith and performed valiantly for the Church because of the example of their mothers. Relief Society has even proved to be the road back for some children. Only a few days ago I met the son of a faithful Relief Society sister. He was eminently successful in his chosen profession but had gone far afield in his religious thinking. Several years ago his mother was called to teach theology in Relief Society. She felt inadequate for such an important assignment, yet she wished to be obedient to her Relief Society call and to serve to the best of her ability. This she did with a high degree of success, teaching the sisters the doctrines of the Church with clarity and conviction until the time of her death.

The son, returning to her home for the funeral, picked up her Book of Mormon as it lay on the table with its passages carefully marked. This he has since studied, reading the book from cover to cover. The other day when I met him he said to me, "The Church must have had great confidence in my mother to call her to teach the theological doctrines. It is evident that she knew and understood them. I have read and re-read the passages she had marked in her Book of Mormon. It has had tremendous influence upon me. In fact, I now know that if I am to have peace of mind I must return to activity in the Church." What a precious reward for the hours of study and faithful service of that mother!

To the woman who serves in Relief Society there comes understanding, enlightenment, and a truer evaluation of her own problems and a wish to solve them in all righteousness.

Service in Relief Society gives to a woman competence in the management of her home and wisdom in guiding and directing her children. It blesses her with an understanding heart and develops within her a testimony that becomes a deep and abiding comfort and sustaining influence as long as life lasts. It makes of her a woman who does justly, who loves mercy, and who walks humbly with the Lord. These are rewards of the highest order.

In Galatians we read: "As we have therefore opportunity let us do good to all men, especially unto the household of faith." (Gal. 6:10.)

In Romans we read: "We then that are strong ought to bear the infirmities of the weak." (Rom. 15:1.)

Through the medium of Relief Society, opportunity is afforded Latter-day Saint women for such service. Relief Society work is, as the Prophet declared, "according to the natures of women," and is a sphere in which she finds satisfaction.

As we share the labors of Relief Society so most certainly we will share in the triumphs of this great Society, and so we will share in the eternal blessings which the Lord will give to his faithful daughters.

RELIEF SOCIETY RELATIONSHIP TO PRIESTHOOD

T HE following steps led to the founding of the Relief Society. They were related by Sarah M. Kimball, a charter member of Relief Society and first secretary of the central (general) board, formed in 1880.

In the Spring of 1842, a maiden lady (Miss Cook) was a seamstress for me, and the subject of combining our efforts for assisting the Temple hands came up in conversation. She desired to be helpful but had no means to furnish. I told her I would furnish material if she would make some shirts for the workmen. It was then suggested that some of the neighbors might wish to combine means and efforts with ours, and we decided to invite a few to come and consult with us on the subject of forming a Ladies' Society. The neighboring sisters met in my parlor and decided to organize. I was delegated to call on Sister Eliza R. Snow and ask her to write for us a constitution and by-laws and submit them to President Joseph Smith prior to our next Thursday's meeting. She cheerfully responded, and when she read them to him he replied that the constitution and by-laws were the best that he had ever seen. "But," he said, "this is not what you want. Tell the sisters their offering is accepted of the Lord, and He has something better for them than a written constitution. Invite them all to meet me and a few of the brethren in the Masonic Hall over my store next Thursday afternoon, and I will organize the sisters under the priesthood after a pattern of the priesthood." (*Centenary of Relief Society*, p. 14, and *Relief Society Magazine*, Vol. VI, March 1919, p. 129.)

An appointment to the office of Relief Society president seems to call for special consideration because of the extensiveness, variety, and often highly confidential nature of her services. She is not only responsible for conducting and forwarding the regular work of the Society as it relates to the recommended meetings, but she is held responsible for personally directing the visiting teaching, which touches every Latter-day Saint family in the ward. She looks after the sick, she ministers where death reigns, and she gives needed encouragement and counsel to despondent and troubled mothers. In the Church Welfare program she is referred to as the "chief assistant to the bishop." Perhaps one of her most important and delicate services is to visit families in need, under the direction of the bishop, and to make recommendations to him for meeting the needs. Also, she has responsibilities incident to temple clothing, often including the handling of authorized pattern garments. In addition she is at times called upon by the bishop to prepare and serve ward dinners or to take charge of other ward projects. Furthermore, it is important that the Relief Society president have the ability to win and hold the love of the sisters of the ward and to unite them, not alone in support of Relief Society, but in support of the bishop and all ward and auxiliary activities. She must be prudent and an example to the sisters of the ward in all things. Hers, indeed, is a responsible calling. She is the mother of the ward. Like the bishop, who is the father of the ward, the requirements made of her are seemingly endless.

RELIEF SOCIETY—DIVINELY ORGANIZED
AND DIRECTED

R ELIEF Society is unique among women's organizations of the world. I recall at one time not long ago being assigned to serve as chairman of the committee to revise the constitution and by-laws of a national woman's organization. I was reluctant to accept the assignment because of the work entailed but was finally prevailed upon to do so. In announcing my chairmanship the president of the organization referred to my reluctance and then she said, "This assignment, however, should not be too difficult for Mrs. Spafford because she has for a pattern the constitution and by-laws of the organization over which she presides and which functions so well." I responded by explaining that Relief Society had no written constitution or by-laws. Whereupon she replied, "Incredible! How is it possible to officer and regulate your far-flung empire without benefit of a constitution and by-laws? It is beyond human comprehension."

Certainly divinely inspired wisdom guided the Prophet in this, as in all matters related to the founding of Relief Society.

The *Book of Records* containing the minutes of the organization meeting was treasured and carefully safeguarded by the sisters of Nauvoo. At the time of the exodus from Nauvoo, Sister Eliza R. Snow added to her few personal belongings which she was to carry across the wilderness this precious *Book of Records,* destined to be a guiding reference for generations to follow. How many secretaries today do you suppose, if driven from their homes and forced to face a long trek across a desolate land, would consider taking with them the record book of a society she was serving? Surely the Lord prompted Sister Snow.

Today this book is safeguarded in the vaults of the Church in the Church Historian's Department. So valuable is it considered by the Church that when we wished to include in the *Centenary of Relief Society* the facsimile of the title page, it was necessary for us to obtain permission and also to receive authorization to have the page photographed in the general board office direct from the First Presidency. The book was delivered to us by a young man especially assigned to this duty by the Church Historian. He waited until the photograph was taken so that he might immediately return the book to its place of safety.

Just as it is my testimony that divine inspiration attended the Prophet and attended Sister Snow in preserving the *Book of Records,* so it is my conviction that divinely inspired insight was given to the early day women leaders as to the place of Relief Society among organized women of the world. They seem to have been given an insight, a comprehension by inspiration, which some of us today have had to gain through the tedious method of experience.

To illustrate: When Sister Sharp and I were preparing the *Centenary of Relief Society,* a pictorial history of the first 100 years of the Society, we did considerable research. From time to time we would encounter such expressions as the following: "Standing as we do at the head of the women of the world," or "In our position as leaders of the women of the world." The *Woman's Exponent* carried on its front page the caption: "For the rights of the women of Zion and the rights of the women of all nations."

Here were these pioneer women closeted away in the vastness of the Rocky Mountains, isolated from women of the world, struggling to establish homes and wrest their daily bread from a desert wasteland, envisioning themselves, by virtue of their position in Relief Society, as leaders of the women of the world.

As Sister Sharp and I would read such statements, we would look at one another and out of our own limited vision we would exchange smiles.

Moved by their vision and lofty concepts of the mission of Relief Society, these women pressed forward. They had been given the religious vote with the organization of the Church. In February 1870 Utah women were granted the right of suffrage. Sarah Young, a grandniece of President Brigham Young, was the first woman to vote in the United States. Mormon women soon became conspicuous figures in the national woman's suffrage movement.

In 1888 a conference called by the National Woman's Suffrage Association convened in Washington, D.C., to celebrate the fortieth anniversary of the first public demand for equal educational, industrial, professional, and political rights for women.

Both national and international women were invited to attend this conference, among them representatives of Relief Society. So important did the First Presidency regard this invitation that, according to the journal of Sister Emmeline B. Wells, the sisters were set apart for the mission.

The chief outcome of the conference was the formation of the National Council of Women of the United States to be made up of national associations within the United States, and the projection of a permanent International Council of Women to which none but national councils would be eligible as auxiliaries.

Relief Society became a charter member of the National Council of Women of the United States and by virtue of this membership an affiliate of the International Council. These Councils have lived through the years.

They have had their good days and bad. Relief Society has continued its membership. At times it has been well considered by the Councils, at other times not so well. The period following World War I was difficult for the United States Council and particularly difficult for Relief Society in its association with this Council. Sister Sharp, who was living in New York, served as a special delegate to one of the biennial meetings. Afterward, she gave a disheartening report about Relief Society's status in the Council.

When I was named president of Relief Society one of the first invitations to reach my desk was an invitation to a biennial conference of the National Council of Women to be held at the Waldorf Astoria Hotel in New York City. Influenced by Sister Sharp's experience, recognizing costs of travel to New York, and pressed by the duties of our new offices, the General Presidency decided to recommend to the First Presidency that Relief Society withdraw from the Council. We carefully typed our recommendation and listed our supporting reasons.

I shall never forget the morning when, unaccompanied by anyone, I presented the recommendation to President George Albert Smith. He read the paper carefully. Then he inquired, "Hasn't Relief Society been a member of the Council since before the turn of the century?" I replied that it had. "And," continued the President, "am I to understand you wish to withdraw?" "Yes," I replied. "We really are not getting anything from the Council." Whereupon, the President tilted back characteristically in his chair and with penetrating gaze said, "You surprise me a little, Sister Spafford. Do you always think in terms of what you get? Don't you think it is well at times to think in terms of what you have to give? Mormon women have something to give to women of the world and I believe they may also learn from the association. Therefore, I suggest that Relief Society continue its membership. Take several of your board members and attend the conference. Make your influence felt."

Greatly humbled, I gathered up my papers and returned to my office. There my counselors were anxiously awaiting the outcome of the interview. Discouraged, I said, "I don't think the President knows what it's all about. We will be obedient and go, but I don't see how we can exert any influence. I doubt that they will even know we are there."

Nonetheless the words of the Prophet stayed with me, and I determined that if it were humanly possible, with the help of the Lord, we would make our influence felt. Time does not permit me to tell the outcome of this conference. Suffice it to say that at the following biennial conference I, as Relief Society's representative, was elected a vice president and served as a vice president as long as I was constitutionally allowed to do so.

In 1954, Relief Society was honored by my appointment to head a 16 woman delegation from the United States Council to the International Council of Women's Triennial Conference in Helsinki, Finland. Thirty-four free nations were represented at this conference. I shall never forget the deeply moving experience which was mine at the official opening of the Helsinki conference.

The meeting was held in the new and commodious auditorium of the University of Helsinki. The building was filled to capacity with representatives of many nations. The ministers to Finland from each of the countries represented, with their wives, honored their respective delegates by being in attendance. The Honorable Jack McFall was the United States Minister. The women wore beautiful evening gowns, the men were in formal attire, wearing their many decorations. It was indeed a glittering audience. In front of the dais was a large symphony orchestra composed entirely of women.

The meeting opened with a prayer for peace, international understanding, and human well-being. Following this impressive prayer lovely Finnish girls wearing native dress and each holding aloft a standard with a large silk flag of one of the countries represented, marched down the aisle and on to the dais of the festival hall and stood at attention. This was followed by the march of the chairmen of the respective delegations. As each chairman reached the dais, she stood in front of the flag of her country and was formally introduced, as the orchestra softly played strains from her country's national anthem. It was my choice privilege to lead the march of chairmen and to be first to be introduced, for they said, "The United States Council was the first member of the International Council of Women, and United States was the leading country of the free world."

My soul was stirred to its depths as I stood that night in front of the glorious stars and stripes and heard my name presented and listened to the stirring strains of "The Star Spangled Banner." As I looked out over that colorful audience I thought, "America is a composite of all this. My beloved Relief Society is a composite of women of many nations." Then there came to my mind with striking force the words of my pioneer sisters—"Standing as we do at the head of the women of the world." There was I, the President of Relief Society, literally standing at the head of the women of the free world. This night I did not smile as I recalled the words of my sisters. Their truthfulness impressed itself upon me with a lasting seriousness.

Nor is our work yet done or our leadership responsibilities completed. In fact at times I feel as though we were only on the threshold of them.

Today there are two great conflicting forces in the world: freedom and slavery; Godliness and Godlessness. Powerful political bodies represent each. Organized women are becoming an increasingly important part of this conflict. Just as the free world has its strong women's organizations dedicated to liberty and opportunity for each individual to realize his full potential, so there are strong communist women's organizations, government-sponsored and financed, active, ruthless, dedicated to the triumph of communism. The main front organization is known as W.I.D.F.—Woman's International Democratic Federation. This organization, under many guises, holds conferences, issues beautifully prepared publications, and aims to influence not only women citizens of the Soviet Union and her satellites, but women of the free world as well, to accept the Godless communist philosophy of life.

Relief Society, with a knowledge of God's divine law of free agency, with a knowledge of the sacredness of the individual and God's plan of life and salvation for his children as revealed in these latter days through his prophets, has a grave responsibility to share its knowledge and shed its influence in promoting freedom and the way of life taught by the Master. There is no organization of women in the world upon whom this responsibility rests so heavily. There is no group to whom the organized women of the world should be able to look with greater assurance for strong and wise leadership. We must work through proper channels it is true, and as authorized by our priesthood authorities, but work we must and give to women of the world the truths we have been given by divine revelation. Accepting through the years its divinely appointed role of leadership, unscathed by time or change, Relief Society must stand a bulwark against the forces of evil striving to engulf women. It must be as a beacon light and guiding star to women.

President Smith was right. Mormon women have something to give to women of the world. It is my firm testimony that Relief Society has the greatest potential for leadership in influencing aright the opinions and actions of organized women of any group of women on the face of the earth today. It is the Lord's organization for his daughters through which they may most effectively serve him and teach and exemplify truth to womankind. May the Lord give us the wisdom and the strength to fulfill our divine mission.

THE DIVINITY WITHIN RELIEF SOCIETY

THE First Presidency, at the time of the centennial of Relief Society, reminded us: "We ask our sisters of the Relief Society never to forget that they are a unique organization in the whole world, for they were organized under the inspiration of the Lord bestowed upon that great Prophet who was divinely called by a visitation of the Father and Son, in person, to open up this, the Last Dispensation, the Dispensation of the Fullness of Times. No other women's organization in all the earth has had such a birth." (*Centenary of Relief Society*, p. 7.)

Sister Eliza R. Snow, in a speech recorded in the *Women's Exponent*, Vol. 9, page 167, declared, "A society of this kind has always existed whenever the Priesthood has been upon the earth, and the allusion of the elder to the 'elect lady' as recorded in the New Testament, means one who presided over the society in his day."

Without doubt, Sister Snow was referring to the second epistle of John, wherein the Elder speaks unto "the elect lady and her children" of whom he says, "I love in the truth." He further says, "I rejoice greatly that I found thy children walking in truth." Then he urges them to continue walking after the commandments of the Lord.

It is not difficult to imagine the message given in this

scripture as being given by one of the leading elders of this day to the Relief Society sisters.

It is noteworthy that the term 'elect lady' was used in the revelation given through the Prophet Joseph Smith to Emma Smith, the first president of the Relief Society in this dispensation. This revelation declares: "Thou art an elect lady whom I have called." (D&C 25:3.)

The Prophet Joseph Smith said: "I gave much instruction and read in the New Testament and Book of Doctrine and Covenants, concerning the elect lady and showed that the elect meant to be elected to a certain work, etc., and that the revelation was then fulfilled by Sister Emma's election to the Presidency of the Society." (*DHC* Vol. IV, pp. 552-553.)

The Apostle Paul, explaining the organization of the Church to the Corinthian Saints, mentions the members which God hath set in the Church. He explains that there are "many members, yet but one body." He asserts, "And God hath set some in the church; first, apostles; secondarily, prophets; thirdly, teachers; after that, miracles; then gifts of healings, helps, governments, diversities of tongues." (1 Corinthians 12:20, 28.) Paul spoke to the Ephesian Saints also about the offices, mentioning apostles, prophets, evangelists, pastors and teachers. Elder Spencer W. Kimball, in an article published in the *Relief Society Magazine*, poses these questions with regard to Paul's words to the Corinthians: "What did the Apostle Paul mean by 'helps and governments'? Could the governments be the Priesthood leaders who govern and direct all the work in the Church, and could the 'helps' mean the helping organizations, such as Relief Society?"

Whether there was a formal organization such as that of our present Relief Society in the early Church remains for the prophets to tell us, but it is not difficult to believe that the sisters were called to do such work as is now assigned to Relief Society.

THE DIVINITY OF RELIEF SOCIETY

THERE are excellent campus Relief Societies. I have visited some of them and other members of the general board have visited them. Always the reports are the same—outstanding leadership, conformity to the regulations of the general board, enthusiasm for the work. As I have visited the stakes of the Church in faraway places, I have seen young women whose first introduction to Relief Society work came on a university campus holding positions of leadership and influence in the organization and greatly influencing the lives of their associates. I have seen this in the Middle East, I have seen it in the Far East, I have seen it in the United States, Mexico, and other places. I feel that our campus stakes are a training ground for Relief Society leadership.

I hope I may convey to you the strong conviction I have of the divinity of this great women's organization. I am not unaware of the fact that young men as well as young women are here. I know that young men may not be members of Relief Society. Young men, however, should be concerned with Relief Society because from the group of young men who are here today will come bishops, stake presidents, high councilmen, mission presidents, missionaries, yes, even general authorities of the Church.

Every man holding such a position becomes concerned with Relief Society. He needs to understand the divinity within it; he needs to know its procedures; he needs to know the programs which implement its purposes; and he needs to know how to guide and direct it. So I make no apology today in speaking of Relief Society to a group of men and women.

A number of years ago when I was on a boat to Honolulu I met a group of young missionaries. We all joined together to have breakfast. At this time I was a member of the general board, and following breakfast I invited the group to meet with me on the deck of the ship. I said, "I'll tell you young men a little bit about Relief Society." One young well-dressed boy in a dark blue suit said, "Sister Spafford, if you don't mind I would like to be excused. I really have no interest in Relief Society, and I certainly don't intend to ever work in it. I see no need for me to sit and listen to talk about something with which I want no identification." About a year and a half later I again went to the Hawaiian Islands. I visited a branch where this young man was serving. He shook hands with me and asked if I remembered him. I did! He said, "Sister Spafford, I wish you would look at the back of my coat and the seat of my pants. Do you see how shiny they are?"

I thought he was worried because his suit was wearing out, and I said, "Oh, don't worry, your suit isn't wearing out. It's made of blue serge, and blue serge soon becomes shiny. I'm sure it's the blue serge fabric that makes your pants shiny."

He said, "Blue serge nothing! It's sitting all day, every day, in Relief Society!"

I remember that when I was first called to be a Relief Society leader in my ward, we were meeting in the basement of a meeting house under construction. The meeting room was uninviting and many of the women of the ward didn't come; we had poor attendance. I used to visit the sisters in the ward and say, "Oh, won't you please come to Relief Society? We need you." After a while, as my experience broadened, I found myself saying, "Why don't you come to Relief Society? *YOU* need Relief Society!" Now as my vision has been enlarged and my experience further broadened, I say to the women of the Church without hesitancy, "You have an *obligation* to be a member of Relief Society, regardless of what other office you may hold in the Church or what other interests or activities may be yours." The Lord has given us this organization to help us meet our divine mission.

THE GREATNESS OF RELIEF SOCIETY

I AM deeply grateful today for the privilege and blessings of this conference, for the faith, for the unity, and for the spirit of sisterhood that exists among us. I am grateful for the presence of General Authorities of the Church whose direction, support, and encouragement are indispensable to us. It is impossible to overestimate the value to us, as organized women, of having with us in our conference God's chosen leaders. One who has known this blessing feels deeply its lack when attending a gathering of women where priesthood authority is not present.

I am deeply grateful for my membership in the Church and for the knowledge which I have of the divinity of Christ and the truthfulness of the restored gospel; for the blessings and watchcare exercised over me by our Father in Heaven in my daily comings and goings; and at this time I am particularly grateful for the watchcare vouchsafed me as I travel about in foreign lands.

I am grateful for the missionaries who are proclaiming the gospel to the nations of the earth. As I noted the earnestness which the missionaries in Europe were performing their labors, the purity of their lives, and the sincerity of their testimonies, I felt to love them every one. I bring to the mothers of these missionaries their love and their greetings. I assure the mothers of the great importance of the work in which their sons and daughters are engaged.

I am grateful for the lives of the young Latter-day Saint men and women in the armed services overseas, who are upholding the standards of the Church. They too, are performing missionary service. I recall one young man who waited for me after the sacrament meeting in Germany one Sunday. He said, "Sister Spafford, I guess everyone asks you to remember them to someone when you return home; but if it is not imposing, I would surely appreciate it if you would call my mother and tell her I'm fine. I know how anxious she is about me." Then with great earnestness the boy_ added, "Every night I pray God to bless my mother for the good teachings she has given me." God will answer the prayers of that boy and he will bless that mother for teaching her boy the principles of righteous living.

I am grateful to live in this beautiful land of America declared by God's prophets to be a land of promise, a land choice above all other lands; a land of great cities and productive farms; a wonderland of broad rivers, blue lakes, lofty mountains, and expansive plains; a progressive land; A Christian land whose culture is enriched by the contributions from many cultures.

I am grateful for my United States citizenship, for the privilege of belonging to a nation whose citizens are assured basic freedoms by a divinely inspired Constitution —where I may go to the church of my choice, unrestricted. (One who has talked with a young man who was imprisoned and severely beaten for possessing a Book of Mormon and a few gospel tracts realizes the greatness of this freedom.)

I am grateful to belong to a nation where I may express my opinions freely; where I have the right to own property, to work, and save, and make provision for my future; where I may maintain my simple home and rear my children according to my own desires and standards;

where I may go forward and improve my own conditions and pursue the interests that make me happy without any unnecessary fears, restraints, or restrictions—rights guaranteed me by a government in which I have voice.

I am grateful today, perhaps more than any other time in my life, for my membership in Relief Society, for the inherent greatness of this organization, priesthood directed and guided by the light of the gospel.

These are blessings to which most of us have become so accustomed that, at times, we are inclined to take them almost for granted. Only as one sees the absence of them does he fully and deeply sense their magnitude.

And now I would speak of Relief Society and its place among women's organizations of the world. I trust that what I say will in no way seem boastful. I assure you I speak with humility.

I recall in the past reading the old *Woman's Exponent* and noting with interest the title on the front page which read: "For the Rights of the Women of Zion and the Rights of the Women of all Nations."

I also recall a phrase used many times by the early-day Relief Society leaders which engaged my attention. It read: "Standing as we do at the head of the women of all the world."

Picturing those pioneer women, more or less isolated from the world, locked away in the vastnesses of the Rocky Mountains, struggling at the side of their husbands to establish homes and wrest a living from hard and barren soil, trying to build a community that would help them to survive and, at the same time, endeavoring to do their part in the establishment of their little Relief Societies, I smiled that they should envision themselves as "Standing at the head of the women of all the world."

However, as my experiences have been widened, as my perception has been deepened, as my knowledge and understanding have been increased, I no longer smile. Rather, I marvel that, young as was the work and new to

them as leaders, they should have had so enlightened a
concept of the place of Relief Society among women's
organizations of the world and of their position as its
leaders.

During the conference, I have had opportunity to
meet the leadership, to learn the purposes, to become more
or less acquainted with the programs and accomplishments
of women's organizations from many nations of the world.

I pay tribute to these leaders and to the organizations which they represent. The leaders are serious-minded
women dedicated to the accomplishment of good as they
see it. They are organized for instruction to their members, for mutual edification, and service to humanity. It
would take this entire session to present to you, even briefly,
their varied interests and activities. However, there are
some things on which all agree. As an International Council of Women they assert their belief in education, in culture, in the removal of prejudices and misunderstandings
between individuals and peoples, in the preservation of the
dignity of women, in social justice, and in the maximum
spiritual development of mankind.

They subscribe to the belief that the age-old role of
mother and homemaker remains today the primary role
of woman. They regard good homes as the basis of man's
well-being and the fundamental cornerstone of a good society.

They support the contention that moral well-being is
basic to a strong, enduring, and expanding world civilization, and that it is accorded too small a part of the organized
and co-ordinated efforts of countries and their peoples.

They believe that women must be the preservers of
the human and spiritual values in community life. And
now that civilization has reached the threshold of the
nuclear age, it is their contention that women must do
their part in guarding against the misuse of the forces of
nature.

These are all matters we as Relief Society women

hold at heart. But a question arises: Wherein are we different from other women's organizations whose work is animated by goals toward which we ourselves strive? Wherein lies our right to claim pre-eminence among women's organizations? Recalling my feeling as I was introduced at the opening session of the conference, I knew full well our position comes not by virtue of my standing on a platform or by any worldly recognition that might be accorded us.

My feelings led me to consider the elements which go into making a great woman's organization. My contemplation brought me to the conclusion that any society of women to be great must be well founded; its purposes must be important to the well-being of people; its program must be capable of fulfilling its purposes; and its affairs must be administered by capable leadership devoted to its cause.

Countless numbers of women's organizations conform to these standards. Relief Society conforms to them.

What, then, does Relief Society possess in addition to all this? I realize the inadequacy of words to define the elements that give Relief Society transcendency among women's organizations of the world. An understanding of this lends itself to feelings more than to verbal expressions. This knowledge is the testimony of the heart rather than the mind. Nevertheless, I call your attention today to a few things. Relief Society is pre-eminent among women's organizations because it is God's organization for his daughters here upon earth. It was founded under the inspiration of the Lord bestowed upon the Prophet Joseph Smith; it was organized "under the Priesthood and after a pattern of the Priesthood." Relief Society women are women embarked in the service of God, and it follows that they are embarked in the service of their fellowmen. Ours is not a man-made society—a higher power is operating to bring about the fulfillment of the purposes of Relief Society.

The light for which organized women are reaching in many of their programs has been ours for more than a century. The hazy paths along which they are slowly feeling their way are clearly illumined for us by the revealed word of God. The power inherent in them is decreed by human determination. The power inherent in Relief Society is God ordained.

The great disciplines of the gospel of Jesus Christ give to us unbounded strength.

I have seen the power of Relief Society literally transform the lives of women; make of them, as the Lord said to Alma, "new creatures."

It makes their burdens light. In faraway Finland I found Relief Society women who by their own words "had suffered much." They were sweet-spirited, poised, capable in their leadership, and they were radiantly happy women. Just as I saw this in Finland, so I saw it in the other European countries, so I have seen it at home.

I have seen the spirit of Relief Society touch the hearts of women and, rising above the barriers of nationality, race, social and economic position, make of them sisters in very deed, ready to labor and minister to one another as well as to those about them. Entirely forgetful of self, I have seen them tenderly and tirelessly minister to the sick and patiently care for the aged.

I wish you all might see some of the little welfare rooms in the faraway missions filled with neatly packaged, usable clothing and other commodities, representing the labor and the love of Relief Society women, ready to meet the emergent welfare needs of their people. I have attended programs, handwork exhibits, socials; I have listened to Singing Mothers concerts—all a glorious reflection of the power of the society to utilize and develop the talents and the tastes of the women.

Few organizations in all the world have so comprehensive a program as does Relief Society. There is not a worthy interest or a woman's talent that cannot be nourished in this wonderful society. Relief Society reaches into every avenue and touches every aspect of a woman's life.

Personal ambitions so damaging in some women's organizations and so conducive to disharmony among members, have little place in Relief Society. With lines of authority and positions within the society well defined by priesthood authority, Relief Society goes forward practically devoid of this disturbing and often destructive influence. Relief Society is a society of order, regulated by a righteous and inspired priesthood.

My visit abroad has deeply impressed me with the importance and magnitude of the work of the Relief Society. My vision has been enlarged until today, like the early-day sisters, I recognize the true greatness of Relief Society.

Today the Lord has given us influence among women's organizations of the world. It is our responsibility so to conduct our lives and our affairs that this influence may be ever widened for the blessing and the benefit of our Father's children.

In conclusion I say to you—sisters, value that with which you have been blessed. Never underestimate its beauty, its importance, its power, and its influence for good. Make it ever more potent as an organization proclaiming the Master's way.

MEMBERSHIP BUILDING

M EMBERSHIP building in Relief Society is a continuing process. It does not lend itself to the setting of a specific goal which, when achieved, relieves us of further responsibility. As long as there are Latter-day Saint sisters unenrolled, as long as there are sisters joining the Church, as long as there are good non-Latter-day Saint women within the bounds of our respective stakes who are not members of the Society, the work is not completed nor does our obligation end with their enrollment. It extends to their full fellowshipping, their personal development, the enrichment of their lives, the blessing of their homes, and their joyous dedication to the advancement of Relief Society.

While the accomplishment of this goal rests primarily upon the ward president, whose vision of her responsibility must be expansive and who must give wise and tireless direction to this work, every officer and member should aid her.

Relief Society is not just another woman's organization. It was divinely founded. It is an auxiliary of the only true Church on the face of the earth today.

The fact that Relief Society is an essential part of the divine organization of the Church designed for the mature females of the Church, should be reason enough for any Latter-day Saint woman to identify herself with it. Beyond this is the fact that Relief Society is the medium through which the women of the Church collectively are to contribute to the advancement of the work of the Church. This we must do. President J. Reuben Clark, Jr., addressing the Relief Society sisters, made this strong and impressive statement in concluding his address: "And this is your destiny [referring to the sisters] and ours [referring to the priesthood] to save the world."

Salvation comes only through knowledge and full acceptance of the teachings of the Church. We would be comparatively ineffective in fulfilling this mission as individuals. As an organized body, priesthood directed, we are a powerful and far-reaching influence. What Latter-day Saint woman would knowingly wish to be remiss in doing her part in the fulfillment of this great assignment? It was the desire of the sisters of Nauvoo to more effectively aid in the work of the Church that led to the request which resulted in the organization of the Relief Society by the Prophet. These sisters realized, as we do today, that hard as they might work as individuals, their collective, organized, priesthood-directed efforts were needed.

The sacredness of the individual is a basic doctrine of the Church. The Lord loves his daughters just as he loves his sons. Exaltation in the Father's kingdom is for his sons and daughters together. In his wisdom and mercy he has provided opportunities for his daughters to develop their talents, enlarge their souls, and learn his plan of life and salvation. Relief Society is rich in these opportunities. In a letter addressed to the sisters of the Church at the time of the Relief Society Centennial observance, the First Presidency said:

The prime, the almost exclusive, allegiance of every member of this great group runs in this field to their fellow members and to the organization. Members should permit no other affiliation either to interrupt or interfere with this Society. They should give to Relief

Society service precedence over all social and other clubs and societies of similar kinds. We urge this because in the work of the Society are intellectual, cultural, and spiritual values found in no other organization and sufficient for all general needs of its members.

We bring women into Relief Society so that opportunities for growth and development leading to their happiness and eternal well-being might be afforded them.

The Lord has been truly mindful of us in giving us an organization through which we may gain so much of eternal value and whereby we may exert a profound influence for good here upon earth. The organization structure is perfect because the Society was divinely established. Perfect as it may be, however, it would not fully accomplish the purposes for which it was given to us were the women not to properly utilize it, build upon it and strengthen it by individual and collective effort. Everyone receiving a good and useful gift has a responsibility to cherish it, to put it to good and proper uses, to take care of it and not allow it to deteriorate and lose its value. So it is with this precious gift of Relief Society, given by the Father not to a selected few of his daughters but to all. Therefore, each one among us has a responsibiliy to the Society to maintain it as the great instrument for good which our Father intended it to be.

It is my conviction that Latter-day Saint women who fail to affiliate with Relief Society do so largely because they have not understood its divine mission and their obligations to it. This understanding comes to women through membership. Therefore, there is imposed upon every one of us who has this understanding an obligation to put forth effort to see that sisters who lack it may enroll and be brought into full activity. To be content and happy in the blessings which are ours as Relief Society members, to be thankful for this choice gift with no special desire or effort on our part to share it with others for whom it was equally given, is to fail to meet a great responsibility.

I often think of the meeting held in Nauvoo on Saturday, March 16, 1844. Referring to this meeting, the *Centenary of Relief Society,* page 18, states:

> Probably no one present realized that this would be the last meeting of the Society in the beloved city of Nauvoo, for in closing President Emma Smith said that she would like to have all the Society present together when a place could be obtained.

Even though the spirit and genius of Relief Society lived on in the hearts and acts of the members as they crossed the great plains, it was seven years before the sisters again had opportunity to meet together in an organized Relief Society meeting, and even then there were only temporary organizations in a few wards and surrounding places.

How do you think you would feel if, at the close of your next ward Relief Society meeting, the president said that she would advise you as to where and when the next meeting would be held, and then no opportunity came for such a meeting for seven years? Would you miss Relief Society? Would your life seem void of something good and precious? Would its influence be missed in your home? Would you be less able to cope with life's vicissitudes? Countless similar questions I could ask. To all of them I believe you would say, "We would indeed."

Think then, sisters, of the good women who do not now enjoy these blessings, not because there are no Relief Society meetings but because they have not discovered the beauties and great worth of the organization. Help them. Bring them in.

VISITING TEACHERS—THE SALT OF THE EARTH

P ERHAPS one of the greatest of all recorded discourses is the Sermon on the Mount given by the Savior to his disciples and devoted adherents who followed him to a mountain near the Sea of Galilee in order that they might hear more of his teachings. These were people who had been attracted by the power of his matchless words and by the miracles he had performed. They felt constrained to forsake their all and follow after him. In this great sermon, the Savior declared he had not come to destroy the law (the law of Moses) but to fulfill it. He taught the higher law—the law of love, ". . . Love your enemies, bless them that curse you, do good to them that hate you, and pray for them which despitefully use you, and persecute you." (Matt. 5:44.)

The beginning of the Sermon on the Mount sets forth the essence of true religion and its attendant blessing. Then in a mode of direct personal address, the Savior pronounced those disciples who sat listening to be the worthy benefactors of mankind. He declared: "Ye are the salt of the earth . . ." (Matt. 5:13.) This is an interesting analogy. Salt is the great preservative. It prevents deterioration and spoilage. It freshens and sweetens. It serves as a corrective, a purifier. It brings out flavor and gives pungency. In using this analogy, the Savior made clear that the small band of righteous disciples would be as a condiment that would arrest corruption, purify mankind, and bring desirable flavor to earth life.

Along with this pronouncement, however, the Savior sounded a warning note as he continued, "but if the salt have lost his savour, wherewith shall it [the earth] be salted? It is thenceforth good for nothing, but to be cast out . . ." (Matt. 5:13.) With his warning, the Savior demonstrated his recognition of the tendency of man, including the so-called righteous, to lose his purifying qualities. He raised the pertinent question as to how, then, corruption should be stamped out and the earth be purified. Thus he emphasized the urgency of his disciples' remaining steadfast.

Through the years, the phrase "the salt of the earth" has been appropriately applied to individuals and to groups whose character, purity, and nobility of life have inspired, and benefited others.

Often I find myself applying the phrase "the salt of the earth" to the great body of women who are Relief Society visiting teachers. Righteous in their lives, faithful in service, these sisters go forth month after month in fair weather or foul, in their calling as representatives of Relief Society. They uplift, bless, and exercise sisterly watchcare over the mothers and homemakers of the Church.

Theirs is not an easy assignment. It involves conscientious study, prayer, countless hours of time, unselfish effort, and the strict regulation of their individual lives in order that they more fully may meet the requirements of the calling.

Regardless of the demands made of them, however, these sisters go forth devotedly on their mission of love and mercy. Many sisters do so year after year, in some instances for a length of time that is almost equal to the span of life.

During the past year I attended a stake visiting teacher convention. Seated on the front row were some of the most angelic looking women one might ever expect to see. They ranged in age from 23 to 92 years. All were visiting teachers who were being honored for their service. They had served in this calling from three to 64 years, respectively. I thought, "How unlimited has been the good these sisters have accomplished." Could it have been precisely measured and then compiled with the records of tens of thousands of others who likewise have served, what an overwhelming account of righteous accomplishment would be revealed!

These sisters, however, do not give this service out of a desire to make a record or for personal recognition. Such motives would not lead to the achievement of the worthy purposes for which the program is designed. What, then, does prompt them to so serve? May I suggest one or two of the major reasons:

1. Respect for Church calling
2. The spirit of the gospel which animates their lives
3. The compassionate nature of the work which is according to the nature of women
4. The genuine need for such a program.

While it is true that the great bulk of visiting teachers give dependable and qualified service, we must recognize that there are times when enthusiasm declines and effort grows lax, when indeed, "the salt begins to lose its savour." At such a time, we remind ourselves of the words of the Savior spoken to his disciples, ". . . if the salt has lost his savour, wherewith shall it be salted?" (Matt. 5:13.)

So the wise Relief Society president is alert for evidences of this problem. She asks herself, "What are its evidences, and how may they best be dealt with?" We suggest a few of the evidences: Declining enthusiasm for the work; the attitude that it is merely a routine duty to be performed or a favor conferred upon or concession made to the presidency; irregularity in attendance at visiting teacher meetings, and even in making visits; a shift in the compelling motive of the visit from rendering a needed and qualified service to a striving for a record in number of visits made; a tiredness on the part of the visiting teacher; and even a questioning of the worth of the program.

The key person in helping the visiting teacher to maintain the freshness and vitality of the service and to find joy and satisfaction in the calling is the ward Relief Society president, supported and wisely counselled by the stake Relief Society president. The general board, too, feels concern and offers its suggestions: Let there be a closeness between the ward Relief Society president and the individual visiting teachers so that the president may be aware at the outset of adverse attitudes or unproductive efforts. Let her see her responsibilities in motivating the sisters to fruitful and happy effort. Let her so act in the very beginning by following approved procedures in making the call. Let her frequently emphasize to the visiting teachers, individually and collectively, the lofty purposes of the program. Let her occasionally inquire of the visiting teachers individually as to how they are enjoying their work, thus affording them opportunity confidentially to apprise her of problems or, better still, to be strengthened by bearing testimony of their love for the calling. Let her be sensitive to the relationship of compatible women who more or less complement one another. Upon occasion, it may be wise for the president to consider the desirability of a change in district assignments. Let her be unafraid to acknowledge individual as well as collective accomplishments, and to express appreciation for the devotion and the quality of work that brought them about. Let the teachers feel her personal faith and confidence in them and her competence in dealing with the work because of her broad knowledge and understanding of the program and her strong personal conviction of the divinity that guides it.

As we consider the type of women who make up the visiting teaching group, as we contemplate the motives which lead them to make visits, as we ponder the uplift and comfort that have been brought into Latter-day Saint homes through their service, as we consider the gospel principles they have taught through precept and example, as we take into account the hands that have been strengthened and the homes that have been blessed, it does not seem inappropriate to refer to the visiting teachers as "the salt of the earth." So important, however, is the program that at no time or under any circumstance should those of us who are in charge of the work allow the salt to lose its savour because of laxity on our part. We bear in mind always that the important factor in helping any sister to maintain the savour in any Relief Society calling is to keep her testimony alive and growing. Active participation in all aspects of Relief Society work is the open doorway to this goal.

VISITING TEACHING—A GREAT WORK

Visiting teaching was instituted by inspiration given to President Emma Smith in 1843 to meet an urgent need of Latter-day Saints in Nauvoo. The program has been continued well over a century in response to the continuing needs of our people. Times have changed, the circumstances of our people have been altered, but the basic human needs which the program is designed to meet have remained constant.

Let us glimpse for a moment conditions in Nauvoo in 1843. From research done by Sister Faye Tarbock we read:

In this city thousands of people were living, some of them in pretentious homes, and others so new in Nauvoo that they depended upon charity for a night's lodging. Daily the slow prairie schooners and the crawling river boats were bringing new citizens—a few with gold in their pockets, but more with the idea that now they had found Nauvoo and "Brother Joseph" that all would be well.

The needs of the people in Nauvoo are attested in the *Centenary of Relief Society,* which states that the continuous arrival in Nauvoo of converts to the Church from other parts of the United States and from foreign lands (for the missionary program was in full action) imposed upon

Relief Society the responsibility of making certain that no illness or suffering was overlooked. The expulsion of the Saints from Missouri also had brought with it problems of great need.

A graphic report of conditions recorded by Eliza R. Snow is contained in the *Centenary*:

> The first winter after the Society was organized was exceedingly cold and severe. Many, in consequence of exposure and hardship in their expulsion from the State of Missouri and the unhealthiness of the climate of Nauvoo, had been reduced by sickness to destitution and if it had not been for the timely aid of the Female Relief Society, would have suffered very much and probably some would have perished.

Under such circumstances the Relief Society president required the assistance of an organized group of women, wisely directed, if she was to meet her responsibilities as leader of the newly organized society, whose basic objective has been declared by the Prophet Joseph Smith to be ". . . to seek after objects of charity and administer to their wants."

I think those first 16 women called to serve as the "Necessity Committee" must have been carefully and prayerfully chosen from among over 1300 members. I wonder how they must have felt to be chosen for so responsible a calling. Surely they were honored, but must they not have felt also humbled and earnestly desirous of meeting the obligations of the calling to the best of their abilities? Must they not have felt great dependence upon the Lord for inspiration? I think they could not have felt otherwise.

Today civilization has brought us countless conveniences and luxuries. We are not being called upon to conquer a wilderness or to establish an unpopular church. We are not being called upon to bear the hardships of wicked persecution. Our standards of living are high and our life experiences interesting and broad. The marvels of our day are a source of constant interest to us. What is new today is often almost outmoded tomorrow. Life is exciting.

Nonetheless life is strenuous and our people are not without need. With all we enjoy, there are still those who are brushing elbows with poverty. There are still the insecure, the heartbroken, the frustrated, the disconsolate; there are the sick, the lonely, the homebound aged. There are those whose faith is weak, who need the strengthening influence of scriptural truths applied to their individual lives in an intimate setting. There are those who need the influence of a testimony of a sister who speaks with conviction and whose message is given completely devoid of selfish motives. Many a woman has been brought into activity in Relief Society and even into the Church through such teaching and testimony.

The strains and pressures of life today call for the exercise of sisterhood as fully as at any time in the history of the Society. There is no program of Relief Society wherein sisterhood is more ideally exemplified than in the visiting teaching program.

Visiting teaching is also an effective organization builder. It has been so through the years. The general board is concerned when a new organization is formed if the leaders lack vision of the potential of the visiting teaching program in building the organization. Also, today this program is proving to be an asset to Relief Society in its support of the missionary and fellowshipping program of the Church.

The visiting teaching program has stood the test of time with few modifications. In fact I know of only two. The name has been changed from the "Necessity Committee" to visiting teaching, and with the advent of the so-called Church Welfare Program the sisters were relieved of administering direct relief, which removed the necessity for collecting of charity funds. This latter change was a trial to some of us. It seems that changes usually bring some pain and misgivings. I recall hearing it predicted that without the motivation of collecting funds for charitable purposes, visiting teaching would soon die out. One sister, a devoted Relief Society leader, gave the program two years to die. But visiting teaching was a divinely inspired program, designed to meet basic human needs through the spirit of the gospel and through the framework of the Church. It was not destined to die. When the Prophet gave to the Society the commission "to seek after objects of charity and administer to their wants," there was nothing in his words that directed the Society to administer to material wants through an organized system of collections from the homes. The charity collection aspect of visiting teaching was merely a means devised in the early days to meet a financial emergency in order that the Society might fulfill the objective set for it by the Prophet. When another plan was adopted by the Church to meet temporal needs, it was entirely right that the visiting teaching collections be discontinued.

It was interesting that with the discontinuance of charity fund collections the visiting teaching program seemed to take on new and greater dimensions. The sisters seemed to see it in clearer focus as a program designed to serve and bless families, rather than as a help-seeking, fund-raising program. They saw it as something designed for the benefit of every family, not merely the few in temporal need. It became the Society's program of watch-care over Latter-day Saint households—the link in the chain that bound every mother to Relief Society.

Sisters who had been reluctant to accept the call of visiting teaching suddenly were willing to serve. Because sisters were impressed with their mission to serve the home rather than to seek help from it, the quality of teaching improved and the number of visits rose phenomenally.

In some stakes, the need of families for visiting teaching may not appear as vital as in some other stakes where greater temporal needs exist. In some stakes temporal needs may be rare or even nonexistent. But other individual needs exist. Furthermore, the obligation of Relief Society to exercise watchcare over Latter-day Saint families was imposed upon it by the Prophet Joseph Smith and the prophets who have succeeded him and must be met.

Ward Relief Societies require continual strengthening and they must do their part in the missionary and fellowshipping programs. Without a well-established visiting teaching program ward Societies would find themselves devoid of an effective way to accomplish these purposes.

Just as in the Nauvoo days there was need for visiting teachers with a spirit of humility and dedication, for women honored to be chosen for this calling and ready to honor it, so there is need today. In going into a home, a visiting teacher remembers that she is an official representative of a great, powerful, and divinely organized Society. Behind every visiting teacher are the vast resources of the Society. This is not so when one goes as an individual to call upon a sister. Going as a representative of Relief Society imposes upon visiting teachers a responsibility, no matter how well they may know the sister visited, of conducting the visit with dignity and as directed by the Society. It places restraints upon them. There are certain things they do and do not do as visiting teachers. It is expected that both words and conduct will reflect the standards and teachings of the Society. Visiting teachers go prepared by prayer and by study. Regardless of whether a sister being visited may hold high social, civic, or Church position, the relationship between the visiting teacher and the sister is that of an official representative of Relief Society calling upon a ward member for specific purposes.

It is hard to precisely measure the results of visiting teaching, particularly for individuals. An endless chain of letters and other communications reaching the general board bear testimony to its value in meeting human needs and in serving women and, through them, their families in today's uncertain world.

May I read from two letters recently received:

Tonight I am walking on air. The bishop just called me to say that the Heyworth children attended Primary today and that their new baby will be blessed the first Sunday of the month. This is a family in our visiting teacher district which we have nursed with special care. I realized the first time we went there that, though they were not active, they were not hopeless. They invited us in to sit by the fire with them. It was a dismal, rainy day and we had spent some time locating the place, so we were glad to be invited in for a brief visit. The sister was expecting her fourth baby and we could see that she had many little problems. So with each visit we tried to be as helpful as possible to her. When the new baby came, we made a point to drop in and be especially helpful. Then for some unknown reason we suggested that the baby should be blessed in the Fast meeting and we explained the procedure. The suggestion fell on fruitful ground. This was the beginning. Now the ward teachers and Senior Aaronic leaders are helping to bring the family into full activity in the Church. Now why all this? Just to let you folks there at headquarters share some of the happy experiences of two visiting teachers, far removed from Church headquarters.

This second example has an element of humor in it but makes a good point.

One day a couple of weeks ago we called on two older sisters who feel they cannot get out. The first one is a sweet, tidy, and lovely person to visit, but she explained that at the age sixty-two one just can't get out to meetings. The next sister doesn't seem to know many of the basic principles of cleanliness. We have tried to be as tactfully helpful to her as possible. The other day she made the remark about how she appreciated our visits and our helpfulness. She said to me, "Why are you so helpful?" "Well," I said, "when I am old, I'll be glad to have someone call on me, and be helpful to me." She then told me she was sixty-two years old. "Sixty-two," I exclaimed, "why, I am sixty-five." The sister has a good sense of humor. She looked at me a minute and said, "Then why are you visiting me and cheering me and helping me?" For a brief moment that's what I wondered, but of course I knew the answer. "It was just because it is so much fun, so satisfying, and because it is my calling as a representative of Relief Society."

We cannot expect startling results from every visit, nor from every month's work, nor even from every year's work, either for the organization or the individual whom we visit. Often, too, our most successful efforts go un-measured and unknown to us. I sincerely believe, however, that an honest appraisal of her work must be satisfying to every visiting teacher who honors her calling and who is honored by it. Such a teacher cannot help but enjoy a generous degree of success and feel herself an effective supporter of the organization.

To me there is no more important work in which one could be engaged than to build Relief Society and to help make life more tolerable, more understandable, more pur-poseful, a bit happier, and more secure for our sisters. This is the great work of visiting teaching.

"SEARCHING AFTER OBJECTS OF CHARITY"

A T the initial meeting of Relief Society, the Prophet Joseph Smith addressed the sisters: ". . . To illustrate the object of the Society that the Society of sisters might provoke the brethren to good works in looking to the wants of the poor, *searching* after objects of charity and in administering to their wants." (*Centenary of Relief Society*, p. 15.) Note that the Prophet did not say that the object of the Society was to help those who came to us seeking assistance; rather, he used the words "searching after objects of charity." The word *search* means "to go forth or look through carefully in seeking to find something." The propriety of appointing a committee for this purpose was suggested by Emma Smith on March 24, 1842, and the following year her suggestion became a reality. Building upon this, we have today our great system of visiting teaching. While visiting teachers today do not administer direct relief, the visiting teaching plan provides that every Latter-day Saint family in every ward of the Church, irrespective of station or wealth, shall be visited once a month. Under the inspiration of their calling, vested with authority, trained in procedures, imbued with the spirit of love, and with a sisterly solicitude for those visited, visiting teachers are in an ideal position to be made aware of needs within a home, which they, in turn, report to their respective Relief Society presidents.

With such a program the material or spiritual requirements of no Latter-day Saint family need go undiscovered. Viewed from its welfare aspect, the visiting teaching program is ideal. It is complete in coverage. If the program was functioning fully, no Latter-day Saint family would be missed. It is right in purpose and in spirit. It is right in principle and in method of performance. No family is singled out as recipients of welfare assistance from the Church because visiting teachers are seen going to the home. All families are visited regardless of circumstances. All matters related to a home are kept strictly confidential except those which are reported to the Relief Society president.

President Stephen L Richards referred to this important aspect of visiting teaching in an address at general Relief Society conference:

I feel that the Lord loves them [the visiting teachers] as we do for their loving service to humanity. Their reward is assured ... I know of no one better situated to secure an intimate knowledge of home situations than are these dear women. In order to help a family intelligently, a knowledge of conditions is necessary. Our visiting teachers go into the home usually when the husband is away, often the children also. The lady of the house is alone. She receives these kindly people, and they soon establish with her, through their *friendly solicitation,* an atmosphere of *understanding* and *confidence.* It is not difficult in their ministrations for the teachers to discern trouble and anxiety of spirit. Perhaps the lady has felt great need for a confidant to whom she might unburden herself. Here is the opportunity, *unsolicited,* generally, but now welcomed. We can trust these friends and they can help us. (*Relief Society Magazine,* Dec. 1954, p. 797.)

We know the Relief Society president is the bishop's chief assistant in administering to the needs of those in distress, and reports of visiting teachers regarding families in need are made to bishops through the Relief Society president under whose immediate direction they work.

This is the approved procedure.

A second important aspect of visiting teaching is to strengthen Latter-day Saint homes.

President David O. McKay at a Relief Society general conference said: "I urge that increased attention be given and more intensive effort be put forth by the women of the Church to perpetuate the truth that home is the true foundation upon which is built the structure of true, civilized Christian society."

President J. Reuben Clark, Jr., addressing a general Relief Society conference in 1949, said: ". . . This is your real mission—to build a home where love shall be, serenity, peace, quiet, culture, and all the things that go to make a home." He prayed that God might give to the women of the Church the vision of the true homemaker, that they might be able to save by this course not only Zion but the whole world. "And that is your destiny and ours," said President Clark to the sisters, "to save the world."

Not only must we strengthen homes through watch-care over material needs but we must contribute to the spiritual well-being of the home. Homes today are greatly affected by the uncertainties of the world in which we live. There are anxieties and heartaches, insecurities and worries with which we all must grapple. Concern for their homes and children often leaves mothers feeling unsustained and insecure.

Many visits a year to Latter-day Saint families, each made in the spirit of love, each bearing a message of truth from our sacred scriptures, and each characterized by a spirit of cheerfulness, comfort, and friendship, cannot help but strengthen our Latter-day Saint homes.

Also, we must not lose sight of the fact that when a pair of visiting teachers call at a door they offer not the lone services of two good women, competent and sisterly as they may be, but behind them is a great and powerful Church auxiliary concerned with the home and ready to serve it. The two visiting teachers are its representatives, its emissaries.

There is a third aspect of the program. Who can measure the strength and power that comes to the Society itself, both the local organization and the general organization, through the visiting teaching program? Month after month, the year round, the women of the wards and branches of the Church are kept aware of Relief Society through the visiting teachers. They are made acquainted with its activities; they are invited to attend its meetings. Can you conceive of any more effective method of keeping our work before the women of the respective wards? We all agree that there is no substitute for a personal visit to interest a person in any program one is trying to promote.

When we wish the sisters of the ward to be made acquainted with some special program or activity, the assignment can be given to the visiting teachers with the assurance that it will be well fulfilled. Occasionally, very important special assignments come to Relief Society as a whole. These would, as a general rule, be difficult to fulfill were it not that we have a functioning visiting teaching program. For example, we all recall when the Church authorities assigned to Relief Society the responsibility for collecting clothing to be sent to the needy Saints in Europe following the close of hostilities after World War II. We were able to fulfill this assignment with efficiency and dispatch. The same was true when we were requested by the Church authorities to circularize the Church with family hour leaflets at a time when the Brethren felt a pressing need to awaken parents to their responsibility in building greater family unity.

At one time a national officer of the Women's Christian Temperance Union came to solicit the cooperation of Relief Society in distributing temperance literature. She commented that she was not a covetous woman, but that there was one thing in Relief Society which she sincerely coveted. It was not the governing board, nor the stake boards, nor the local boards, because, she explained, her organization had these to varying degrees and referred to as national, state, and local chapters. But she said she coveted the last vital link in our organization chain, the link that made us unique and strong. It was the link that bound the Society to every one of the Latter-day Saint homes—the visiting teaching program.

Fourth, we must not lose sight of the benefits and blessings that have come to individuals through visiting teaching. These are beyond calculation. Countless numbers of women have born testimony of the personal blessings that have come to them through the visits of visiting teachers.

Countless visiting teachers have born testimony to the blessings and benefits that have come to them through the fulfillment of their calling.

It would seem that the purposes of visiting teaching are well defined and that they are of sufficient importance to justify the requirements we are making of the sisters. However, we must remember that all of these goals will not be realized just because we have these goals and because we have a program whereby we may achieve them. They will not be realized just because we make a certain number of visits. The accomplishment of the purposes of visiting teaching rests, in large measure, with the visiting teachers themselves. Their attitudes must be right; their vision of the work must be large; they must recognize the importance of the calling; they must prepare themselves through study, through attendance at the visiting teacher meetings, through prayer, and through righteous living. They must have a sincere interest in those whom they visit. They must time their visits so that they will be welcome in the homes when they make a visit. Their personal appearance must be neat and modest. They must use wisdom and good judgment in what they do and say in the homes and so conduct themselves as to inspire confidence. They must avoid an attitude or a spirit of self-righteousness, criticism, or inquisitiveness. They are not social welfare investigators. They must hold sacred what they see and hear in every home visited. Visiting teaching, when properly done, is not an easy assignment nor is it merely a duty to be performed. When viewed properly, it is a sacred and an important calling, contributing significantly to the most basic and worthy purposes of Relief Society.

THE ROLE OF RELIEF SOCIETY IN THE
WELFARE PROGRAM

T HE Prophet Joseph Smith made clear that one of the Society's basic purposes was "to relieve the poor, the destitute, the widow and the orphan, and for the exercise of all benevolent purposes." He admonished the sisters that they were "not only to relieve the poor, but to save souls." Experience has taught us the close correlation between sound practices in relieving the poor and the saving of souls.

The Prophet further said: "This is a charitable Society, and according to your natures; it is natural for females to have feelings of charity and benevolence." And, indeed, it is within the nature of womankind to give "love-inspired, benevolent service." For one and one quarter centuries the sisters of Relief Society have walked along the path laid out by the Prophet Joseph Smith and redefined by the Presidents of the Church who have succeeded him. Their tender, compassionate services to those in distress have been manifold.

Relief Society has adopted the motto: "Charity never faileth." The meaning which we attach to the word "charity," however, is not that which the world has come to accept. To us charity is the expression of unselfish love which builds up and strengthens not only the physical but the spiritual in our people, and helps the individual and the family to realize their full potentials.

The term "welfare" also has special meaning for us, differing from the connotation presently attached to it by the world. We accept the true meaning of the word "welfare" as a state of faring or doing well. It is a condition of health, prosperity, happiness, a condition of well-being achieved through living according to the teachings of the Church. With reference to this, we are reminded of the words of King Benjamin:

> And behold all that he requires of you is to keep his commandments and he has promised you that if ye would keep his commandments ye should prosper in the land; and he never doth vary from that which he hath said; therefore, if ye do keep his commandments he doth bless you and prosper you. (Mosiah 2:22.)

President J. Reuben Clark, Jr., in outlining measures for our security and welfare, said: "First and above and beyond everything else, let us live righteously, fearing God and keeping his commandments, that we may claim his blessing as of right and not as of mercy only."

The meaning which we attach to the term "welfare" greatly enlarges the scope of Relief Society welfare services, encompassing many activities not ordinarily regarded as welfare activities. It influences our approaches, our procedures, our goals in helping people. It brings to our services the spirit and the blessings of the Lord.

In all of its activities, Relief Society works under the guidance and direction of the priesthood. The Prophet Joseph Smith instructed the sisters in the beginning: "You will receive instructions through the order of the Priesthood which God has established . . . to lead, guide and direct the affairs of the Church." This directive, of course, would be meticulously applied to its welfare services, which are among its most important activities.

Through the years, as Relief Society has pursued its tender, merciful ministration, it has been able also effectively to meet the special requirements brought out by the differing circumstances of each succeeding era. The Nauvoo period was characterized by the administration of direct temporal relief. In this, the sisters were supported by the Prophet, who, at the founding meeting of the Society, after contributing a $5 gold piece, stated, "All I shall have to give to the poor, I shall give to this Society."

With the inauguration of the Church Welfare Plan, Elder Marion G. Romney pointed out that the Relief Society was relieved of administering direct temporal relief and of maintaining a separate charity account, and the Society became strictly a service organization. Its services, however, were expanded in a number of ways. The sisters were called upon more fully to devote their time to watching over the female members of the ward family. Emphasis was placed on training them to sew and cook and develop greater ability in all the arts of homemaking. With adroitness, mothers and other homemakers were taught how to get the most out of the means at their disposal. With consummate skill, mothers with special or more pronounced homemaking problems, were taught how to overcome these problems through the Relief Society homemaking meetings, and as often as deemed advisable, through special help in their individual homes. In addition, full support was given by the Society and its members to other facets of the Church Welfare Program as assigned to the Society by the priesthood.

May I call attention to the purposes of the Church Welfare Plan? I quote from the First Presidency:

Our primary purpose was to set up, in so far as it might be possible, a system under which the curse of idleness would be done away with, the evils of a dole abolished, and independence, industry, thrift and self respect be once more established amongst our people. The aim of the Church is to help the people to help themselves. Work is to be re-enthroned as the ruling principle of the lives of our Church membership. (*Conference Report*, Oct. 1936, p. 3.)

Now, with regard to these purposes and Relief Society —the dissolution of the curse of idleness; the dispelling of the attitude that it is all right to get something for nothing;

the establishment of the spirit of independence; the encouragement of industry and thrift, with their resultant self-respect; the need to glorify work as the ruling principle in the life of an individual, if he would be happy and productive—all of these have their beginnings in the attitudes, standards, and practices of the home. Indeed, the foundations of individual and family welfare are built in the homes.

In a day when the Church is re-emphasizing that the home is the training and governing center in the lives of family members, we must keep in clear focus the importance of the cardinal principles of human welfare as defined in the purposes of the Welfare Program, and the need for the home to meet its responsibilities toward them.

Mothers are intimately involved in the attitudes and patterns of life adopted by their families in the homes. Relief Society, therefore, has the responsibility to guide, teach, and train the mothers in these fundamentals of good living. This, to me, is a vital welfare service of the Society. Relief Society is not a "load lifter" alone. It is also a great educational institution. It is clearly within the realm of Relief Society welfare to educate the sisters in the arts of homemaking, money management, home storage, thrift practices, legal responsibilities to insure protection and security for themselves and their families, and similar skills.

Mothers also need help in child guidance, including how to provide opportunities for children to carry responsibility and to be productively employed. Children must be taught to value work through having incentives for doing it and through joyfully participating in it. Emphasis needs to be placed on adequately preparing children for life through education and training in order that they may favorably compete in today's highly competitive society and live self-maintaining, self-directing lives.

Mothers must also be taught how to plan for fruitful days for themselves when family members are no longer with them, and also to prepare themselves for the so-called aging years by developing worthwhile interests that will engage their time and keep them active and productive. Otherwise, these aging years may become years of idleness and frustration.

WELFARE—GOD'S PERFECT PLAN

M ANY have the concept that the Church Welfare Program was inaugurated in 1936. Actually the Church Welfare Program as we know it today offers nothing new in the form of aims or fundamental principles than has existed since the days of the Prophet. To assist the bishops to meet the problems of increased numbers needing assistance during the 1930's and to more fully comply with the Lord's instructions to the Church insofar as its responsibility for the care of the poor is concerned, the Welfare work was more fully organized on a Church-wide scale in 1936 with a General Welfare Committee and Welfare committees in regions, stakes, and wards. These coordinative steps are perhaps the only thing essentially new.

The Lord, in the very beginning, by revelation through the Prophet, commissioned, directed organization, fixed responsibility upon the bishops, defined procedures, advocated storehouses, set forth basic governing principles of helping those in need among us.

Let me read you a few quotations in support of what I have said:

And behold, thou wilt remember the poor and consecrate of thy properties for their support. . . . And they shall be laid before the bishop of my Church and his counselors. . . . If there shall be properties in [their] hands . . . more than is necessary for the support [of the poor] after this first consecration . . . it shall be kept in my storehouse to administer to those who have not, from time to time, that every man who has need may be amply supplied according to his wants. (D&C 42:30-31, 33.)

. . . it must needs be that there be an organization of my people in regulating and establishing the affairs of the storehouse for the poor of my people. (D&C 78:3.)

To the people he gave profoundly basic instructions.

To the rich man:

Wo unto you rich men that will not give your substance to the poor, for your riches will canker your souls; and this shall be your lamentation in the day of visitation, and of judgment, and of indignation: The harvest is past, the summer is ended, and my soul is not saved! (D&C 56:16.)

To the poor man:

Wo unto you poor men, whose hearts are not broken, whose spirits are not contrite, and whose bellies are not satisfied, and whose hands are not stayed from laying hold upon other men's goods, whose eyes are full of greediness, and who will not labor with your own hands! (D&C 56:17.)

And again—"Thou shalt not be idle, for he that is idle shall not eat the bread nor wear the garments of the laborer." (D&C 42:42.)

These quotations set forth the fundamentals of Church Welfare.

In a revelation regarding the temporal affairs of the people, the Lord admonishes the people:

That through my providence, notwithstanding the tribulation which shall descend upon you, that the church may stand independent above all other creatures beneath the celestial world. (D&C 78:14.)

If we are to stand independent we must be able to produce all things necessary to meet our essential needs. This the Church is striving to do through the Welfare production projects.

The objectives of the program are two-fold, immediate and long term; i.e., to give immediate relief to those in need; to rehabilitate families, to help them to be self-directing, and self-maintaining.

Both of these objectives are daily being realized.

The program is spiritual as well as temporal.

When I contemplate the greatness of the program and realize that it is God's perfect plan for the care of his people and that he has given to each one of us commandments in relation to it, I know that we can ill afford to withhold in any degree our support.

COMPASSIONATE SERVICE—A FUNDAMENTAL
WORK OF RELIEF SOCIETY

RELIEF Society is great because of the greatness of its birth. Under divine inspiration, a Prophet of God, one chosen to be the instrument through which the gospel was to be restored to earth, gave to latter-day women this Society, and he personally taught them correct procedures and what their several activities would embrace. Throughout its history, the Society has been guided, directed, and protected by the influence of that sacred power given to men holding the holy priesthood. It has been blessed in both the local and general organizations with the leadership of women of vision, faith, courage, understanding, and diligence. Its membership has been made up of devoted, self-sacrificing, hard-working women, rendering free-will service because of an inner conviction of the truth of the gospel and the importance of caring for the children of our Father and of contributing to the Master's work. A great underlying spirit has motivated all of its activities, the spirit of the gospel. This is the unifying, compelling force that has carried it ever onward and upward.

The work of Relief Society is soul-enriching. It calls for self-sacrifice, but it offers self-fulfillment. Through its program, Latter-day Saint women have experienced a century of self-development and self-refinement. The Prophet turned the key that knowledge and intelligence should flow down from that time henceforth. Whatever a woman's talents may be, Relief Society offers opportunity for her development. Since the turn of the century, a formal educational program has been carried forward where "subjects that tend toward the elevation and advancement of women in many lines of thought and action" have been taught. Through the educational opportunities of the Society, thousands of women have become more adept in homemaking, and have been better able to intelligently participate in the civic and social life of their respective communities. Withal, they have maintained a spiritual equilibrium.

Relief Society has been rich in this service-power, as its works bear testimony. Love-inspired service is the thing for which Relief Society is best known and most highly respected.

One caution I would offer Relief Society women today, however. We must be alert to preserve, strong and active within this Society, this precious, vital element, lest modern trends and influences dull it or retard its expression.

I wonder if we are doing this, or if the recent tendency of Relief Society has not been to emphasize our educational activities and to be less attentive to our compassionate services. Then, too, I wonder if we have not been somewhat influenced by the trend of the times which has been toward professional service in meeting human needs.

Conditions today seem to warrant a re-emphasis on compassionate service as the fundamental work of Relief Society. Evil forces are stalking the earth, spreading sorrow and distress. There is an ominous murmur of additional trials and sorrows ahead. Advanced as we are in many fields, today's world is not free from distress and suffering. There are still sorrowing hearts that need to be comforted; there are still the discouraged and weary who need to be given new heart; there are still those who are ill, needing a few hours of practical nursing, for whom no nurses are available; there are still motherless homes needing the softening touch and capable hand of a good woman; there are still homebound persons among us who, through a friendly visit, need to be brought into contact with the current of life; there are still the aged with their manifold infirmities and problems calling for attention.

Relief Society women, awake to their duties and working under the direction of men holding the Holy Priesthood, can be effective in alleviating these distresses among our people.

Relief Society women today must guard their trusts carefully. They must not let the hours and days slip by, unmindful of time's swift passing, insensitive to the needs and the opportunities about them, unheeding to the dangers lurking ahead. But, walking in the paths marked out for them by our latter-day prophets, holding fast to gospel truths, strengthened and reinforced by the knowledge and intelligence gained through the educational opportunities of the Society, they must advance the fundamental purposes for which this Society was established.

In this trying, chaotic day, may our Latter-day Saint mothers unite as one and, clothed with the armor of faith, may we pray that the hand of evil will be stayed and that the hearts of men and nations will turn unto the ways of the righteous, that suffering, fear, sorrow, and hatred will loose their hold upon the earth.

THE MOTIVATING SPIRIT OF RELIEF SOCIETY

IN Relief Society work there is a great underlying spirit, as deep and as broad as the work itself, which motivates all of our activities. It has characterized the work of the Society for nearly one hundred years. It has been exemplified in the lives of thousands of women who have affiliated with the organization. It has been the unifying, compelling force that has carried us forward and enabled us to succeed. It was this spirit which prompted 18 women to request the Prophet Joseph Smith to organize them into a society for human betterment.

It was the same spirit which kept the organization alive in the hearts of women when they were unable to attend regular meetings because of the difficulties incident to crossing the plains and establishing the Saints in the valleys of the Rocky Mountains. It is this same spirit which has caused the organization to grow and flourish until today its influence is felt far and wide.

It is the same spirit which so recently caused a Relief Society president living in a war-torn country to travel a distance of 60 miles on a bicycle to succor her sisters whose city had been ravaged and whose homes had been destroyed by war. This Relief Society president did not carry to her stricken sisters baskets of food and new clothing.

She was unable to restore the shelters which had been so ruthlessly demolished. She did not carry a purse full of money to purchase material comforts for them. I do not believe she was conscious of her own efficiency in the conduct of her work nor was she concerned about individual or organization credit. Her one concern was the spiritual welfare of her people. She wanted them to know that they were not alone in their time of trouble. She wanted to encourage and bless those whom she loved. She carried to her sisters something of greater worth than food, clothing, shelter or money; she carried to them the greatest restorative in the world—the true spirit of the gospel. Her genuine love for her fellow men and the activities which it prompted were motivated by the spirit which underlies and motivates all of our worthy activities.

To the degree that the spirit of the gospel characterizes our work we will be successful, and we will fail to the degree that it wanes or is found lacking.

The Apostle Paul gives us the key. He says, "None of us liveth to himself," (Rom. 14:7.)

Peter further says:

Be ye all of one mind, having compassion one of another, love as brethren, be pitiful, be courteous:

Not rendering evil for evil, or railing for railing: but contrariwise blessings; knowing that ye are thereunto called that ye should inherit a blessing. (1 Pet. 3:8-9.)

It is the spirit of the gospel which enables us to render our most effective service. Service thus rendered is a selfless service devoid of any thought of recompense. Personal sacrifice and effort are discounted. All consideration of personal gain is effaced. Recognition and praise for what we are doing are disdained. Everything becomes subservient to the genuine desire to help one another and promote the work of the Lord.

The most important thing in Relief Society is to keep this spirit alive. It should dominate all of our activities. If the work of our capable leaders is animated by the spirit of the Lord, the lives of Relief Society women will indeed be enriched, the work of the organization will progress, and those who are called to serve will enjoy the greatest luxury in the world—the luxury of doing good. This is true success.

RELIEF SOCIETY—A BULWARK AGAINST EVIL

F ROM a letter dated April 6, 1961, written by the president of a ward Relief Society in London, I quote:

Last Sunday morning a very nice lady came to Hyde Park Ward just to see what we were like . . . This is how she got to know of the Church. She was walking down Fleet Street just a few days before and was window gazing when she saw a wonderful display of pictures of the Singing Mothers group, with pictures of the Hyde Park Chapel. They were taken during the dedication days and were exhibited by the Daily Telegraph. This lady said she was entranced. She just couldn't get over the happiness that radiated from the singers, so she decided she must find out about them. She made her way to the Hyde Park Chapel. I showed her through the place and invited her to attend the services. She later became a member of the Church all because she saw over 250 happy women in a picture.

At the time the *Centenary* was in the course of preparation there came to my attention a letter written by Sister Emma Morris in Nauvoo in May 1842 relative to her membership in the Society. I quote from this letter:

I have been to Relief Society meeting. It was a busy day, but I enjoyed it thoroughly. It pleased me to no end though it did not surprise me to see how able are the women leaders. I was shown very special attention, being formally introduced and accepted as a member by vote of the sisters present. My human vanity made me enjoy this, but my great happiness comes from knowing that I have joined with other good women in good works.

From a Salt Lake City Relief Society member comes this statement written in 1942:

From old family records I have learned how dearly great grandmother prized her place in Relief Society. She believed that the plan came from God, that it would be a mighty instrument in enlarging women's sphere of usefulness. She sensed that the individual efforts of many women could be greatly magnified through the power of organization, that she could not possibly have appreciated the tremendous potentialities of over 100,000 women a century later, nor could she possibly have foreseen that the Society that she helped to pioneer would bring to me, her granddaughter, the incomparable joy I experience as a member of this Society.

Relief Society today holds a position of influence and respect among organized women of the world. Relief Society, with a knowledge of God's divine law of free agency, with a knowledge of the sacredness of the individual and God's plan of life and salvation revealed in these latter days through his prophets, has a grave responsibility to share its knowledge and shed its influence in ever-widening circles in the promotion of freedom and the way of life taught by the Master. There is no organization of women in the world upon whom this responsibility rests so heavily. There is no group to whom organized women of the world should be able to look with greater assurance for strong and wise leadership. We must work through proper channels, it is true, and as authorized by our priesthood authority, but work we must and give to women of the world the truths we have been given by divine revelation. Relief Society must stand as a bulwark against the forces of evil striving to engulf women. It must be a beacon light and a guiding star to women of many nations. To meet our obligations we must be strong in numbers, strong in faith, strong in courage, and strong in good works.

The Relief Society was small in 1842 compared to its numbers now. The Prophet foretold great things concerning the future of this organization, many of which I have lived to see fulfilled, but he prophesied many things which remain yet to be fulfilled, and I rejoice in the contemplation of these things daily, feeling that the promises are sure to be verified in the future as promises have been in the past. I trust the sisters who are now laboring and who will in the future labor in the interest of Relief Societies in Zion will realize the importance attached to the work and comprehend that upon them a great responsibility rests. President Joseph Smith had great faith in the sisters' labors and ever sought to encourage them in the performance of the duties which pertained to the Society. "These duties," he said, "were not only for benevolent purposes and spiritual improvement, but were actually to save souls."

I, too, have great faith in the sisters of Relief Society. I know that great and glorious things still lie ahead. But let us not forget a single woman in our respective wards who needs Relief Society and whom the Society needs. This membership building program is not ours alone. It belongs to the past, it belongs to the present, it will belong to the future. It is the Lord's work and He will bless our efforts as he has always done.

A DAY OF REJOICING

THE minutes of our meetings, in which are recorded the activities and experiences of the sisters, have served well as precedent for the Society to act upon. From time to time the general board minutes, which include reports of Relief Society activities and experiences Church-wide, are carefully reviewed and evaluated and form the basis for the rulings, policies, procedures and recommendations whereby the Society is governed. For the convenience of the sisters, these are recorded in the *Relief Society Handbook of Instructions*, which book is priesthood approved.

These regulations are not given to circumscribe the sisters in the conduct of the work of the Society nor to arbitrarily regulate or rule over them. They are given because time, experience and inspired wisdom declare them to be sound and for the well-being and advancement of the Society. They have been prepared in harmony with the Prophet's directive: "The minutes of your meetings will be precedent for you to act upon."

It was never intended that our Father's organization for his daughters should be operated according to whim or desire, but according to his will as made known through his inspired leaders.

Thus the divine purposes of the Society are accomplished; the character of every Relief Society organization is the same regardless of its size or where it may be located; every sister, irrespective of nationality or circumstance, may receive the same benefits and blessings; every branch and ward in the Church may receive from its Relief Society the same type of helpful service. It has been my privilege to visit Relief Society organizations in many states of the United States, in Canada, Mexico, the Hawaiian Islands, in faraway New Zealand, in Great Britain and many of the countries of Europe. I have visited Relief Societies large and small with the sisters speaking differing languages. I have visited them in small hamlets as well as in great cities. Impressive, indeed, has been the fact that regardless of the size of the organization or the language spoken by the sisters, the Relief Societies have all been alike in character, purpose, procedure, and spirit. The strength, power, and value of this uniformity cannot be overemphasized.

National And International Reports
And Addresses

AFTER EIGHTY YEARS

(Eightieth Anniversary Luncheon Meeting of the
founding of the National Council of Women of the United
States, April 1, 1968, Waldorf-Astoria Hotel, New York
City, N.Y.)

A NEWSPAPER columnist, speaking recently of the
present day, referred to it as "woman's era—her triumphant day of achievement." Certainly it is a
day when, in most countries of the world, discrimination
against woman because of her sex has in large measure
been removed. Today she is a person of consequence in
national and international affairs. In our own great nation,
doors of opportunity are invitingly open to her in business
and the professions, and she is steadily making inroads into
the top policy-making levels of government. There is
scarcely any field of human endeavor she may not enter
if she wills to do so. Her opinions are sought and respected
and her influence on national attitudes, programs and
practices, on American home and family life, as well as on
social and economic conditions generally, is potent.

While woman points with justified pride to her position of dignity and influence today, she is not unmindful
that this position was hard won, that it was not conferred
upon her merely through the good graces of change. She
knows that each forward step has been taken over a rough
and rocky obstacle course. She knows, also, that preceding
her was another woman whose vision, courage, and de-

termination enabled her to carry the lighted lamp and level the rugged ground.

It seems appropriate as we observe the 80th Anniversary of the founding of the National Council of Women of the United States and also the International Council of Women, that we look back a moment at the road that has been traveled and at the woman of yesterday whose efforts brought us to this triumphant day. It is appropriate inasmuch as one of the avowed purposes of the Councils was to unite as a body of women to "devise new and effective methods of securing equality and justice for woman."

In the early part of the 19th Century, a woman's world, in large measure, was her home and her church with, perhaps, a few humanitarian services extended to her immediate community. Life for the average woman was hard, and many shackles bound her in the development of her talents and in the exercise of her abilities, as well as in the exercise of her God-ordained free agency.

There were rigid barriers of law against property holding and guardianship of children. Most industries refused to employ her and those which did employ her offered only routine labor with long hours and low pay. The taboos of society on education and public expression, along with the prevalent superstition which held, "the weak, feminine brain, incapable of serious thinking . . ." shackled her personal development. The advantages of education were extremely limited. Colleges of higher learning did not admit her.

The political privileges of woman were nil. There had been sporadic women's clubs of a sort—neighbors meeting together for sociability and the exercise of their minds— with some groups working in a haphazard fashion for the public good. These clubs were poorly organized, however, and affairs were largely controlled by husbands of the members.

In 1833, a few bold women formed the first woman's club with a political purpose—the Philadelphia Female

Anti-Slavery Society. The furor which this act aroused is described in the book *Angels and Amazons*, issued by the National Council of Women of the United States. It states that the woman who identified herself with this group was regarded as bold and unwise indeed, for a respectable woman did not speak in public, nor did she organize in behalf of any political cause. At the first convention held by this group, a mob roared outside the meeting place, and following the meeting the building was burned.

Woman was not to be deterred, however, in her efforts for emancipation. Early in 1848, Elizabeth Cady Stanton joined with Lucretia Mott, Martha C. Wright, and Mary Ann McClintock in calling what is regarded as the first Woman's Rights Convention. It was held July 19, 1848, in the little Wesleyan Chapel at Senecca Falls, New York. In the book *Angels and Amazons* we read that the word "convention," as a term for this meeting, "expressed hope rather than fulfillment. . . . It was practically a small assembly of neighbors." It thrashed out, however, the first public "Declaration of Independence For Woman." This "Declaration" was the offspring of the pen of Mrs. Stanton, who was the chief agent in calling the convention.

Forty years later came that highly significant event— a convention convened March 25, 1888, in Alboughs Opera House in Washington, D.C., to observe the 40th Anniversary of the first public declaration of women's rights. The convention was called by the National Women's Suffrage Association. Two giants of the early suffrage movement— Elizabeth Cady Stanton and Susan B. Anthony—were the key figures. Their primary purpose in calling the convention was to further the cause of woman's suffrage. So strong were the convictions of Mrs. Stanton on the importance of woman's suffrage that according to one of her biographers, Theodore Tilton, ". . . she would willingly give her body to be burned for the sake of seeing her sex enfranchised;" while Susan B. Anthony, according to one of her biographers, Ida H. Harper, "stood ready to sink all personal feelings . . . for the sake of promoting this cause which she placed above all else in the world." It was a day of rejoicing for these two great advocates of woman's rights when Frederick Douglass, a respected and influential community leader of the day, who had been invited to speak at the convention, wrote: "The cause of woman's suffrage has under it a truth as eternal as the universe of thought, and must triumph if this planet endures."

Invitations to the 1888 Washington convention were issued to 77 women's organizations selected as being of either national scope or national value. Of this number, 53 accepted. In addition to the delegates from the United States, there were representatives from England, France, Norway, Denmark, Finland, India, and Canada. Eighty speakers addressed the convention.

The central figure proved to be Susan B. Anthony. In her black dress and pretty red silk shawl with her gray-brown hair smoothly combed over a regal head, she was every inch a stateswoman.

In addressing a meeting preliminary to the convention, Susan B. Anthony, with all the earnestness of her strong nature and in a voice vibrating with emotion, set forth far-sighted views with regard to the platform—views which maintain today in the National Council of Women. Said Mrs. Anthony:

We have now come to another turning point and, if it is necessary, I will fight forty years more to make our platform for the Christian to stand upon. Whether she be a Catholic who counts her beads or a Protestant of the strictest Orthodox creed . . . these are the principles I want to maintain: that our platform may be kept as broad as the universe; that upon it may stand the representatives of all creeds and of no creeds—Jew or Christian, Protestant or Catholic, Gentile or Mormon, Pagan or Atheist.

(It may be of interest to you who know the price of your seat at a table today to learn that for the opening session of the 1888 Washington convention 25¢ was charged with 50¢ for seats in the reserved section.)

In *The Life and Work of Susan B. Anthony,* by Ida Housted Harper, published in 1898, the Washington convention is referred to as "the greatest women's convention ever held."

Certainly, we must concede that this convention remains among the greatest women's conventions ever held as we contemplate that it was utilized as the springboard for the formation of the National Council of Women of the United States and the International Council of Women, whose continuing influences over a period of 80 years have reached into hamlet and city, touched for good the lives of people of many nations and all races, helped win for woman in our own beloved nation the right of suffrage through the adoption of the 19th Amendment to the Constitution in 1920; helped woman in other nations toward suffrage; helped open for woman doors of opportunity and service; effectively contributed toward lifting woman to a position of dignity, trust, and responsibility in community life and world affairs; and perhaps most important of all, helped woman to realize her own potential as a thinking, feeling, producing, and contributing human being in a world where such is sorely needed.

So today we pay tribute to those stalwart women who launched the so-called "women's movement"; we honor those who called the 1888 convention; we revere those whose foresight and genius conceived the Councils of Women and set the sails that bid them where to go: Susan B. Anthony, Elizabeth Cady Stanton, Lucretia Mott, Lucy Stone, the Grimkie sisters, Frances Willard, Clara Barton, and others of immortal memory.

We pay tribute to those other women of lesser prominence who caught the vision, played well their respective parts in the founding of the Councils and in the advancement of the cause of woman. Without them the convention could have failed in its purposes. These were the delegates who came, who listened, who were convinced, and who went forth to act in their respective spheres of influence. They, too, were women of stature—enlightened, courageous, tireless in their dedication to the cause they espoused.

One such woman was Emily S. Tanner Richards, the offficial delegate to the convention from the organization which I represent. May I present a brief word picture of Mrs. Richards, with the hope that in my so doing, you may also see the other delegates, how they worked, and the magnitude of their contribution.

Mrs. Richards' home was in Salt Lake City in the heart of the Rocky Mountains. By nature she loved freedom and by environment she enjoyed it. Her husband was an attorney whose affairs took him often to Washington D.C. Mrs. Richards usually accompanied him. While in Washington, she had rare opportunities to be instructed and inspired by the great suffrage leaders. These influences, together with the teachings of her Church which at the time of its founding granted woman the religious vote, made of her a strong advocate of the rights of woman and a consistent believer in the obligations that accompany these rights. Her supporting voice was clearly lifted at the Washington convention. Upon her return home, she was appointed by the National Suffrage Association as chief organizer for Utah. With intelligence and courage, she led this organization, rallying to her many prominent and capable women dedicated to the cause of national suffrage. With conviction as to the place of women in public service, she organized women's charity societies, establishing in that early day a child placing service. She organized a political education society known as the Utah State Council of Women. There then came into being the organization of The League of Woman Voters to which she lent her great administrative strengths. She won appointments to school and library boards, and helped other women of competence to do so as well. She influenced legislation. Step by step, she and her associates established in community leaders a confidence in the ability of woman to take her place at the side of man.

At length she received responsible assignments and special honors from Utah's governors.

Thus did Mrs. Richards advance the so-called woman's movement in Utah. Similarly, it was advanced throughout the width and breadth of the land by other delegates to the Washington convention.

We also pay tribute to the National Council of Women of the United States and to the International Council, which for 80 years have consistently made their organized contributions to the achievements of woman. We honor them for the way in which they have held to the original concept of an aggregation of organizations extending their influence and power by uniting as a single body on matters of common concern. We respect them for their integrity with regard to suffrage, and for their readiness to lend their influence in its behalf wherever it has been denied to woman. We admire them for their achievements and for their continuing concern for human well-being. True, new interests and activities engage the Councils as times and needs change, but throughout the years they have held firm to a body of principles patterned by Elizabeth Cady Stanton, who penned the first "Woman's Declaration of Independence": Good home and family life, proper care of children, temperance, woman's suffrage and the widening of woman's sphere, indignation against all forms of oppression, love of liberty and love of justice, respect for human rights and human dignity.

Just as the beginning years of the woman's movement claimed great and enlightened woman leaders, so have the advancing years. We pay tribute today to such brilliant and distinguished women as May Wright Sewell, Dr. Anna Garland Spencer, Mary McLeod Bethune, Eleanor Roosevelt, to mention but a few. Nor do we lose sight of the dedicated leaders among us today who generously devote their time, energies, talents, and means to the great purposes of the Council.

In a day referred to by the columnist as woman's "triumphant day of achievement," let us rejoice in the accomplishments of the past and the good of the present, and let us look with clear vision toward the future. None would deny that we are living in a day of turmoil, upheaval, and confusion and that the action of today will leave its mark on the world of tomorrow. Let us then remind ourselves that the struggles and sacrifices that have brought woman to her present position of influence and power require that she shall use these strengths to dissipate hate and prejudice, allay fear, promote understanding; that she shall engage in intelligent and well-directed action that effectively will contribute toward building a better world. Today our focus must be on our responsibilities rather than on our rights.

Power is in our hands. How best to use that power is the challenge before us. Can we not meet this challenge with the same degree of success that the women of the past met the challenges of their day? Can we not do so with confidence, working unitedly under the aegis of the National Council of Women which for 80 years has performed with integrity and honor? I believe we can.

THE ROLE OF MEMBER ORGANIZATIONS —
PAST AND PRESENT

(National Council of Women Annual Luncheon Meeting, October 9, 1963.)

O NE Christmas Eve, a few years ago, there came to my home a member of our Relief Society bringing a beautifully wrapped Christmas gift. I knew instinctively that she attached great value to the gift. Her eyes were alight and her face aglow as she presented it. The unwrapped package revealed a well-used book entitled, *History and Minutes of the National Council of Women of the United States, 1888-1898*. It was certainly not the commercial value of the book that made the gift precious to her and to me, for she had purchased it for a nominal sum at a book store dealing in used books. Its value lay in the fact that it recorded, in the form of minutes of meetings and verbatim accounts of addresses of leaders, the story of the founding of the National Council of Women of the United States and the International Council of Women, along with the thinking and action during the first 10 years of their existence, which established them on firm footing.

This Relief Society member's mother and grandmother had each served as delegates to meetings of the two Councils. They had taught her that the concept and establishment of a council of women "committed to the overthrow of all forms of ignorance and injustice, and to the applica-

tion of the Golden Rule to society, custom, and law," was
a precious heritage which should be preserved.

In the preface of this book, Louise Barnum Robbins
writes:

> It has been my inspired duty and happy privilege to place
> in this volume the record of the harmonious union of a large
> number of organized bodies of women.
> It is a history of learning the forgetfulness of the things that
> divide in remembering the greater things that unite.

The story of the founding of the two Councils is familiar to all of us. The occasion of the observance of the fourth
decade of the woman's suffrage movement, sponsored by
the National Woman's Suffrage Association under the leadership of Elizabeth Cady Stanton and Susan B. Anthony,
was utilized as the springboard for the founding of the
National Council of Women of the United States and the
International Council of Women.

Invitations to attend an eight-day conference, to con-
vene March 25, 1888, in Albough's Opera House in Washington D.C., were extended by the National Woman's
Suffrage Association to 77 women's organizations, selected
as being of either national scope or national value. Of this
number, 53 accepted and 24 did not. Invitations were also
extended to a number of women "who as individuals were
considered representative of lines of work not yet organized."

The history of individual memberships in the National
Council of Women is an extremely interesting one. We
might well look back upon it as a guide for today. That
they have had their place and made their contribution to
the accomplishments of the United States Council and, at
times, even to the continuation of its very existence is evident as one reviews their history.

We remember, however, that we study history not
alone to determine what has contributed to our strength,
but to acquaint us with problems and pitfalls which should
be avoided if possible. While history reveals the value of

individual membership affiliations within the Council, it also pinnacles the problem of proper and balanced recognition of these members in relation to organization members, both in the areas of Council administration and in program planning and activity. It creates an awareness of the limitations of individual members, as compared with organization members, in implementing action and programs endorsed by the Council, and warns of the need to maintain proper balance between the two.

My assignment today, however, is not to dwell upon individual membership affiliations, but rather to deal with the role of member organizations in the Council.

The organization which I represent came into the Council as a charter member, as did the young women's organization of our church, the YWMIA, along with a number of other organizations, because of an absorbing interest in suffrage. It was neither intended nor desired, however, that discussions in the new Council should be limited to questions touching the political rights of women. This is attested by the fact that invitations to attend the founding meetings were issued to representative organizations in every department of women's work: literary clubs; art and temperance unions; labor leagues; missionary, peace and moral purity societies; charitable, professional, educational, and industrial associations; and on through a long line of groups with diversified interests. "Each," says the record, "were to be offered equal opportunities with suffrage societies to be represented in what should be the ablest and most imposing body of women ever assembled."

It is fascinating to read of the varied causes which, in addition to suffrage, challenged the Council during the first 10 years of its life. To mention one or two—national divorce reform laws; equal wages for equal work to be paid by the government in all departments of its service; with consideration as to efficiency and not sex; the appointment of women on all committees set up by churches for the revision of their creeds; the emancipation of women from irrational dress and the acceptance of hygienic and modest dress that would meet the demands of health, comfort, and good taste. The report of the committee on dress reform is delightful. I read a sentence or two from this report:

> The executive committee, and the committee on dress agree in deprecating anything in the nature of a uniform for women; our recommendations will allow large liberty for taste and judgment. Our hope is to deliver women from certain hard and fast lines with which fashion has confined them.
>
> Utility and beauty, of which proportion is an essential element, demand freedom of outline, and outside dress should conform to this principle and enhance the personal attractiveness of the wearer.

Thus, today, we are heirs not only to the great concept of the Council of Women—the concept of an aggregation of organizations extending their influence and power by uniting as a single body on matters of common concern—but we are heirs to the pattern of organized women acting unitedly on broad and diversified matters, many of which might be outside the realm of the immediate purposes for which the respective organizations exist.

In addition, we are heirs to some sound governing regulations that have stood the test of time and made it possible for organizations with rigid policies and firmly established governing regulations of their own, to nevertheless participate in the Council as active members without conflict with their own governing policies and laws.

May I cite one of these outstanding Council regulations. In the beginning it was stated as follows:

> This Council is organized in the interest of no special propaganda, and has no power over its auxiliaries beyond that of suggestion and sympathy; therefore, no society voting to become auxiliary to this Council shall thereby render itself liable to be interfered with in respect to its complete organic unity, independence, or method of work or to be committed to any principle or method of any other society, or to any utterance or act of the Council itself, beyond compliance with the terms of this Constitution.

The by-laws of our Council, today, have declared this same principle, although in different words.

I might say that Relief Society, as a church auxiliary, and by action of its own governing board, is bound by rigid policies and regulations. Yet, in all the years that it has been a member of the Council, its delegates have not been placed in a position where they felt pressed to take action counter to the policies and regulations of the organization which they represented.

Three quarters of a century now have passed since the Council was founded, its basic purposes and governing principles defined, and its pattern of interests and plans of action established. Like all institutions which endure for long periods of time, the Council has had its good days and bad. The war years were trying years. Had it not been for the devotion of a few women of clear-sighted vision whose belief in the potential of the Council was unshakable, the Council could have lost its mooring and drifted into oblivion. Whether the ideal would have ever again been recovered and given shape no one knows. But the Council was not destined for oblivion. In time, its honored traditions drew to it other capable leaders with faith in its potential. World upheavals due to war moderated, vitality was restored, and progress in a new era of time began.

Today the Council holds a position of influence and prestige. The recent 75th anniversary of the founding of the two Councils, the National Council of Women of the United States and the International Council of Women, brought together a large and representative body of women from many Councils of the free world, with our own Council acting as host. I am sure all who attended the meetings recognized the prestige of the United States Council and the esteem in which it is held. I am sure you will agree that delegates saw in our present leaders, women of outstanding ability, courageous in thought and action, hospitable, gracious women of modest demeanor, yet alert, purposeful, and energetic. A Council with this type of leadership and one with a record of so much worthy accomplishment should command the respect of all women who believe in

growth and extended service through organization, whether
or not they accept the Council's method for this growth and
services for themselves.

The 75th anniversary conference brought into clear
focus areas which today need the energies of the respective
Councils. Delegates were given a renewed awareness that
this is a day of extreme world unrest—a day of nuclear fis-
sion; of fast means of communication and transportation
that have made the world small; a day of emergence of
newly-independent nations with an array of problems incident to their development and stabilization; a day of racial
conflict; a day of complex social change and relaxed moral
values; a day of communistic philosophies and subtleties—
bringing with it special problems demanding attention.

Well-considered resolutions directed the attention of
Council delegates to specifics. Above all, we were brought
face to face with the fact that this is indeed a day of influence and power for women, a day demanding strong, clear-
sighted leadership and wise direction.

Early in its history the Council took the position that
what affects women anywhere affects women everywhere.
Therefore, our Council lends its support to matters of international concern. In so doing, however, it does not lose
sight of its responsibility toward our own national needs.
President Kennedy, in a major address on foreign policy in
Salt Lake City wove through his message the theme of
national self-interest. So pronounced was this theme that
great emphasis was given it by our local press. Said the
President, "National interest is more powerful than ideol-
ogy." He quoted Palmerston to the effect that "friendships
may rise or wane, but interest (self-interest) endures."
Self-interest, it would seem, begins with our own housekeeping and from there extends to the world community.

Today there is before us, as a nation, the serious issue
of integration. The Council took a position on this issue in
1888 and stands firm today.

The so-called problems of juvenile delinquency have

been by no means stamped out in our nation. A recent study of children assigned to our Church social services agency by the Juvenile Court revealed that the problems of 59 per cent of these children are home and family oriented. This leads me to ask: Do we need to take a look at our American home and family life? Is all well in this area so important to national well-being? Do we as a Council need to enter into programs designed to emphasize the values that contribute toward stable family life and the inculcation of good character traits in family members? Which should be of greater concern to us—a strong national economy with emphasis on women in the labor market, or a strong national character with emphasis on the responsibility of mothers toward their homes and toward building within their children a discriminating sense of the true and enduring values of life—values that result in good character?

What of the general moral standards of our nation—integrity in public office, honesty in business, fair play in sports and in our relationships one with another? What of the spiritual strength of America? What is happening to our great American tradition of prayer? Are we not encouraging by our remisses in gatherings such as this a disregard of the need for communion with God through prayer? I remind you of the words of Tennyson in his "Morte D'Arthur": "More things are wrought by prayer than this world dreams of."

In the face of automation, does the Council have any responsibility toward employment for girls and women, particularly young women during the school vacation period and older women whose family situation leads them to desire to return to the labor market? When we operated the Salt Lake Relief Society Employment Department, serving women and girls in a limited geographic area, we had in excess of 3500 girls seek help in job finding during one school vacation period. Only about 30 per cent of them were placed. Many were inadequately qualified for available jobs. Approximately 100 excellent job openings were not utilized because of inadequately qualified applicants.

Is there a need to develop stronger attitudes toward safeguarding our individual freedoms as citizens of this great nation? This subject opens an endless array of concerns.

I have mentioned but a few areas which might challenge the efforts of the Council—matters which should be of deep concencern to us. Truly, there is a world of work for this national Council to do if we would help preserve the greatness of our nation.

The Council, strong as it is, still needs added strength to meet the demands of our day. I know of no better way to bolster Council strength than to enlist as members a larger number of influential organized bodies of women—groups which can implement effectively the work of the Council.

Do I hear, "This is easy to say, but difficult to do"? True, real problems present themselves. Many national organizations have international affiliations of their own. They must be helped to see that through Council affiliation, the base of their service to society is broadened, they meet their responsibility toward general national and international well-being, and they can command a larger hearing for their own program than when working alone. Many organizations today have their headquarters outside New York. Distance from Council headquarters becomes a deterrent in the minds of some leaders. Distance, however, is not the handicap one would think, as Relief Society can attest.

The enrollment of more organizations as members opens up a whole area of study for the Council and is something I believe we must eventually undertake. I offer a few suggestions.

The excellence of Council performance with its attendant increased prestige has a real drawing power. Everyone likes to belong to a going concern. Let us not hide our light under a bushel. Let us take steps to make our good works better known.

Direct and serious membership invitations from the Council itself may prove effective. Invitations to open sessions of conferences, social events, and similar activities open the door for follow-up membership contacts. The effectiveness of this method of enrolling organizations was proved by our early-day leaders.

Active solicitation by individual member organizations who know the Council and its worth and who are held in esteem by the solicited group is effective. This effort seems to me a responsibility of member organizations.

There must be demonstrated on the part of the Council an adequate recognition of member organizations in administrative posts and in the programs and activities of the Council. Our early records reveal that when a press association was solicited for membership, the appeal was made that they would frequently have opportunity to be "on the program."

There must be a sensitiveness to the purposes for which the respective organizations are maintained and a demonstrated readiness on the part of the Council to promote and support individual organization's purposes. These purposes may be readily ascertained by review of the reports given at the annual meeting.

Above all, there must be equal consideration of all organizations.

In closing, may I suggest that as members of the Council, which is in many ways unique among women's organizations, we must dissipate the attitude that once we have elected officers, it is their duty to devise ways and means whereby they may maintain the Council, increase its influence and power, and serve and hold us as members. Rather, we must see ourselves as a united body of women working together to serve society, equally responsible with our elected officers for the maintenance and success of the Council to which we belong.

RELIEF SOCIETY AND THE WOMEN'S
MOVEMENT

(National Council of Women Biennial Meeting, 1952)

A REVIEW of the history of Relief Society leaves one deeply impressed with the foresight, the courage the judgment, and the progressive action of our early-day leaders. Imbued with the spirit of the gospel, eager to bring about righteousness and the well-being of their fellows, counseled and directed in their activities by the priesthood, they not only advanced the cause of Relief Society but they stepped to the fore in such fields as nursing, medicine, industry and the arts, winning for themselves a place among the noteworthy. They early identified themselves with national movements among women of the United States, foremost of which was the suffrage movement.

The women of Utah having been granted the right to vote in 1870 and having enjoyed the religious vote from the founding of the Church had deep-seated feelings with regard to national suffrage. As early as 1879 they sent delegates east to attend a woman's convention. From that time Mormon women regularly attended the national suffrage conventions. In 1888 a Council was called at Washington, D.C. by the National Women's Suffrage Association to represent all nationally organized work by women in this and other lands. Relief Society was represented. This meeting adopted the plan of forming a permanent International Council of Women and a permanent National Council of Women. Three years later, in 1891, at the first triennial meeting of the National Council of Women of the United States, with the advice of President Wilford Woodruff, Relief Society became a charter member of the National Council of Women. This affiliation, entered into by our early-day leaders, has continued through the years, and the Society is active today in the affairs of the Council. While national suffrage has long since been won, other worthy causes have held the interest and enlisted the support of the Council, perpetuating it for more than 60 years.

The Preamble of the Constitution of the National Council of Women written by its founders in 1888 is the active principle which guides the work today:

We, women of the United States, sincerely believing that the best good of our homes and nation will be advanced by our own greater unity of thought, sympathy and purpose, and that an organized movement of women will best conserve the highest good of the family and the State, do hereby band ourselves together in a confederation of workers committed to the overthrow of all forms of ignorance and injustice, and to the application of the Golden Rule to society, custom and law.

The 1952 meeting brought together trained, widely-experienced, serious-minded women whose desire to work toward a better world, and whose courage in attacking what they regarded as evil were very evident. A spiritual quality pervaded the meetings. I opened the conference by prayer and each session of the three-day meet, including each luncheon session, was called to order by prayer.

The general problems with which the women were concerned were: declining moral standards; the breakdown in home and family life; the lack of religion and fundamental knowledge of truths in the family; the need to strengthen the spiritual life of the nation with less emphasis upon material things; the need for the educational system to be more effective in the training of children; and the failure of society in its responsibility to youth.

Problems such as the need for better programs for the aged and the mentally ill were considered. There was pronounced concern over the devastating and spreading influence of communism and the growing strength of communist women's organizations.

In the round-table discussion "The Defense of Moral and Social Values" the premise was accepted that moral right is that which is true, ethically good and proper, and in conformity with Christian moral law. Eminent authorities declared that what *was* morally right *must remain* right regardless of changing times and circumstances—right is immutable. They deplored the growing moral lassitude on the part of people generally, the increasing tendency to accept as expedient in public life things we personally condemn in private life, such as slander, graft, dishonesty, and abuse of confidence and trust. They declared that national sensitiveness appears to have been dulled into a calm acceptance of such evils without an awareness of the demoralizing effect upon the nation. There was a feeling that permeating our entire social strata is a growing disregard for the fundamental virtue of integrity. Sex immorality and the increasing use of narcotics by the youth of the nation evoked a strong plea for preventive as well as corrective measures in dealing with these evils.

In the round-table discussion on "The Defense of Physical and Environmental Values," panel members decided that "social consciousness with well-directed action" seems the way to meet the physical and environmental values in a world in turmoil. Our aging population, the increase in mental health disorders, and other such growing community problems were considered in detail, with concrete examples given of what could and should be done. It was agreed that there is no arbitrary chronological age at which people become old and unfit to work and a program which would involve persuading employers to give work to people as long as they have productive capacity would be worthwhile. In the field of mental health,

"mental parolees" and a possible program for their benefit were discussed. The importance of music, literature,
and art in the development of children and as hobbies for
older people, affording opportunity for creation and expression, were brought out forcibly in this round table.

At the third round-table, "The Defense of Socio-
Economic Values," it was pointed out that "it is not the
world that is in turmoil, but the people in it." The challenge to women today is: What can they do as women
to stabilize social and economic principles? Discussants
supported the thesis that good human relations which dig-
nify the worth of the individual and promote the values
which have enabled civilization to endure constitute a
sound approach. Social values of the past were contrasted
with those of today. It was pointed out that when the
nation was young and human beings themselves were
the sole instruments of communication, self-reliance was
a necessity and teamwork alone made it possible for people
to obtain the things in which they believed. This in turn
demanded good human relations for the common welfare.

The home was related to world human relations. It
was the opinion of panel members that no home is good
unless its human relations are good. First comes a good
husband-and-wife relationship, next a good parent-and-
child relationship. The good home was declared to be
the "key" to a good society.

The economic status of the family as it affects its well-
being was also considered. Women were urged to concern
themselves about private and public debt, about taxes, and
about "spending binges," particularly of young couples who
buy on time payments, thus inviting many problems and
creating for themselves unnecessary difficulties.

The need for women's organizations in the United
States to be alert to propaganda of the European Communist's women's organizations was shown in reports of
both standing committees and member organizations. Impressive indeed were the remarks of the representatives

of the Free Ukranian Women of the United States and the Free Czechoslovakian Women of the United States, both new member organizations of the Council. Council delegates were given a vivid picture of conditions behind the iron curtain. Speakers deplored the fact that in the twentieth century women behind the iron curtain are subject to terror and slavery that breaks up homes and violates every fundamental human right. The Council remembered with gratitude and admiration the many years of service and cooperation of the now abolished National Council of Women of Czechoslovakia and other countries behind the Iron Curtain.

Many special courtesies were extended the Relief Society delegates both during and outside meeting hours. That Relief Society is held in high esteem by members of the Council, there is no doubt. That the work of the women of our Church is appreciated is without question. Our many years of identification with the Council have brought understanding and friendship. Relief Society women have been able to contribute to the Council and benefit from it. The affiliation entered into by our early-day leaders more than 60 years ago continues today a fruitful association.

OUR HOMES IN THE ATOMIC AGE

(American Mothers Committee, Corvallis, Oregon, December 8, 1967)

THE American Mothers organization is a vital, growing organization with clearly defined objectives. It has already had considerable success in reaching its goals, but as the need for its work increases, so must its influence be extended.

Originally, the American Mothers program was incorporated in the Golden Rule Foundation. In 1933 it became a separate division of the Foundation, with these declared purposes: To strengthen the spiritual and moral foundations of the home; to strengthen the role of the mother in the home; to give to the observance of the annual Mother's Day a spiritual quality.

It is of interest that the first honorary chairman was Sarah Delano Roosevelt, mother of our former United States President, Franklin D. Roosevelt. In 1935, Mrs. Roosevelt designated the first American Mother—Mrs. Lucy King Johnson of Georgia. Mrs. Roosevelt remained honorary chairman until her death in 1941. The next honorary chairman was Mrs. Mamie Eisenhower.

The American Mothers organization embraces all faiths and looks with favor upon the pooling of their viewpoints and the coordinating of their efforts in behalf of home and family life that will produce happy, productive citizens who will be able to accommodate themselves to the changes and stresses of our time.

Five major programs have developed to implement the basic purposes of the American Mothers organization:

1. The naming annually of the American Mother of the Year as a feature of the observance of Mother's Day. The American Mothers organization has been designated as the official sponsor of Mother's Day by the United States Chamber of Commerce.

2. The Young Mothers program, designed to awaken young mothers to their responsibilities and to provide discussion opportunities on child guidance and homemaking.

3. The promotion of prayer groups in the interest of advancing faith in a supreme being with over-ruling power, and prayer as a means whereby women may unitedly appeal to that supreme being for world peace.

4. An international relations program through which leaders of the American Mothers organization who are traveling abroad may give helpful service in the effective observance of Mother's Day in other countries.

5. Representation at the United Nations, through which the American Mothers organization may be kept apprised of opinions and actions which affect homes and families world-wide.

May I enlarge upon these programs. First, the annual naming of the American Mother of the Year is designed to hold before the mothers of America the ideals of motherhood. The chosen mother must exemplify those virtues which internalize in family members' spiritual strength, moral fortitude, and a sense of civic responsibility that leads toward worthy life accomplishment by her children.

The American Mother is selected from among the fifty state mothers by a competent secret jury, each of whom was chosen for state recognition from a large number of mothers nominated by various organizations, groups, or even individuals within the state.

Well-authenticated biographies on the women selected to be state mothers by the respective states are submitted to national headquarters for review by the jury. Selection of the American Mother, however, is not based exclusively on the biography. During the Awards Week when the mothers are assembled in New York, the jury members observe the mothers, talk informally with them without being known to them as members of the jury. Jury members ascertain their viewpoints, attitudes, and observe their personalities prior to the actual selection of the mother.

The six basic qualifications for the American Mother are:

1. That she be a successful mother as evidenced by the character and achievements of her individual children.

2. That she be an active member of a religious body.

3. That she embody those traits highly regarded in mothers: courage, cheerfulness, patience, affection, kindness, understanding.

4. That she exemplify in her life and conduct the precepts of the Golden Rule.

5. That she have a sense of responsibility in civic affairs and be active in service for public benefit.

6. That she qualify to represent the mothers of America in all responsibilities attached to her role as the national mother.

In order that the virtues and characteristics of the American Mothers shall not be lost sight of with the passing of the Awards Week activities, as sometimes happens under such circumstances, the organization publishes a book entitled, *Mothers of Men,* containing the biographies and achievements of the National Mothers. Through this book the influence of these mothers can be carried into countless American homes on a continuing basis.

With regard to the second purpose, a wise man has said, "Desire alone cannot bring accomplishment. One must have discipline, training, example." So the American Mothers has brought into being its Young Mothers program.

As to the Prayer Group program, may I read a statement from Doctor Malcolm Duncan Winters, Jr., a Captain of the United States Air Force and an eminent specialist in internal medicine who formerly practiced at the Mayo Clinic: "The problem of the scientific validity of religion can be stated more correctly in the form of this question, 'Is there a God and is he personally interested in man?' I consider that question basic—basic to our very existence. . .

"This question affects all of us to such an extent," said Doctor Winters, "that we have been influenced to think about this in various ways since early childhood. . . . The question can only be answered by a step of spiritual faith . . . Faith in God is the basis for belief in him." Certainly prayer is the expression of that faith.

A prominent Canadian physician who practices in the United States and England defined faith as "the one great moving force we can neither weigh in the balance nor test in the crucible."

It is my personal conviction that children brought up in a certain set of beliefs will continue to adhere to them. The child brought up in an atheistic home is likely to remain atheistic; if brought up in a praying home, he is likely to remain a praying individual in adult life. The individual in today's life is sorely in need of the sustaining power of prayer, of belief in God and the conviction that he has an interest in his children. For these reasons, the American Mothers Committee advocates prayer in the home and encourages prayer groups among the mothers.

With regard to the fourth and fifth purposes of the American Mothers organization, they deal with the great principle of the brotherhood of man. They embody the admonition set forth in the second great commandment, "Thou shalt love thy neighbor as thyself." (Matt. 19:19.) Through its international program and its identity with the United Nations, the American Mothers organization is able intelligently to extend its work beyond its own home borders.

Now let us consider for a moment the implications of what I have said. First, it is that the home in which there is an intelligent and spiritually strong mother wields the greatest single influence on the spiritual and moral strength of the individual.

Second, it is that with all our scientific advancements and startling developments designed to bring about a better life for man, there is still need, perhaps a greater need than ever before, for the spiritual values of love, understanding, cooperation, unselfishness, peace, and faith— faith in oneself and faith in a supreme being. There is urgent need for conformity to the traditional rules of right conduct—uprightness, fair play, honesty, integrity that merits confidence and contributes significantly to the building of a good world.

I am not a crier of doom, nor do I feel the world is falling apart. On the contrary, I believe we live in a better word today than at any time in history, regardless of the tensions, pressures, insecurities, social upheavals, and endless changes to which we must adjust. We are heirs to a progressive civilization. The richness, the hope, the promise of life today is wonderful indeed. Nonetheless, we need stout hearts and strong characters to meet the future, a future pregnant with unborn events, big with possibilities, stupendous in its demands, and challenging in its problems. We know that persistent climbing levels the hills and gives added strength to travel on. We know, also, that a good tomorrow is dependent upon the same human forces that have brought us a good today—spiritual strength, integrity in private and public life, a sense of social responsibility on the part of every individual, with a willingness to positively engage in activities which promote human well-being.

It is true that with the impact of change, attitudes and patterns of life have been altered. Much that was traditional and good is now regarded as outmoded, and the new sometimes leaves us questioning, for we know that that which is new is not always good. New standards of accepted behavior appear almost daily on the horizon, often leaving us off balance. Some types of behavior leave us bewildered and confused. In today's atomic world, there is, I believe, an urgent need for organized effort to help mothers see clearly and to meet their basic responsibility of inculcating in their children the basic and eternal values of a good life.

The strong convictions which are mine that the home is the basic institution in the establishment of spiritual and moral strength are influenced in great measure through the experiences of the organization over which I preside in dealing with young people in trouble.

The Church maintains in Utah, Arizona, Nevada, California, and Idaho, social service agencies licensed by the respective states to engage in care of unmarried mothers, adoption placements, foster home care for children, and similar services. These agencies are staffed by highly-trained and experienced social case workers, and they must meet the regulations of the respective states in their standards and practices.

Among the programs of special interest which are conducted is one referred to as the Youth Services program. This program deals with children who are in conflict with home, school, church, society, or the law, and whose problems are of a somewhat serious nature. Referrals come from juvenile courts, the schools, the clergy, the family, and there are even some self-referrals. (Imagine if you will, a fourteen-year old girl seeking out a case worker at midnight because her mother locked her out for remaining at a social past the hour that they had set for her to return home. The hour she returned home was not unreasonably late.) Records verify that the children come from families of varied income levels. A study of 400 families revealed 25 percent had an income of $8,000 or more; 10 percent of the fathers were in the professions; 45 percent were in skilled or semi-skilled occupations. Only 3 percent were unemployed. Certainly children from the lower economic groups were not in the majority.

With few exceptions, these children are found to come from disturbed homes or have home-related problems. Twenty-five percent of the mothers of the 400 families and 16 percent of the fathers had second or third marriages. Consider the adjustments for children under these circumstances.

Originally in dealing with children where home problems were pronounced, they were placed in foster care; now this is not thought to be the best solution for most children. At the present time, only 4 percent of the children are in foster-care homes. The child is kept in the home of his natural parents if at all possible and intensive case work, including group work is done with the child, the parents, and even with other members of the family. Often a multiple approach of several disciplines is required—the home economist, the psychologist, the psychiatrist, the nurse, the clergyman, the school teacher who would tutor a child having school problems. Always work is directed toward developing the spiritual values—understanding, patience, love, family cooperation, peace and order in the home, easy communication between child and parents. Also, the moral values must be dealt with—the avoidance of deceit, lying, and cheating, and the development of strict honesty and fair play.

Through this approach, considerable success has been achieved. I read a brief letter in point: "Dear Mrs. Spafford:

It has been just a year since custody of ....
was returned to us.   He did fairly well during the spring
months, with only one or two upsets.   Now he is doing
fine and we are happy about it.   He is a good boy as the
case workers told us.   We know this, now.   His problems
were not all his fault.   I think they were mostly mine.   I
didn't teach him when he did wrong—I just yelled at him
in a rage.   His father used the belt, sometimes brutally.
We do love the boy and now we are not afraid to say so.   We
are proud of him and he knows it.   We love Mr. Proctor
and others who helped our boy, and who helped us.   Now
life is better for all of our eight children.   Thank you—and
bless you." (The letter was signed by the boy's mother.)

I have been speaking of professional *corrective* work.
The American Mothers program is *preventive*.   Both corrective and preventive work are needed if we would live
well in today's atomic age.   I leave to your judgment which
is of first importance.

SECTION SEVEN

Special Messages

THE SPIRIT OF CHRISTMAS

T HE true spirit of Christmas is the spirit of the Master whose birth we observe on Christmas day. It is this spirit which prompts acts of thoughtful kindness, binding people together in love and friendship.

It is true that our Christmas giving is not always done in the true spirit of Christmas. Sometimes it becomes shallow and even burdensome. Sometimes it becomes extravagant indulgence, nourished by commercialism. The *Deseret News* made reference to this editorially. It asked the question: "What is Christmas all about? What is it coming to? Sometimes it seems to be mainly about who can spend the most money for the most extravagant present. This year the situation seems to have gotten further out of control than ever before." Then the editorial cites examples of what it terms 'Yule extravagance:' dinner pajamas for ladies, $275; a girl's white cowboy outfit, $1,875; a satin blouse, $90; a kidskin belt, $30; men's leopard skin gloves, $125; neckties, $50 each. A radio commerical lists a lipstick at $47.50. The editorial continues: "The dizziest gift of all is listed as a 'nothing box,' something like a music box with an image on the lid with eight eyes that wink in no definite pattern. 'It offers no

special use,' says the advertisement, 'but it is very unusual,'—price $200.' "

We know these ridiculous extravagances exist and
those who buy such gifts do not always do it in the true
spirit of Christmas. I still believe, however, that for most
people the true spirit of Christmas, the spirit exemplified
by the Master whose birthday we observe, holds sway,
and gifts are thoughtful expressions of love and good
will.

Recently I had an interesting experience. I had taken
my seven-year-old grandson to a department store to shake
hands with Santa Claus. A very long line of children and
parents awaited their turn. Immediately in front of us
was a tiny mite of a girl, also with her grandmother.
The little thing kept hold of the grandmother's hand and
was as patient as my young charge was restless and im-
patient. My boy twisted, turned, whined, and bombarded
me with exasperating questions: "Why does Santa Claus
take so long?" "All the candy canes will be gone before
we get there!" "Why didn't you come for me earlier? I
was ready," and so on. Finally, when we were just a few
children removed from Santa Claus, a woman with a little
brood of youngsters crowded in ahead of everyone. Santa,
apparently unconcerned as to her proper place in the line,
took one of the children on his lap and proceeded to visit
with it. This was more than my boy could stand. He burst
out, "Those kids are cheats, and I'm sick of Santa Claus."
Whereupon, the little girl turned with the most startled
look, and in a thin little high-pitched voice said, "Oh, my!
Don't you know this is Christmas time. Everybody is
supposed to love everybody and to be good, good, good.
Else it won't be a true Christmas." This little child, not
more than five years old, had captured the true spirit of
Christmas—love, unfeigned unselfishness, and a desire to be
good.

Charles Dickens wrote: "It is good to be a child sometimes and never better than at Christmas, when its mighty
founder was a child himself."

The centuries roll on; seasons come and go; circumstances change; Christmas observances differ; Christmas extravagances bloom and fade, but the beautiful story of the birth of the Babe of Bethlehem will always influence men to love one another, to be less selfish and to be "good" as the little girl said. From this great event generates the true spirit of Christmas; in this is embodied the deep significance of Christmas giving.

WHAT DOES CHRISTMAS MEAN TO YOU?

Words are strange things—an articulate sound or combination of sounds which symbolize an idea. They take on meaning in the light of the life experiences of the hearer; for example, the word "mother" brings a certain picture to one person while to another it may recall something quite different. Words have fine connotations; what may be "honest" to me may not be "honest" to you. Words have great power: they stimulate the intellect; they stir the emotions; they influence behavior.

Probably no one word is exerting a greater influence upon our emotions, our thinking, our planning, and our doing at the present time than the single word "Christmas." What does "Christmas" connote to you? Does it bring to mind a virgin mother, a tiny babe, a lowly manger? Do you picture shepherds keeping watch over their flocks by night, the glory of the Lord shining round about them, an angel choir praising God and saying, "on earth peace, good will toward men"? Does your heart fill with gratitude for God's greatest gift to man? Are you stirred with a desire to serve him more devotedy, to love his children more sincerely? Thousands there are the world over to whom the word "Christmas" suggests such thoughts. Christmas to them is "observance."

To other the word conveys a distinctly opposite picture—one of hilarious debauchery, the gratification of extravagant wants, reckless spending, the overindulgence of physical appetites, excessive eating, intemperate drinking—excesses which can only bring distress, remorse and a general lowering of the quality of the individual. Christmas to them is "celebration."

Many there are to whom the word suggests excitement, overwork, anxiety, worry, self-denial. The day looms before them as something which must be met, which must be lived through, but which will be a "good thing over with."

The majority of individuals, however, find their hearts beating in joyous anticipation in response to the word "Christmas." It means giving, receiving, sharing, sacrificing. It is a happy, joyous time—a time when all are made glad. Like the streets and the shops, hearts are light, made bright by an inward flame of love for mankind.

So pronounced is the feeling of love, so generous are hearts, that wisdom does not always dictate our Christmas expressions. Often sacrifices are made out of proportion to the requirements of the day. People deny themselves important things that they may be lavish in their giving. All too often debts are incurred which become a burden as we move into the New Year, and Christmas joys are made dull by the heavy load. This is particularly true in the case of parents providing for their children. Children have so many wants, so many desires, in this day. Parents can scarcely bear the thought of denying the child his Christmas wants; in many cases great sacrifices are made to gratify them. Sacrifice is good—it stamps out selfishness, it develops the individual, it brings its compensations. But should parents always be the ones to make the sacrifice? Would it not be a wholesome thing for the child to make sacrifice also, to forego some of his desires? In making too great sacrifices, may we not be indulging the selfishness of our children, denying them one of the greatest gifts parent can give—the opportunity for character development?

Cooperation is a sound principle of happy living. Why not apply it in our Christmas observance? Let the family plan and work together, each making his contribution in the form of sharing, giving, and sacrificing. Then the great gift of self-development, family unity and stability, true happiness, will come to all.

A happy Christmas must be dominated by intelligence as well as emotion. It will always remain a challenge to the best that is in us. It should not be a time of indulgence nor of stress and strain because of our imperfect approach to it. It should not debase the fundamental ideals of Christianity.

Let us not place too high a value upon the things which money can buy. Let us develop an appreciation for the immaterial as a source of happiness and satisfaction. Let us emphasize the type of happiness which no amount of money can ever buy. Then the word "Christmas" will have its proper connotation—peace, good will, love, joy.

THE LATTER-DAY SAINT CONCEPT OF CHRISTMAS

MANY beautiful legends have grown up accounting for the giving of gifts at Christmas. One of the best-known is the legend of the Bishop of Myra, which accounts for Santa Claus as the giver of gifts and the inspiration for giving.

About 1600 years ago, according to this legend, there lived in Asia Minor a man named Nicholas, who in the course of time, became the Bishop of Myra. He was a rich and generous man who loved humanity, and delighted in making everyone happy, but he preferred that his beneficences remain secret. It was his practice to make gifts to the poor by throwing toys and various articles of usefulness and beauty through people's window, or by leaving money and food at their doors at night. He was so thoughtful of children that he was referred to as the "guardian of children." Their joy as recipients of his favors was his greatest happiness. For a long time his identity remained a secret, but at length he was discovered dressed in his splendid bishop's robes of red, trimmed in ermine, carrying a great sack of gifts on his back.

As the years passed, various stories were told about him until he was credited with performing miracles. His stories spread from country to country and so popular did

this character become that at length December 6, the date
of his death, was set apart in honor of St. Nicholas. Later
the custom of observing St. Nicholas Day was absorbed
into the Winter or Christmas Festival of December 25, and
the name St. Nicholas was corrupted to Santa Claus. For
hundreds of years this gay. and generous character has
lived in the hearts of adults and children alike as the symbol of Christmas. Thus, concludes the legend, was born
the Spirit of Christmas.

Beautiful and impressive as is this legend, however, it
does not satisfy the Latter-day Saint concept of Christmas.
Ours is an exalted concept and to us Christmas giving is of
far-deeper significance. Our concept is based on the divine
mission of the Savior, and the spirit of giving is the intensified spirit of the Master, active in our individual lives.

Without Christ and his atoning sacrifice, life for man
would have been hopeless and death permanent. Because
of the transgression of Adam, all men were sentenced to a
two-fold death—death of the body, and spiritual death, or
separation from God through sin. The atonement of Jesus
Christ was the supreme gift of God to man. Through it
man was redeemed from the Fall of Adam. The supreme
sacrifice of the Savior brought the hope and promise of the
resurrection, life everlasting, eternal joy and endless
progress to all who accept its benefits. The blessings of
the atonement of Jesus Christ are free gifts to all men, in
part without regard to their own action, and in full by
their obedience to the laws upon which the blessings are
predicated. At this Christmas Season we remember the
atonement of Christ, knowing it was indeed the supreme
gift to mankind.

With reference to this, John the Beloved Apostle
said, "Herein is love, not that we loved God, but that he
loved us, and sent his Son to be a propitiation for our
sins." (I John 4:10.)

A very special gift that is given to confirmed members
of the Church is the Gift of the Holy Ghost, which quick-
ens all the intellectual faculties.

We remember also at this Christmas season that to each has been given an individual gift by the Father to help him through life—a gift of the Spirit. Three volumes of scripture attest this truth—the Book of Mormon, Moroni 10; the Bible, I Corinthians, 12; and the Doctrine and Covenants, Section 46.

These gifts are from God, says the scriptures, and they are given by the manifestations of the Spirit of God unto men to profit them. To one is given that he may teach the word of wisdom; to another that he may teach knowledge; to still another exceeding great faith; to another the gift of healing; to another the gift of prophecy; to another the gift of working mighty miracles, and so on through a long list of spiritual gifts. (D&C 46.)

I am always impressed with the account in the Doctrine and Covenants:

And unto the bishop of the church, and unto such as God shall appoint and ordain to watch over the church and to be elders unto the church, are to have given it unto them to discern all those gifts lest there shall be any among you professing and yet be not of God. (D&C 46:27.)

Referring to these individual gifts of the spirit, the scripture reminds us: "And ye must give thanks unto God in the spirit for whatsoever gift ye are blessed with."

The greatest and most marvelous gift of the Father to his children in this dispensation was the restoration of the gospel through the Prophet Joseph Smith. One hundred fifty-six years ago on December 23 was born in Sharon, Windsor County, Vermont, a child destined to be the instrument in the hands of God through which the world might once again be given the gospel truths in all their purity and strength. Again, in this latter day came Christ's message of hope and promise and truth for the world. And now, as of old, heralds of that message call upon the heavens to witness, and the earth to give ear, for God again speaks to his children through his ordained leaders, and "it behooves the Universe to listen when God speaks."

Two persons, the Savior and the Prophet Joseph Smith, have exerted the greatest influence upon our lives of any personalities ever to live upon the earth. None of us could have the concept of Christ which we now have were it not for the revelations which come through the Prophet Joseph Smith.

It is of interest how much the lives of these two great personalities parallel one another. The divine mission of both was foretold by God's prophets. In the days when Christ lived upon the earth few appreciated him, save the very few who adhered to the cause he espoused. The same was true of the Prophet. Christ was crucified. The Prophet Joseph Smith was martyred. Yet, today more than one-fourth of the world's people declare themselves to be Christians; and tens of thousands of people in many parts of the world accept the divine mission of the Prophet Joseph Smith and adhere to the teachings of the gospel restored through him.

Among the theological doctrines of the Church there is perhaps none more sublime or dearer to the hearts of parents than the eternity of the family unit. Tonight as Latter-day Saint parents tuck their excited, anxious little ones in bed, rejoicing in the happiness the dawn of Christmas will bring to them, they also rejoice in the knowledge that these little ones may be theirs eternally. There will be a prayer in the hearts of Latter-day Saint parents that all of the good gifts of the gospel of Christ will be given their children through their adherence to the teachings of the Gospel.

The knowledge which is ours through the ministries of the two chosen sons of God whose birthdays we observe at this season make Christmas more significant to Latter-day Saints than to any other people upon the earth.

A CHRISTMAS MESSAGE

O NE Christmas my visits took me where visible expressions of the day were sharply contrasted. I visited homes where luxuriant and costly gifts were everywhere in evidence. I visited homes where gifts were simple and scarce. The happiest home visited was that of a widowed mother with two little boys about 10 and 12 years of age. The children, proud and excited over their gift of a cross-cut saw, told how many logs they had gathered prior to Christmas in anticipation of the gift. They told how much wood they could saw and cut during the holidays. They explained how the coming winter would not find them cold while mother worried about fuel. The mother radiated happiness, not superficial, momentary enjoyment but a deep and grateful happiness. A Christmas tree stood in the corner of the room and a warm fire burned in an open grate. Special Christmas extravagances, I am sure. But the real warmth in that home was the warmth of love and unity of interests. This little family had captured the Christmas spirit.

The Yuletide brings parents an opportunity to establish family traditions and customs that fasten the family together in lasting bonds of love and perpetuate family ideals from one generation to another.

I know of a mother who began with her first child a custom that became dear to each succeeding child as he joined the family circle. It has now been passed on to the children of those children, strengthening the family ties and deepening the appreciation of the true significance of Christmas. On Christmas Eve, the very last thing before the children are tucked into their beds, the mother, father, and children sit before the fireplace where the stockings are hung, or in front of the Christmas tree, and listen to Christmas carols. Then the mother reads the sweet but simple story of the birth of the Christ child. Even the tiniest child, too young to understand the full import of the story, knows the pictures and knows that Christmas is celebrated not only because of Santa Claus, but, more important, because the birth of the "baby Jesus" is commemorated on that day.

As we review our own Christmases of the past, it is not the details of any gift that remain to make the occasion dear to us. Rather, it is the feelings that surged within us —the eagerness of planning, the joy of united effort, the gladness of expectancy, the happiness of association with friends and loved ones. It is the spirit of Christmas that remains with us as the most real thing connected with the day, and it is this that we would enjoy again and again.

STANLEY GOES ON A MISSION

(Missionary Farewell Address for Stanley Spafford, April 21, 1963)

IT is with a sense of responsibility that I occupy time on the program tonight, for this is an important occasion—important to Stanley, to his parents, and to the Church. The mission which lies ahead for Stanley and countless other Stanleys throughout the Church will exert a lifelong influence upon him.

Recently I attended a meeting where a distinguished judge and lecturer was the speaker. It was not a Latter-day Saint meeting. In introducing the speaker reference was made to his legal training, his academic achievement, his wide experience, the unique opportunities that had come to him, all of which had contributed to his outstanding success as a public figure. In response to the introduction the speaker said that one of the finest and most important influences in his life had been omitted. He had filled a three-year mission for the Latter-day Saint Church. He regarded this as of foremost importance in whatever degree of success had come to him, either in his personal or public life. Countless men and women bear testimony to the good influence upon their lives of missionary experience.

Few things more deeply affect Latter-day Saint parents or more favorably influence a family than to have a boy or girl go into the mission field. Endless families have

testified to the fact that the home and family experienced
untold and unusual blessings while a member was in the
mission field.

To the Church, missionary work is of foremost importance. I recall a viewpoint expressed one time by a
member of the First Presidency, who said in substance
that the work of the Church falls into three great divisions:
First, the work for the baptized members, such as sacrament meetings and auxiliary work, designed to enlarge
their knowledge of the doctrines and to increase their
understanding of the plan of life and salvation and keep
testimonies growing and strong;

Second, the missionary program whereby the gospel
is carried to the elect of the Lord out of every nation upon
the earth;

Third, the vicarious work for the dead, that all may
have the blessings and privileges of the gospel.

Thus, in the final analysis the work of the Church is
all missionary work.

At the present time a greatly accelerated missionary
program is going forward. Nineteen-year-olds are doing a
glorious work and making a special appeal by their youth,
the purity of their lives, and the sincerity of purpose which
they exhibit. It has recently been my privilege to visit the
New Zealand South Mission and also the South Australian
Mission. The success of the missionaries in both of these
missions, as in other missions of the Church, is exciting.
Many young people, that is, young men and women between the ages of 15 and 25, are accepting the gospel and
are enthusiastic over Church programs. What a powerful
influence for good they will be in the world of tomorrow!
Converts of but a few years are holding positions of leadership and trust.

The readiness of people in many parts of the world
is imposing great responsibilities upon missionaries going
out at this time. They must prepare themselves perhaps
as never before by study and prayer. They must labor

unceasingly. They must organize their time and so live as to enjoy the Spirit of the Lord and his divine guidance at all times.

Like so many missionaries, Stanley comes from a family who have prepared him for a mission by holding before him the ideal of a mission by their teachings and by the example of their lives. They believe in missionary work. Stanley is not going into the mission field unwillingly or with a clouded view of what is expected of him. Throughout his life he has been a faithful church-goer. His entire life has been one of teaching and training in the ways of the gospel. He is familiar with the program of the Church and with Church procedures. He knows the importance of keeping the commandments. He has a testimony of the truthfulness of the gospel. He believes in prayer, in administration of the sick; he recognizes the power and the authority of the priesthood. This is the equipment of which good missionaries are made.

Undoubtedly there have been times when his young, inquiring mind and limited life experience, as with many young people, have caused him to question or even to ask for proof. This is to be expected of a thinking, growing, searching mind, but I am confident that even at such moments, if put to the test, his testimony would have asserted itself with strength.

We occasionally hear a young man or woman going into the mission field express doubt as to the reality of his testimony. He feels he doesn't have a testimony, especially one sufficiently strong for missionary work. It is my opinion that such feelings are prompted by lack of understanding of what constitutes a testimony rather than by lack of a testimony itself.

A certain degree of sacrifice is incident to missionary service. By sacrifice I mean a surrender of some desirable thing in behalf of a higher or more pressing objective. This has always been true of missionary work. When the missionary work was opened in Europe in 1839, the Lord

chose by revelation the most stalwart and select men in
the Church for this work—the Twelve. B. H. Roberts, in
his book, *The Rise and Fall of Nauvoo*, relates the circumstances of the departure of the Twelve following the
revelation wherein the Lord said: "Let them depart to go
over the great waters and there promulgate my Gospel
and bear record in my name." And that is the sole purpose
of missionary work.

Elder Roberts vividly describes the illness and poverty
of the elders and the sacrifices incident to their missionary
service. For example: "Elder [Heber C.] Kimball left his
wife in bed shaking with ague, and all his children sick.
It was only by assistance of some of the Brethren that
Heber himself could climb into the wagon." "It seemed
to me," related Brother Kimball afterward, "as though my
inmost parts would melt within me at the thought of
leaving my family in such condition, as it were. almost
in the arms of death. I felt as if I could scarcely endure it."

Brother Roberts summarized in these words:

> In sickness, in poverty, without purse and without scrip,
> leaving their families destitute of the comforts of life, with nothing
> but the assurance of the people who were as poor as they them-
> selves, that they would be provided for, the Twelve turned their
> faces toward Europe to preach the Gospel to the world, never
> looking back or complaining of the hardships or sacrifices they
> must endure for the Master's sake.

This spirit has characterized missionary work since it
was instituted.

Even though Stanley's sacrifice and that of other missionaries today differ from the sacrifices of those first
missionaries who went to Europe, nevertheless many missionaries today surrender some very desirable things in
behalf of a mission call. Schooling is sometimes interrupted. They must set aside the comforts of a good home,
the association of a close-knit family. Sometimes they must
learn a new language and adjust to new ways of life,

All young men and women are not willing to make

the necessary sacrifice. Only the other evening I inquired of an active Latter-day Saint couple as to whether their son was contemplating a mission. The mother replied, "Oh, he couldn't go on a mission now. He must go to college. If he wishes to go after his college is completed, he might consider a call."

This has not been the case with Stanley. To him and his family a mission call comes first.

Stanley is going to a well-established mission. In a letter he recently received, the Relief Society president of this mission stated, "The work is moving forward in our mission. It is a source of joy and gratification to see the converts to the Church entering so capably upon the work of building the Kingdom."

Stanley will not be left to his own resources in meeting the requirements of his mission. The promise made by the Lord to Parley P. Pratt and to Ziba Peterson in 1830 when they were called to labor as missionaries among the Lamanites applies for all missionaries:

> And I myself will go with them and be in their midst; and I am their advocate with the Father, and nothing shall prevail against them.
>
> And they shall give heed to that which is written and pretend to no other revelation, and they shall pray always that I may unfold the same to their understanding.
>
> And they shall give heed unto these words and trifle not, and I will bless them. Amen. (D&C 33:3-5.)

Stanley will go into the mission field equipped as was Brigham Young when he went forth on a mission saying, "Truth is my text; the Gospel of Salvation is my subject, my assigned field of labor is my circuit."

Tonight I am reminded of these prophetic and impressive words of the Prophet Joseph Smith written in the classic letter to John Wentworth, the letter of which the Articles of Faith are a part:

> No unhallowed hand can stop the work from progressing; Armies may assemble, calamy may defame, but the truth of God

will go forth boldly, nobly, and independent, until it has penetrated every continent, visited every clime, swept every country, and sounded in every ear, till the purposes of God shall be accomplished, and the Great Jehovah shall say, "The work is done."

A young person's call to a mission makes him a part of all this. He has been called by the Lord by his chosen and appointed leaders. He will go forth proud in the cause he represents, sure of the truths he teaches. He will plant the gospel in the hearts of those who will listen. He will teach people to obey its divine mandates and to be governed by its sacred truths. There is no more important work in which a young man could be engaged.

My earnest prayer is that Stanley may be blessed with every needed blessing and that his family may prove a supporting influence for him in his great calling, and I ask it in the name of Jesus Christ, Amen.

REMARKS AT THE FUNERAL SERVICE
OF AMY BROWN LYMAN

(Tuesday, December 8, 1959)

I N speaking at this service today, I feel a deep sense of responsibility to Sister Lyman herself, to her family and friends, and to Relief Society, over which she presided as its eighth general president, and whose affairs she influenced as a member of the General Board for many years.

This is an important and sacred occasion. It marks the close of earth 'life for one of our Father's favored daughters. Sister Lyman has completed her earthly work. She has fulfilled her mission and now goes on to a new sphere of action, rich in the experiences of earth life.

Sister Lyman has lived an eventful and colorful life here upon earth. Born amid the rigors of pioneer days in the little village of Pleasant Grove, nestled at the foot of Mount Timpanogos, a village which she loved, she has made her earth life a fruitful one. It has been rich in experiences, progressive in viewpoint, extensive in service, and broad in influence. She has met each day with interest in its affairs, and with judgment and courage she has responded to the requirements each day has made of her.

Sister Lyman, I believe, was born generously endowed with talents and leadership capacity. These she has continuously enlarged upon. They have cast her into roles of leadership, both within and without the Church.

I believe I speak advisedly, however, when I say that among the many organizations and groups to which she gave her talents and leadership abilities, none superseded Relief Society in importance in her mind and heart. Relief Society was her great love. Just as she loved Relief Society, so she loved Relief Society women. She has said of her work in Relief Society and of the sisters, and I quote:

> I am grateful for the opportunities I have had of serving my Church . . . particularly in the Relief Society, where during most of my mature life I have worked so happily and contentedly with its thousands of members. I have visited in their homes, slept in their beds, eaten at their tables, and have thus learned of their beauty of character, their unselfishness, their understanding hearts, their faithfulness and their sacrifices. I honor beyond my power of expression this great sisterhood of service.

Sister Lyman was called to the General Board in 1909, during the presidency of Sister Bathsheba W. Smith. Prior to this time, she had been a member of the society in her own ward, and in her childhood home, she had been taught to honor this organization as a great humanitarian society. As a member of the General Board, her special talents were soon recognized, and in 1911 she was named assistant general secretary, a position she held for two years, after which she was appointed general secretary. In this responsible post she served for fifteen years, being relieved only to take over the responsible duties of first counselor in the general presidency. She served as a counselor for eleven years until she was called by President Heber J. Grant, in January, 1940, to become general president of Relief Society, an office she held for five years.

A total of thirty-six years she gave to the work of the Relief Society general board—testimony enough of her love for Relief Society and her belief in its divine mission.

During the thirty-six years she identified herself with the general board, she took part in many interesting developments in the work of Relief Society and played an important part in the expansion of its programs. Time permits mention of only a few of these activities. Under the direction of President Clarissa S. Williams, she took an active part in modernizing the business affairs of the society, including those of stakes and wards. When she assumed the duties of general secretary, Relief Society headquarters were not equipped as they are today. There were no typewriters, no filing cabinets, no adding machines or mimeograph machines. There was no typist and no bookkeeper. It was not long, however, until necessary equipment for efficient work was obtained and good business and bookkeeping procedures established.

During her time as general secretary, uniform ward record books and visiting teacher report books were introduced. These were important, not only in standardizing the record keeping, but the work itself.

For more than thirty years she was associated with the business management of the *Relief Society Magazine*. For parts of two years she acted as magazine editor. She loved and supported the magazine to the hour of her death, referring to it as "a dearly beloved child" to her. Indeed she must have loved it always, for in the days of its beginning, days of abject poverty for it, she and Sister Jeanetta Hyde went from business house to business house soliciting advertising in order to finance the magazine, and with the help of their children, they wrapped and mailed the publication.

She was active in the development of good educational programs and served as chairman in the preparation of the first Relief Society Handbook published in 1931.

I am sure she is happy today that the singing mothers are represented here. It was through her great vision and foresight and wise action that the singing mothers program was guided into one of ward and stake choruses, which could be combined for general Relief Society conferences, rather than having one central chorus. This has been a strength to Relief Society and brought happiness and development to thousands of Relief Society sisters whose sweet voices have inspired us and brought a spirit of worship into our meetings.

The division of Relief Society work with which Sister Lyman seems to be most intimately identified, however, in the minds of most people who know of her work, is the founding in 1919 and the nurturing and development of the Relief Society Social Service and Child Welfare Department, under the direction of Sister Clarissa Williams and upon advice of President Joseph F. Smith. This department continues today, an extremely important division of Relief Society work, offering standardized case work services which require license.

Sister Lyman's work in social welfare has not been confined to the Church. She has extended it nationally and even internationally. She credits her first interest in social work to a summer class in sociology which she took at the University of Chicago, at which time she also did volunteer social work with the Chicago Charities, which brought her into contact with Hull House, the famous Chicago settlement house established by one of the nation's great social workers, Jane Addams. She also took a special course in 1917 in family welfare work in Colorado which, she maintained, further stimulated her and created in her a strong desire to fully participate in social welfare, utilizing the highest standard of practices. She maintained that this schooling in Colorado provided her with basic preparation for her later work. It is my opinion, however, that regardless of all this, she would have been a good social worker. Her work was primarily prompted by her innate desire to help her fellowmen.

We have always considered Sister Lyman as a link which bound the present to the beginnings of Relief Society. She was called to the General Board during the presidency of Bathsheba W. Smith, who was the youngest among the eighteen original members, and the fourth general president of Relief Society. Sister Lyman often recalled visits to Pleasant Grove when she was a child, of Sister Eliza R. Snow and Sister Zina D. H. Young. She was familiar with the character and work of these two great woman leaders, the second and third general presidents of Relief Society. She served under the leadership of Sisters Emmeline B. Wells, Clarissa S. Williams, and Louise Y. Robison, the fifth, sixth, and seventh general presidents respectively. She herself became the eighth general president. Today, I wish to express my sincere appreciation for the opportunities and training which she gave me, the ninth general president, during the three years I acted as her counselor in the general presidency, and prior to that as editor of the *Relief Society Magazine* and a member of the general board.

This connection with all of these leaders has been of interest. It has made her a veritable treasure house of information. With her remarkable memory, delightful speaking style and her keen sense of humor, an hour with her, listening to her tell interesting, intimate, unrecorded bits in the history of Relief Society was both informative and delightful.

Sister Lyman loved history. A good record keeper and historian herself, she taught others of us the values and delights of these activities. Relief Society has benefited from this.

As a Relief Society representative, Sister Lyman brought credit to the society through her activities in the National Council of Women of the United States. She was recording secretary, auditor, and third vice president of the Council, and represented the Council three times as a delegate to the International Council of Women meetings —once in Washington, D. C., once in Yugoslavia, and once in Scotland. At a recent National Council of Women biennial meeting held in New York City, a former president spoke to me in high esteem of Sister Lyman's work in the Council and sent with me a message of love and appreciation to Sister Lyman.

Her own years of presidency were war years, characterized by disturbed times. The work had to be conducted under difficult, trying, and exceptional circumstances. The centennial observance, which fittingly fell during her term of presidency, and into which she had put so much of her heart, had to be greatly curtailed. But, with characteristic courage, she met the situation. With wisdom, skill, and obedience to those presiding over her, she turned what might have been an extremely disappointing occasion to the sisters of the Church into one long to be remembered for its sweetness, simplicity, and impressiveness.

Sister Lyman has not confined her work to Relief Society. She has been interested in public affairs and has been a civic leader of distinction among women. Among her important civic activities was membership in the Utah State House of Representatives. She served on many local and state welfare boards, notably the Utah State Training School. She was on the governor's committee of five to select a site for this institution and served on the board for many years. She was one of nine persons appointed as a committee on the organization of the Utah State Conference of Social Work. I was with her at the recent annual meeting of this organization when she was honored for her great work in behalf of the organization, as well as for her contributions to social work generally throughout the state.

Sister Lyman traveled widely, spreading her influence wherever she went. From 1936-1938 she presided over the women's organizations of the European Mission. She referred to this work as "a joy, a satisfaction, and an inspiration throughout."

It is to be expected that a person of Sister Lyman's abilities and scope of activities would receive many special honors—among such honors were the Brigham Young University Distinguished Alumnus Award and the election by the Salt Lake City Council of Women to its Hall of Fame.

As I knew Sister Lyman (and I believe I knew her

well) she could be described very much as she described her own mother—"forceful, dynamic, and efficient; wise, far-seeing, and of good judgment." She was a woman's woman. She was a good speaker and an interesting writer. Her messages were always well-organized and presented with clarity and conviction. Her autobiography, *In Retrospect,* delightfully preserves her own history and gives interesting accounts of incidents related to the history of Relief Society. She was a prodigious worker, a good teacher, a great leader, and a choice friend.

In her autobiography, there is inscribed on the fly leaf her simple and sincere testimony of the truthfulness of the gospel and its meaning in her life. It reads:

I am grateful for the gospel and especially for my testimony of its truthfulness. This testimony has been my anchor and my stay, my satisfaction in times of joy and gladness, my comfort in times of sorrow and discouragement.

Sister Lyman's admirers are legion. Her friendship and life will be a cherished memory. In the Book of Revelation (14:13) we are told: "Blessed are the dead which die in the Lord from henceforth: Yea, saith the Spirit, that they may rest from their labours; and their works do follow them." Sister Lyman's work will follow after her. May her family be blessed through their beautiful memories of her abundant and useful life. May the love she has shown them and their own tender loving ministrations to her return to bless and comfort them, and may they be sustained in their hour of sorrow in the knowledge that she lives eternally.

A NEW YEAR'S GREETING

To each Relief Society sister we say, What will be your choices this new year? Will you choose to rid yourself of encumbering and non-essential activities which complicate your life and interfere with your joy in living? Will you choose to be more sensitive to the desires, hopes, and needs of your husband and your children? Will you choose to devote yourself more fully to the rewarding labors of your home? Will you choose to expand your friendships and deepen those with which you are already blessed? Will you choose to reach out more frequently and more willingly to help a neighbor in distress? Will you choose to become better acquainted with what the Lord would have you do, and in appreciation for his goodness and the abundance of his blessings, will you choose to serve him more devotedly? Having made these choices, will you exercise the will to act in harmony with them?

If so, the new year will be a fruitful and a happy one for you. Peace will reign in your heart. The evil impacts of life over which you have little or no control, life's strains and sorrows which are the common lot of man, will leave you unbowed and unbroken.

RECORDING MADE AT BERLIN

(For broadcasting over Radio-Free Europe from Munich, Germany July 8, 1954 to five of the iron curtain countries)

I BRING to the women of Czechoslovakia, Poland, Bulgaria, Hungary, and Rumania the love and greetings of the women of America. The women of America are concerned about the well-being of women throughout the world, and our sympathies reach out to those who are in sorrow and distress and who are suffering in any manner.

We know the plight of women is not always of their own creation. We also know that women the world over are by nature much the same. We know the spirituality inherent in women and their inner reliance upon God. We know the inborn desires, hopes, and longings of womankind for their homes and their families· We know the love of women for women, the love of women for humanity, the love of women for peace. Those influences which submerge, restrict, and interfere in any way with the free exercise of these traits, are burdensome to women, and the conditions they create leave them distraught and miserable.

So the women of America, understanding your natures, your hopes, your desires, and appreciating your problems, extend to you their love, their faith, and their prayers. We encourage you to make truth and right your watchword, and diligence and faith your staff.

INTERNATIONAL SINGING MOTHERS
CONCERT TOUR

"LET Not Your Song End with Its Singing" was the concluding number of each one of a series of concerts presented in seven large centers of the United Kingdom by a Relief Society International Singing Mothers Chorus composed of 250 singers representing five countries—United States, England, Scotland, Ireland, and Wales.

As this glorious song rang out through the great concert halls of Great Britain, one felt the prophetic nature of its message. The superbly beautiful music of these sweet-spirited mothers will not end in the concert halls, but will go on in the homes, in branches and missions, in wards and stakes of two continents, to sustain and bless our Father's children and to further his work.

In a revelation given in July 1830 to the Prophet Joseph Smith and directed to his wife, Emma, who 12 years later became the first President of Relief Society, the Lord said: "For my soul delighteth in the song of the heart; yea, the song of the righteous is a prayer unto me, and it shall be answered with a blessing upon their heads" (D&C 25:12.)

Throughout its 119 years of history, during which time Relief Society has spread to the far corners of the earth, Relief Society mothers have been singing mothers. They have sung with heart and voice. Yet, in all the long history of the Society, it was not until now that Relief Society members residing in more than one country have been brought together in one choral group. The recent concert tour of Great Britain bears testimony of the blessings of the Lord to his daughters, of the power of music, and of the importance of the Relief Society in the advancement of the work of the Church.

It was not an easy undertaking to bring together for several weeks of rehearsal fifty-seven women from stakes in Utah extending from Provo through Ogden; also to assemble for sectional rehearsals 200 British women; then to transport the 250 American and British sisters to London and from this center to Manchester, to Nottingham, to Cardiff, to Newcastle, to Glasgow, and to Belfast for concerts, and then on back to Liverpool and from thence to their respective homes.

The music repertoire consisted of twenty-three sacred and secular numbers, with both British and American composers represented. Some of Dr. Florence Madsen's own compositions were included. Each number was recognized as being among the finest in choral music. Though difficult to learn, the sisters memorized the songs and presented them with artistry under the masterful conducting of Dr. Florence Jepperson Madsen. The organist, Dr. Frank Asper, the pianist, Zesta T. Geisler, the soloists, Annette Richardson Dinwoodey, Jean Taverner, and Jewell E. Cutler, the violinists, Reva Blair and Blanche Wilson, all lent great talents to impressive and soul-stirring concerts.

As the chorus moved from city to city on its memorable tour, receptive and appreciative audiences greeted the singers. Enthusiastic applause and high commendation for the quality of the singing and the uniqueness of the undertaking were forthcoming on every hand.

Warm welcomes were extended by Lord Mayors in a number of the cities where concerts were given. Some of these distinguished civic leaders honored the Church by attending the concerts held in their respective cities. Other distinguished persons were also present at the various concerts.

Everywhere the press was generous in reporting the event. The Newcastle press reported the concert as follows, under the heading The Singing Mothers Excel:

In the City Hall, Newcastle, last night the International Chorus of Singing Mothers of the Church of Jesus Christ of Latter-day Saints gave a concert of sacred and secular music. This was one of a series of concerts which this body of singers is giving in seven centers in the United Kingdom. The whole concept is remarkable—50 American singers who have come over specially for these events joined with 200 British singers, who have for some time been rehearsing sectionally and they have formed a choir whose performance was an absolute object lesson in choral singing. Apart from the obvious fact that every member was thoroughly cognizant of the music—the whole exacting programme was sung without reference to copies—credit must be given to the expert training and inspiring conducting of Dr. Florence Jepperson Madsen. . . .

The programme consisted of a varied selection of three and four-part choral items, solos by Jewel Cutler (soprano), and Annette Richardson Dinwoodey (contralto), a violin solo by Blanche Wilson and two organ solos. Some of the accompaniments were played on the organ by Dr. Frank W. Asper, who provided adequate support without ever being too loud, in spite of the temptation of the large organ, the power of which he rather devastatingly demonstrated in his solos. The rest were in the hands of the pianist, Zesta T. Geisler, whose playing was excellent. Her accurate accompaniments were helpful to choir and soloists alike.

Of the contribution of the choir to the programme one can only speak in the highest terms.

Helped by the absence of copies, there was absolute unanimity in everything they did, with constant attention centered on their conductor, whose clear and meaningful leadership ensured splendid precision. They sang with artistic expression and never lost vitality, whether in vigorous and strenuous passages or in the quietest parts.

But while praising highly their tone and the general interpretation
of the music, it was that rare quality in singing, splendid enunciation,
which struck me most. Such clarity, such care with adequate stresses,
left the audience in no doubt about the words.

Classical, English, and American composers were represented.
Only to mention a few—Handel's "Come Unto Him" was beautifully
sung, as was Elgar's "The Snow." We were given an unaccustomed
staccato rendering of a Bach chorus, but it was effective. An Irish
song, "I have a Bonnet Trimmed With Blue" was very taking, and
Landon Ronald's "A Southern Song" was given an interpretation
which warranted the repetition demanded.

Dr. Madsen, the conductor, had one composition and two
arrangements in the programme, all bearing the stamp of expert
musicianship, and her "Come, Ye Blessed" was given a sincere and
moving rendering.

A remarkable achievement of Dr. Florence Madsen,
and one which received considerable attention and commendation, was the perfect blending of the English,
Scotch, Irish, Welsh, and Western American accents into
an harmonious oneness. This, however, was not the only
blending. The lives of the sisters were blended as one.
From the hour when the Queen Mary docked at Southamp-
ton bearing the American group until farewells were
spoken at Liverpool, a spirit of love and sisterhood prevailed. The welcoming song, "Come, Come, Ye Saints,"
sung by 60 British singers, came ringing across the water
as the ship docked and was promptly answered by "Now
Let Us Rejoice in the Day of Salvation, No Longer As
Strangers on Earth Need We Roam." This glorious and
heartfelt singing formed a favorable beginning for loving
friendships.

The impressive address of President David O. Mc-
Kay, and the inspired dedicatory prayer pronounced by
him at the Hyde Park chapel, London, will live on in the
hearts of the listeners. His words as he referred to the
Relief Society room made a deep impress upon the hearts
of the Relief Society sisters there assembled:

We dedicate the Relief Society rooms and kitchen and all that
pertains thereto. Bless the Relief Society and the service they are

rendering, the significance of which is now becoming more clearly understood by the people of the world. Holy Father, guide the members and keep close to them, and may all the people realize what it means to have our mothers rendering service, not only to their loved ones and children at home, but through their ability as leaders of the women of the world.

The tour of the International Singing Mothers Chorus appropriately concluded with a special temple session at the London Temple. A spirit of peace and well-being pervaded the souls of everyone and seemed as a benediction upon the momentous undertaking.

There were mixed emotions the morning when sisters of five different countries who had lived together and sung together for a fortnight said their adieus. The sorrows of parting were alleviated only by the joys of returning to home and loved ones, enriched by the experiences and strengthened by the blessings that had attended the sisters throughout the tour. These sisters of different nationalities, but with the same ideals, standards, beliefs, and eternal goals, had formed deep and abiding friendships. In the heart of each was sincere gratitude to the Lord for the opportunity that had come to her to be a part of this unique missionary endeavor. In the heart of each was a deepened appreciation for the gospel of Jesus Christ as restored through the Prophet Joseph Smith, and an increased determination to further the work of the Church. There was a firm resolve in the heart of each sister to rear her children in the love of the truth. There was an awakened desire to further develop her talents and to use them in building strong and ever-growing Relief Societies. There was a greater understanding of the true meaning of sisterhood.

To attempt to measure the values that will accrue from this international singing mothers activity, entered into by invitation of the First Presidency, would be fruitless. Many values already shine out with crystal clearness. Others remain yet to be identified. The full measure of the value of the undertaking must be determined by time and eternity. That the Lord looked with favor upon the undertaking is attested by the abundance of the blessings which he showered upon the sisters as they traveled from place to place on their mission of love and song.

The General Presidency expresses deep felt appreciation to the First Presidency for the glorious opportunity afforded Relief Society singing mothers, and prays that Relief Society sisters may ever be found worthy of the trusts placed in them by the Church.

THE RELIEF SOCIETY BUILDING—
A DREAM FULFILLED

As I study the lives of the past eight Relief Society presidents and review the accomplishments of the Society under their leadership, I am convinced that each was peculiarly suited to her day. Whether she was so suited by virtue of her native endowment or by special endowment of the Lord I do not know. Each carried the day by day load with intelligence; each devotedly gave her energies to the tasks before her; each dreamed dreams for tomorrow's fulfillment—all to the end that Relief Society would grow and expand and that the women of the Church would enjoy richer and more productive lives. Some of the dreams saw fulfillment by the president who dreamed the dream. Other dreams saw fulfillment in the days of her successors. Some of the dreams of these early day leaders remain still to be fulfilled.

Let me tell of one dream that began in the days of Emma Smith and persisted through the years, with the joy of fulfillment coming during my presidency—the dream of Relief Society having its own headquarters building.

The Prophet gave to the sisters in Nauvoo a lot of land on which they might build a house. It is not hard for me to imagine the rejoicing of the sisters as they con-

templated having a house of their own. This house was
never built, however. Nonetheless, the dream lived on.
Pioneer days in the valley kept the dream dormant for a
period of time. Then, in 1896 Sister Zina D. H. Young
brought it to light at Relief Society conference. According
to the records, Sister Young "opened out upon the subject
of a house for the Relief Society to be owned by them."
Counselor Sarah M. Kimball said she "felt it a humiliation
to be without a place of our own . . . we want to have a
house and we want land to build it on, and it should be
in the shadow of the temple." The sisters assembled in
conference that day voted unanimously in favor of the
proposition. But still, the building was not built.

In 1900 the Relief Society under pressure of an unfulfilled dream joined forces with the sisters of the MIA
for the purpose of erecting a woman's building. For eight
years, on into the presidency of Bathsheba W. Smith, the
sisters collected money. But during this period of time,
original plans were changed to include quarters for the
Presiding Bishop—plans for a woman's building as such
had to be abandoned. Relief Society had contributed
$8,000 and was given the north half of the second floor
of the so-called Bishop's Building for its offices. This was
a grave disappointment to the sisters but it did not destroy
the dream. Time moved on with Emmeline, Clarissa,
Louise, and Amy all clinging to the dream and from time
to time bringing it to light.

Just 49 years after President Zina Young called for a
vote of the sisters assembled in general Relief Society
conference as to whether they wished to raise funds for a
home of their own, I, who had caught the spirit of the
dream, called for the self-same vote. Again the voting was
unanimous.

In one year the sisters contributed $600,000. This was
matched by the Church. A choice building site in the
shadow of the temple was given Relief Society by the
Church and in October 1956, President David O. McKay

dedicated this beautiful Relief Society Building. This was the day when in the kind providence of the Lord, Relief Society was to have a home of its own; a day when a dream of 114 years was fulfilled.

"A MONUMENT TO WOMANKIND"

(Relief Society Building Dedicatory Service Address
October 3, 1956)

I
T is a choice privilege to be here today and to participate
in this long-awaited and important event in the history
of Relief Society—the dedication of the Relief Society
Building. It has been 11 years since Relief Society women
took upon themselves, by vote of the sisters assembled in
a general Relief Society conference, the task of erecting a
Relief Society Building, one that should be monumental,
beautiful, and adequate to serve the Society not only for
the present but in the years to come. Even as the sisters
raised their hands in support of the proposal, the magnitude
of the undertaking was recognized, but inspired by dreams
of the past, urged by present needs, moved by devotion to
Relief Society, imbued with indomitable faith and courage
and, above all, having the support and approval of the
First Presidency, the Relief Society sisters launched a
building program that, insofar as I know, has no precedent
among organized women.

Today the building stands completed—strong in its
construction, beautiful in its furnishings, functional in its
arrangement. I invite your attention to the simple elegance
of its classic design, the beauty of the materials of which
it is built—its stones, bronze, marbles, and woods; the
convenient arrangement of its rooms; the expert craftsman-

ship throughout the structure; its artistic decor; its inviting portal; its spirit of love and peace—all uniting to form the kind of Relief Society home envisioned in the long ago.

As the building program has progressed, there have been both happy and anxious days. It was a happy day when the financial goal of one-half million dollars, to be raised by Relief Society members, was reached. We rejoiced when the First Presidency granted to us the choice building site, literally in the shadow of the temple. We were delighted when ground was broken and a year later when the corner stone was set. As we watched the walls rise and the building take shape, our happiness was superseded only by our gratitude.

Anxious days accompanied the study and approval of the building plans, the making of countless important decisions incident to the erection and furnishing of the building, and the management of the trusted funds. Uncertainties assailed us at times. One day we wondered if we had built too large, only to wonder the following day if we had built large enough. The pronounced awareness of the responsibilities entrusted to us and the far-reaching effects of our decisions have been with us continually and have sent us often to our Father in heaven in earnest prayer.

Regardless of the responsibilities and worries, however, there has never been a moment when we have felt to regret the decision to build or when we have wished that we might turn back. Always there has been within our hearts the assurance that the undertaking was right, and the conviction that this was the day when, in the kind providence of the Lord, Relief Society was to have a home of its own.

We have been immeasurably sustained in the undertaking from the beginning by the encouragement, counsel, and support of the First Presidency and the other General Authorities of the Church and by the devotion to the program of the Relief Society sisters.

Talented professional persons, skilled craftsmen, gifted artisans, workmen with expert technical knowledge and proficiency have assisted us in the realization of our goal. I mention the services of Bishop George Cannon Young, architect, and his associate, Brother Richard Wood; the contractors, the late Brother Frank J. Fulmer and his sons, Brother Frank H. Fulmer and Brother David H. Fulmer, with their associate Brother Willard L. Fulmer; also the construction foreman, Brother Harry Mabey. I mention also the services of the decorator, Miss Marian Cornwall. Also I express thanks to the former and present Church Building Committees. We acknowledge with appreciation the assistance given us by the Church Purchasing Department.

Humbling indeed has been the devotion of Relief Society sisters to the program as evidenced by their interest in it and their contributions toward it—all clear and unmistakable evidence of their love for and devotion to Relief Society. Readily they met by individual and collective effort their great assignment to raise one-half million dollars within one year. To this amount has been added voluntarily gifts of funds ranging from a small handful of pennies contributed by a faithful and loving sister to larger gifts from individual sisters, from groups of sisters, and from ward and stake, mission and branch, Relief Societies —all faithful and devoted sisters. These gifts were contributed to the end that there might be in their Relief Society home some special article of beauty or usefulness that otherwise might have been denied. Choice gifts of handwork, even precious heirlooms, have been presented to the building, expressions of love for Relief Society from Relief Society sisters.

Rare gifts of beauty and artistry representative of the culture of the nations of the earth where Relief Societies are organized, adorn the building. These are there because of the love of Relief Society sisters in faraway lands for their organization and because of their desire to have their

Relief Society Building, so far removed from them, reflect the esthetic creations of their homelands.

The building program has been a cohesive, unifying force within the Relief Societies. From the far north lands to the sunny south, from the little villages in the islands of the sea to the great metropolitan centers it has sealed together as one the sisterhood of Relief Society. Out of this program have come untold blessings of immeasurable worth.

The fire of enthusiasm for the program has touched the hearts of many kind friends, not members of Relief Society, whose interest and generosity have been both encouraging and helpful. Many sisters, long since departed from among us, are memorialized by gifts and contributions of funds.

Today we are happy and grateful to present to the First Presidency for dedication, a building which we feel fittingly represents the enduring qualities of Relief Society, one which we feel represents the spirit and character of Latter-day Saint womanhood in its strength, its beauty, and its usefulness.

Humbly and gratefully we express thanks to our Heavenly Father for the completion of our Relief Society home and for his boundless blessings unto Relief Society. We pray that all who shall go forth from our Relief Society home shall enrich the lives and lead toward the eternal well-being of the daughters of our Heavenly Father. We pray that the new building may facilitate the work of our divinely inspired, priesthood-directed Society and enable the sisters to effectively serve as the handmaids of the priesthood in the great work of the Church. That the choice blessings of the Lord may ever rest upon Relief Society, upon this home which we dedicate today and upon each of us, I sincerely pray.

Index

A

Abinadi, 51
Abraham, 19, 86, 95
Addams, Jane, 454
adversity, 96
aged: activities for, 171; care for, 183-86; centers and clubs for, 171; Church activities for, 185; Church philosophy of, 184; Church programs for, 178; courses for, 173; definition of, 168; education for, 172; free time for, 167-75; future for, 174; gospel comforts for, 181; income for, 168; leadership positions for, 172; loneliness of, 180; needs of, 153; professional case work services for, 172; programs for, 180; recreation for, 169; responsibility to, 184; stereotype of, 167-68; value of religion to, 186; visits to, 180; volunteer help for, 177-81; volunteer programs for, 101; work for, 179, 184-85
Alboughs Opera House, 399
Alma, 13, 15, 42-43, 49, 71
America, 107-8
American Mothers, 420-25, 428
Amulek, 29-30
ancestors, 187
anchor, 273
Angels and Amazons, 251, 399
Anthony, Susan B., 131-32, 399, 400, 406
Anti-Slavery Conference, 165
apostles, chosen, 65-67
Aristotle, 134
army, invading, 117
Arnold, Matthew, 155
Articles of Faith, 449
Ashraf, 132, 254
Asper, Frank, 464-65
atomic world, 426
atonement, 440

B

Ballard, Melvin J., 57
Ballif, Ariel, 275

B

Bangkok, Thailand, 268
Benson, Ezra Taft, 112
Bible, 37, 287-88
Bill of Rights, 134
bishop, 178-79 184
Bishop of Myra, 439-40
Blair, Reva, 464
Book of Mormon, 37, 51, 154, 321
Book of Records, 4, 325-26
bread of life, 59
Brigham Young University, 76, 163
Brimhall, George H., 164
brotherhood, 57, 100-101, 423
Brown, Hugh B., 141
Browning, Robert, 174
Bunyan, John, 89
Burns, Robert, 241

C

Cannon, Annie Wells, 306
celestial pattern, 233
Centenary of Relief Society, 357-58
character, 278
charity: collection of, 360, defined, 371; objects of, 13, 365-70; in welfare 179
Chicago charities, 454
children, bearing and rearing; 110
Chile, suffrage in, 132-33
choice, 9-12, 458
chosen, those who are, 65-67
Christmas, 431-44
Church attendance, 61
Churchill, Winston, 191-92
"Citizens' Memorial Preservation Committee, The," 203
Clark, J. Reuben, Jr., conviction of, 20; life of, 78-80; statements on destiny of Relief Society, 348; eternal family, 226; LDS home, 261, length of calls, 75; Relief Society mission, 367; righteous living, 372; three family functions, 238-39; women's duty, 261
Clark, Marguerite, 201
"Code of Personal Commitment, A," 139
Cohen, Audrey C., 269